On Study

"This is a highly inspiring and compelling book. It offers a remarkable and original reading of some of Giorgio Agamben's thoughts, developing them into a profound philosophy of study that challenges the language of learning that has colonized educational thought in the last decades. In a really surprising and provoking way Lewis opens up a route for a (un)timely educational philosophy and theory."
　　　　　—**Jan Masschelein**, Professor in the Faculty of Psychology and Educational Sciences, KU Leuven, Belgium

In this book, Tyson E. Lewis argues that studying is a distinctive educational experience with its own temporal, spatial, methodological, aesthetic, and phenomenological dimensions. Unlike learning, which presents the actualization of a student's "potential" in recognizable and measurable forms, study emphasizes the experience of potentiality, freed from predetermined outcomes. Studying suspends and interrupts the conventional logic of learning, opening up a new space and time for educational freedom to emerge.

Drawing upon the work of Italian philosopher and critical theorist Giorgio Agamben, Lewis provides a conceptually and poetically rich account of the interconnections between potentiality, freedom, and study. Through a mixture of educational critique, phenomenological description, and ontological analysis, Lewis redeems study as an invaluable and urgent educational experience that provides alternatives to the economization of education and the cooptation of potentiality in the name of efficiency. The resulting discussion uncovers multiple forms of study in a variety of unexpected places: from the political poetry of Adrienne Rich, to tinkering classrooms, to abandoned manifestos, and, finally, to Occupy Wall Street.

By reconnecting education with potentiality this book provides an educational philosophy that undermines the logic of learning and assessment, and turns our attention to the interminable paradoxes of studying. The book will be key reading for scholars in the fields of educational philosophy, critical pedagogy, foundations of education, composition and rhetoric, and critical thinking and literacy studies.

Tyson E. Lewis is Associate Professor of Educational Foundations at Montclair State University, USA, where he directs the graduate program in pedagogy and philosophy.

New Directions in the Philosophy of Education Series

Series Editors
Michael A. Peters
University of Waikato, New Zealand; University of Illinois, USA
Gert Biesta
University of Luxembourg, Luxembourg

This book series is devoted to the exploration of new directions in the philosophy of education. After the linguistic turn, the cultural turn, and the historical turn, where might we go? Does the future promise a digital turn with a greater return to connectionism, biology, and biopolitics based on new understandings of system theory and knowledge ecologies? Does it foreshadow a genuinely alternative radical global turn based on a new openness and interconnectedness? Does it leave humanism behind or will it reengage with the question of the human in new and unprecedented ways? How should philosophy of education reflect new forces of globalization? How can it become less Anglo-centric and develop a greater sensitivity to other traditions, languages, and forms of thinking and writing, including those that are not rooted in the canon of Western philosophy but in other traditions that share the 'love of wisdom' that characterizes the wide diversity within Western philosophy itself. Can this be done through a turn to intercultural philosophy? To indigenous forms of philosophy and philosophizing? Does it need a post-Wittgensteinian philosophy of education? A postpostmodern philosophy? Or should it perhaps leave the whole construction of 'post'-positions behind?

In addition to the question of the intellectual resources for the future of philosophy of education, what are the issues and concerns that philosophers of education should engage with? How should they position themselves? What is their specific contribution? What kind of intellectual and strategic alliances should they pursue? Should philosophy of education become more global, and if so, what would the shape of that be? Should it become more cosmopolitan or perhaps more decentred? Perhaps most importantly in the digital age, the time of the global knowledge economy that reprofiles education as privatized human capital and simultaneously in terms of an historic openness, is there a philosophy of education that grows out of education itself, out of the concerns for new forms of teaching, studying, learning and speaking that can provide comment on ethical and epistemological configurations of economics and politics of knowledge? Can and should this imply a reconnection with questions of democracy and justice?

This series comprises texts that explore, identify and articulate new directions in the philosophy of education. It aims to build bridges, both geographically and temporally: bridges across different traditions and practices and bridges towards a different future for philosophy of education.

In this series

On Study
Giorgio Agamben and educational potentiality
Tyson E. Lewis

Education, Experience and Existence
Engaging Dewey, Peirce and Heidegger
John Quay

On Study
Giorgio Agamben and educational potentiality

Tyson E. Lewis

LONDON AND NEW YORK

First published 2013
by Routledge

Published 2016 by Routledge

2 Park Square, Milton Park, Abingdon, Oxon OX14 4RN

Simultaneously published in the USA and Canada
by Routledge
711 Third Avenue, New York, NY 10017

Routledge is an imprint of the Taylor & Francis Group, an informa business

© 2013 Tyson E. Lewis

First issued in paperback 2015

The right of Tyson E. Lewis to be identified as author of this work
has been asserted by him in accordance with sections 77 and 78
of the Copyright, Designs and Patents Act 1988.

All rights reserved. No part of this book may be reprinted or reproduced or
utilised in any form or by any electronic, mechanical, or other means, now
known or hereafter invented, including photocopying and recording, or in
any information storage or retrieval system, without permission in writing
from the publishers.

Trademark notice: Product or corporate names may be trademarks or
registered trademarks, and are used only for identification and explanation
without intent to infringe.

British Library Cataloguing in Publication Data
A catalogue record for this book is available from the British Library

Library of Congress Cataloging in Publication Data
Lewis, Tyson E.
    On study : Giorgio Agamben and educational potentiality /
    Tyson E. Lewis.
        pages cm
    1. Study skills.   2. Learning ability.   3. Education—Philosophy.
    4. Agamben, Giorgio, 1942–   I. Title.
    LB1049.L457 2013
    371.30281—dc23

2012049741

ISBN: 978-0-415-81216-0 (hbk)
ISBN: 978-1-138-64991-0 (pbk)

Typeset in Bembo
by RefineCatch Limited, Bungay, Suffolk

Contents

	Series editors' preface	viii
	Acknowledgements	x
	Introduction: A reconsideration of im-potentiality	1
1	From being willful to being more willing	16
2	Im-potentiality: The ontology of study	37
3	The aesthetics of study: Poetic rhythm, mood, and the melancholic angel	53
	Notch: Night study	68
4	The method of study or collecting signatures	75
5	The time and space of study: Weak utopianism and im-potentiality	95
6	The work of studious play: The problem of transmission revisited	116
	Notch: Stupidity	131
7	Studying with friends	136
8	Public, collective studying as an im-potential political gesture	149
	Bibliography	166
	Index	172

Series editors' preface

In this book Tyson Lewis explores a new direction in the philosophy of education by bringing the work of Giorgio Agamben to bear on key educational issues, most notably the vexed questions of subjectivity and freedom. Rather than providing an explanation of Agamben's work in order then to ask what this might imply for education and educators, Lewis uses some of Agamben's key insights – most notably his theory of im-potential – to go to the heart of contemporary discussions about education, particularly the current trend to make learning into a lifelong duty aimed at realising the 'full potential' of every individual, as we cannot only read in many policy documents but also, and more problematically, in much of the contemporary research literature on education as apparently a lifelong and a life-wide process (see Biesta 2006). Lewis argues that Agamben's theory of im-potentiality actually "enables us to think potentiality against the logic of learning, which reduces potentiality to a 'not yet' that actualizes itself in a 'must be'". He writes:

> Indeed, im-potentiality does not simply separate potentiality from impotentiality (thus sacrificing contingency for necessity, possibility for impossibility), rather it recognizes that the subject emerges precisely in the gap that separates and binds together opposite forces in the atopic space existing between desubjectification and subjectification. If learning separates, rendering processes of desubjectification and subjectification "indifferent" (Agamben 2009b: 21), then a new notion of the educational subject is necessary that does not divide but rather sutures together negative and positive poles of subject formation. This new process would mean overcoming the apparent necessity of learning and the impossibility or infeasibility of alternatives.

The device Lewis uses to open up a different way to think about education and a different space for education is the idea of 'studying' which is introduced as the "paradoxical state between education for subjectification and learning for desubjectification, between possibility and impossibility, between contingency and necessity". Lewis argues that studying can be seen as a 'remnant of education' that exists between these possibilities and that the life of the studier "is a *precarious* life of one who is neither the learner nor the student". Throughout the chapters Lewis shows that studying for Agamben is not reducible to education broadly conceived or learning more specifically but becomes "the zero-point for critically examining both the logic of necessity that characterizes the current age of biotechnological control and the proposed alternatives". What is exciting about this exploration – which Lewis describes as "returning the studier to a pure experience of im-potentiality" – is that it offers a radically different notion of educational freedom.

What makes this book powerful is not just the careful, detailed and creative way in which Lewis explores the different dimensions of the argument, but also the fact that he does so in discussion with a wide range of authors, both those 'located' more strongly within philosophy and philosophical writing and those 'located' more strongly in education and educational writing. There is therefore also the sign of a different way of doing philosophy of education, one that emerges more from the space in between both fields. In this sense the book provides a new direction in the philosophy of education in a number of ways and at a number of different levels, not in order to reach a firm conclusion but, as Lewis puts it, to bring us to a threshold "that returns us all back to the labyrinth for more tinkering".

Michael A. Peters and Gert Biesta

Acknowledgements

I would like to begin by thanking Gert Biesta and Michael Peters not only for including me in their book series but also for their ongoing support in general. I must also acknowledge the fundamental role that my ongoing dialogues with colleagues such as Jan Masschelein and Eduardo Duarte have played in the development of my thinking. While our understanding and appreciation for Agamben and for study differ in certain respects, these differences have pushed my thinking the most, catalyzing my deeper investigations into the mysteries of study. And finally, I would like to thank Anne Keefe (my wife, editor, and intellectual muse), Daniel Fisherman, David Backer, and Florelle D'Hoest for taking the time to read over early drafts of this manuscript. They were all, in their own ways, excellent study partners who gave generously, always seeing the potentiality in my writing.

I could not end here without also acknowledging my mother, Allyson Lewis, who always struggled to make sure I had the time and space to study. For this, she has been my most loyal supporter and my best teacher. With love, I dedicate this book to you.

Introduction

A reconsideration of im-potentiality

> Nothing makes us more impoverished and less free than this estrangement from impotentiality.
>
> Giorgio Agamben

> The law, if no longer practiced, but exclusively studied: this is the gate of justice.
>
> Walter Benjamin

Potentiality is an important educational concept that repeatedly appears in practice, policy, and theory. For instance, in practice, it is not uncommon to hear pre-service teachers, active practitioners, as well as parents, principals, and even university presidents make statements such as "I want to help students fulfill their unique potentials in life." Indeed, in a course which I regularly teach titled Philosophical Orientations to Education, one of the first assignments I have students write is a critical analysis of their own beliefs concerning the nature of education and its aims. Countless times, I have received essays that, in one form or another, endorse the widely held, common-sense view that education *should* help students realize or fulfill their individual potentials. In fact, a "good" teacher is someone who is capable of pinpointing a student's potential, and in turn, can help that student actualize this potential in relation to an educationally productive end.

This common-sense notion of potentiality is reiterated in a host of policies and in national debates concerning the broad aims of educational institutions. For instance, the rousing crescendo to the executive summary of George W. Bush's No Child Left Behind Act reads as follows: "In America, no child should be left behind. Every child should be educated to his or her full potential" (2001: 3). Similarly, when introducing his national educational reform strategy, Race to the Top, President Barack Obama made the following statement:

> America will not succeed in the 21st century unless we do a far better job of educating our sons and daughters ... And the race starts today. I am issuing a challenge to our nation's governors and school boards, principals

2 Introduction

and teachers, businesses and non-profits, parents and students: if you set and enforce rigorous and challenging standards and assessments; if you put outstanding teachers at the front of the classroom; if you turn around failing schools—your state can win a Race to the Top grant that will not only help students outcompete workers around the world, but let them fulfill their God-given potential.

(24 July 2009)

It would seem that any visionary statement concerning education must, at some point, gesture to the concept—no matter how vacuous—of fulfilling potentiality. In fact, the main charge repeatedly leveled against school systems often turns on precisely this point: education is not helping students fulfill their "God-given" potential. The simultaneous gesture toward both the secular economy and the sacred should not be overlooked in the above statement, for fulfilling potentiality is just as much an economic duty as it is a divine right. And it is education that must fulfill a task bordering somewhere between holy mystery and profane (if not crass) material competitiveness.

Symptomatic here is the *instrumentalization* of potentiality in educational reform movements in both the United States as well as across Europe. A major policy initiative in Great Britain titled 21st Century Skills: Realizing Our Potential states, "The aim of this national Skills Strategy is to ensure that employers have the right skills to support the success of their businesses, and individuals have the skills they need to be both employable and personally fulfilled" (Clarke 2003: 11). Within the skills framework, potentiality is linked directly to the question of economic viability and human capital. To realize one's potentiality is to actualize it in terms of a clearly identifiable skill set that serves an economic function within a globally competitive market. Potentiality is transformed into a commodity that is to be managed in order to be made productive for a predetermined, economically driven end. All potentiality that counts as potentiality must be translatable into utilizable skills. In other words, skills training and fulfilling potentiality become completely synonymous. Importantly, 21st Century Skills realizes that the learning of skills does not end with graduation. Rather, what is presented is a lifelong process. Thus we read that:

People are the key to a successful economy. We must put in place a framework that gives every young person a firm foundation and gives adults opportunities to develop their skills throughout their working lives. But learning and skills are not just about work or economic goals. They are also about the pleasure of learning for its own sake, the dignity of self-improvement, the achievement of personal potential and fulfillment, and the creation of a better society.

(Clarke 2003: 59)

Skill training is of national interest and of strategic importance for maintaining global competitiveness. Skills must be managed throughout one's entire life-cycle. This perpetual educational mandate for skills collapses economic ends, personal potential and fulfillment, and social improvement into one equation. As such the Skills Strategy offered here integrates productivity, social justice, and self-cultivation. There is no room for the possibility that potentiality might resist the process of managerial control and skill-based implementation, or that the pleasure of learning might not coincide with the fulfillment of potentiality in the form of measurable, identifiable, and commodifiable skills, or that social betterment might lie outside the framework of perpetuating a successful economy within global capitalism. While 21st Century Skills does provide a marginal nod toward the concept of learning for learning's sake, what is most interesting is that this activity is *only included as an exclusion* from personal growth or social justice.

And higher education is not immune to the discourse of potentiality either. This is especially true for vocational universities that target non-traditional, working-class students. For instance, ITT Technical Institute often employs the slogan "helping students reach their full potential" in a host of advertising media. Also, DeVry University's 2012 academic catalogue speaks directly to the hopes and aspirations of students in a struggling economy with these reassuring words: "The university is firmly committed to helping you reach your full career potential." While unemployment rates rise and economic recession seems to be a constant reality, these for-profit universities connect learning to employment as a sound marketing strategy for reaching students who have been reconceptualized as potential customers buying a product: their own potentiality sold back to them. Thus the question of potentiality and its consistent appearance in the marketing strategies of universities suggests that the contemporary crisis in higher education (Giroux 2007; Schrecker 2010) cannot be divorced from the desperate attempt to commodify and "put to work" the potentiality of the student. Indeed, *to be an educated person means to get the most out of one's potentiality*. In the current economic climate, educational institutions ranging from kindergarten to college are desperately attempting to harness potentiality as a means to another end, transforming it into a resource to be made productive.

If potentiality rests at the center of the debate that links together the economy, personal achievement/self-realization, and social betterment, then it is to the question of potentiality that we, as critical theorists, must turn in order to understand the educational logic of learning that now subsumes most if not all levels of schooling. Not only has learning come to colonize schools and universities, but it has extended its reach beyond these institutions, transforming society as a whole into a kind of schoolhouse and workers and citizens into perpetual learners who must be continually schooled and re-schooled in order to remain competitive and flexible on an open market. As such, questions of learning are not merely secondary or superstructural issues but lie at the very heart of the logic of biocapitalism. Stated differently, learning is *the educational logic of biocapitalism*. Drawing on the work of Clayton Pierce (2013), I argue that biocapitalism is a particular form of capitalism that does not depreciate or use-up one's labor power so much as continually invests in the production and

4 *Introduction*

reproduction of such power through a total integration of one's potentiality into an economic/learning structure that emphasizes continual reskilling in order to survive within competitive global markets. Within this logic, social and economic problems become *learning* problems, and, vice versa, learning problems become problems in the management or governmentality of social and economic systems to maximize productivity. One symptom of biocapitalism is the "quantified self movement." Conceptualized by entrepreneur Gareth MacLeod, this movement utilizes biotechnologies to transform one's life into a constant data stream to build a holist, personalized profile. Various apps are designed to monitor a variety of daily activities including brushing teeth, sleeping, sexual relations, mood, and so on. In this model, life becomes reducible to quantifiable numbers that can be compiled to facilitate the maximum output of our various potentialities. In other words, self-knowledge and self-study become forms of self-management and self-governance within an overall biotechnological framework concerned with optimization of life-resources.

The connections between governmentality of the self and learning in the contemporary moment have been articulated by Jan Masschelein and Maarten Simons, who argue that "the word 'learning' has come to be indispensable for speaking about ourselves, others, and society" (2008: 391). On this view, learning is not some sort of universal and necessary aspect of the human condition but rather a specific, historically contextual set of concepts, practices, and institutional norms. For Masschelein and Simons, the four fields that together form the intersecting dimensions of the learning apparatus of biocapitalism include "the necessity of learning for a knowledge economy, the importance of learning in order to guarantee freedom in a changing society, the educational expertise concerning learning and instruction, and the importance of the employability of learning results" (ibid.: 396). Stated simply, employees are now transformed into lifelong learners who must renew their skills in order to remain competitive within a flexible, knowledge-driven economy. Lifelong learning emphasizes perpetual reskilling in order to maximize self-actualization and ensure ongoing employability.

The decentralization and pluralization of learning sectors throughout civil society indicates a growing interest in learning as self-regulation and self-management, or, in Foucauldian terminology, the governmentality of the self. As with Foucault's description of neoliberalism, Masschelein and Simons describe how lifelong learning is part of a "withdrawal of the state" that shifts responsibility for governance to private individuals, thus transforming economic, political, or educational problems into individual problems. For Foucault, "educational investments" (2008: 229) by the neoliberal state transform us into entrepreneurial individuals who can organize our own learning for maximum economic outputs. The battery of tests that the individual undergoes throughout a lifetime help to identity, classify, train, and actualize untapped resources within the population. In sum, learning, as portrayed in a host of policies including 21st Century Skills, becomes "disconnected from issues of education and schooling" to become "a kind of capital, as something for which the learner him- or herself is responsible, as something that can and should be managed (and is the object of expertise), and as something that is employable" (Masschelein and Simons 2008: 402). Governmentality of the self for global, economic productivity works through the "freedom" of the self to regulate and manage its own process of reskilling through lifelong learning. In this sense, the quantified self movement is just one more appendage to the learning apparatus that remakes subjects into self-monitoring, entrepreneurial learners who must constantly *test* and *evaluate* their performance in order to maintain and/or improve their social and economic situations. In all cases, learning is *commanded* by the logic of biocapitalism—it is a command to the individual to *command his or herself* through willful production.

While Masschelein and Simons provide a penetrating analysis of the various discourses, practices, and institutional norms that collectively form the learning apparatus, they neglect the centrality of the question of potentiality within this schema. *Potentiality is what must be actualized over and over again through the learning of skills*. Learning is, in other words, the putting to work of potentiality in the name of self-actualization and economic viability. The investment into the self that is demanded in lifelong learning is an investment into the *capitalization of potentiality*. Learning has thus become a biotechnology for managing and measuring the nebulous force, power, or will of potentiality. While potentiality remains undefined in these documents, it is the *untapped reserve of creative energy* needed to expand the knowledge economy through the dual processes of employability and enterprising skills. Although vague, potentiality nevertheless has a certain *structure* that is absolutely essential for the omnipresent dominance of learning: it is a constituting "not yet" that "must be." Stated differently, the logic of the learning society is a logic of investment into economically profitable potentialities that must be actualized according to the needs of the market. Learning rules out the possibility of other possibilities, which must be canceled in order to maintain efficiency and productivity. While learning institutions often couple an optimization metric with the imperative to "stay flexible, and keep options open," these options are nevertheless the options dictated to the student by certain economic needs. Flexibility is therefore decoupled from potentiality that resists any predetermination. The logic of flexibility is more aptly phrased as "stay flexible, and keep options open, *as long as* these options are measurable, marketable, and ultimately profitable." Through the logic of learning, even flexibility becomes a kind of absolute necessity.

Yet the notion of potentiality as the "I will" of the self-initiating, self-regulating entrepreneur is highly limited. From *De Anima*, Giorgio Agamben argues that Aristotle enables us to think two kinds of potential: generic and effective. A generic conceptualization of potentiality explains how a child is able to grow up to be a particular type of person with a particular role in society (a statesman for example). Through education, the child suffers an "alteration (a becoming other) through learning" (Agamben 1999c: 179) where "the passage from the act implies an exhaustion and destruction of potential" (Agamben 2005b: 136). It is precisely this model of potentiality that currently

6 *Introduction*

informs discourses of the learning society, which emphasize investment into potentiality in order to fully actualize this potential in the form of constant measurement of performance outcomes. Here the ontology of the child is structured according to the strict logic of "not yet": not yet an adult, not yet a citizen, not yet a productive member of society. Thus the child must suffer an alteration through learning that destroys the "not yet" in order to fully actualize a latent potentiality for adulthood, citizenship, or productivity (i.e., transform the "not yet" into the necessity of the "must be" of the professional, employable adult). In all sectors of the learning society, emphasis is on measuring and quantifying the effects of learning inputs, including school accountability, university accreditation, economic performance, citizenship involvement, and so on. Yet to fully actualize potentiality is to destroy it, transforming a contingency into a necessity. As much as learning desires to constantly replenish potentiality for the never-ending extraction of its powers, nevertheless, its very logic attempts to continually deny the gap between potentiality and actuality by insisting on constant surveillance and evaluation of performance. In this schema, potentiality becomes subordinate to actuality—it is in some senses what makes the actual possible but also what must be eliminated in order for the passage to the act to be complete and for the learner to rightfully take a place within the allotted order of things (either in relation to the economic, the political, or the social). To fulfill potentiality is to destroy it in the name of efficiency and effectiveness, *commanding and controlling* the possibilities offered by potentiality according to a sovereign logic (the logic of biocapitalism). The contingencies of potentiality are what must be sacrificed in order for the child to learn x skills for x purposes predetermined in advance by experts in the field of educational research and economic development. The result is a notion of the human as capable of only a select few behaviors, skills, and actions easily assignable to a specific function within the overall division of labor. In other words, the logic of learning is anchored in an ontology of generic potentiality as a "not yet" that "must be" made manifest in measurably determinate, socially useful, and economically manageable skill sets. Learning, in short, concerns *deadlines*—or lines that end with the death of potentiality. Tests are therefore grave markers—not markers of what has passed out of actuality but rather of what *has passed into actuality*.

The problem of the learner's subjectivity is the direct result of an ontology of generic potentiality that constantly transforms the "not yet" into the "must be." Rather than producing a subject within a meaningful world of actions, apparatuses of learning result in a special kind of *desubjectification*. At first this may seem paradoxical, for discourses and practices of learning seem to emphasize self-motivation, self-directed action, and self-management. Yet the emphasis on the self within the learning society speaks to an underlying *crisis* in the very self that is constantly being commanded to self-actualize its latent potentiality. For Agamben, desubjectification is a process informed by the dual logics of necessity and impossibility. When fused together, these logics "divide potentiality from impotentiality" (Agamben 2002: 147). In other words, desubjectification is a process that insists on the world *as it is* (necessity) and that alternatives *cannot possibly occur* (impossibility). The subject is captured as a resource for the world; his or her choices become nothing more than reflexes of the needs of the world to replicate itself. It is my contention that learning is the first initiation into the rituals of desubjectification. Agamben writes, "What defines the apparatuses that we have to deal with in the current phase of capitalism is that they no longer act as much through the production of a subject, as through the processes of what can be called desubjectification" (2009b: 21). Agamben then proceeds to give the example of the cell phone apparatus. "He who lets himself be captured by the 'cellular phone' apparatus," warns Agamben, "cannot acquire a new subjectivity, but only a number through which he can, eventually be controlled" (ibid.). Although this example seems to be rather trite if not reactionary, it reveals that contemporary processes of desubjectification are inscribed into the most mundane aspects of everyday life. Through control and capture, the world takes on the appearance of necessity and impossibility. Within the learning apparatus, desubjectification reduces students to nothing but impersonal data points to be aggregated and disaggregated according to standardized matrixes of measure. The result is an "identity without an identity" (Agamben 2011b: 52), or a desubjectification of the student as an irreducibly unique singularity to a statistical fact, an abstract quantity of human capital, or a generic skill set of an entrepreneurial self.

Opposed to the reductive notion of generic potentiality and the resulting desubjectification of the student, Agamben argues that there is a second notion of potentiality in Aristotle's work that can be referred to as "effective potentiality" in that it represents a "conservation of potential in the act and something like the giving of potentiality to itself" (2005b: 136). This is the type of potentiality that interests Agamben the most. Those who have knowledge are *in potential*, meaning that they equally have the capability to bring knowledge into actuality and *not* bring knowledge into actuality. Agamben then gives the example of an architect who "is in potential insofar as he has the potential to not-build, the poet the potential to not-write poems" (1999c: 179). By conserving itself, potential remains impotential (*impotenza*). *Im-potentiality* (which indicates the symbiotic relation between potential and impotential) is not simply impotence, but is an active capability for not-doing or not-being. Agamben summarizes: im-potentiality is the "*capability* of the act in not realizing it" (1998: 45) and thus "permits human beings to accumulate and freely master their own capacities, to transform them into 'faculties'" (2011b: 44). Rather than a stumbling block that must be continually denied, repressed, or overcome, Joanne Faulkner argues that Agamben's theory of im-potentiality "refers not simply to incapacity but rather to a being-able that abstains from doing" (2010: 205) that permits a new relation to one's own impotency. Rather than a simple lack or deficit, im-potentiality is a privation in the sense that im-potentiality means one has potential but prefers not to actualize it in any specific form. Thus, all theories of potentiality must also and equally be theories of the impotential, for it is im-potential that enables freedom to flourish—not the freedom of "I will" as a

8   *Introduction*

power of self-production according to economic imperatives or socially predetermined norms so much as an ontological openness to new possibilities.

In fact, it is the giving of potentiality to itself that is the experience of freedom. Agamben writes, "Here it is possible to see how the root of freedom is to be found in the abyss of potentiality . . . To be free is, in the sense we have seen, *to be capable of one's own impotentiality*" (1999c: 183). What makes us human, according to Agamben, is precisely the capability to *not* be, to remain im-potential. It is this paradoxical existence that opens history to contingency—to the potential to act otherwise or to be otherwise. Evil in this sense is derivative of a flight from an indetermining im-potentiality into the logic of pure or complete actualization for a predetermined end (complete necessity). It is a denial of the constitutive link between growth and impotence. Citing Agamben, "Evil is only our inadequate reaction when faced with this demonic element [our impotential], our fearful retreat from it in order to exercise—founding ourselves in this flight—some power of being" (1993a: 31–32). Thus enabling students to experience their potential means that they must be given the chance to experience their impotence, their capability not to be. In the learning society, education has become obsessed with the measure of what someone *can do* in order to fulfill a particular role within the economy, yet for Agamben, this obsession with assessment and verification of actualization is itself a form of evil that destroys our freedom to be *rather than* precisely because it denies our ontological indeterminacy. His theory of im-potentiality enables us to think of potentiality against the logic of learning, which reduces potentiality to a "not yet" that actualizes itself in a "must be." Indeed, im-potentiality does not simply separate potentiality from impotentiality (thus sacrificing contingency for necessity, possibility for impossibility), rather it recognizes that the subject emerges precisely in the gap that separates and binds together opposite forces in the atopic space existing between desubjectification and subjectification. If learning separates, rendering processes of desubjectification and subjectification "indifferent" (Agamben 2009b: 21), then a new notion of the educational subject is necessary that does not divide but rather sutures together negative and positive poles of subject formation. This new process would mean overcoming the apparent necessity of learning and the impossibility or infeasibility of alternatives.

We can now summarize Agamben's critique of neoliberal democracy—and in turn the discourse and practice of learning in all its manifestations (from 21st Century Skills to the quantified self movement). The problem with neoliberalism is that

> today's man believes himself capable of everything, and so he repeats his jovial "no problem," and his irresponsible "I can do it," precisely when he should instead realize that he has been consigned in unheard of measures to forces and processes over which he has lost all control. He has become blind not to his capacities but to his incapacities, not to what he can do but to what he cannot, or can not, do.
>
> (Agamben 2011b: 44)

Introduction   9

It is this Promethean hubris that bothers Agamben—a hubris that is also found in the biocapitalist logic of infinite expansion and profit generation. In the short aphorism "The Idea of Communism," Agamben argues that neoliberal democracy and pornography share a similar form of evil: the empty promise of total fulfillment and gratification of our desires. Agamben writes, "naturally it is not a matter here of fulfilling something; nothing is more boring than a man who has fulfilled his own dreams: this is the insipid social-democratic zealousness of pornography" (1995: 75). The lie of contemporary democratic hubris as well as pornography is that happiness can be and must be fulfilled. Hubris is therefore founded upon the necessity of what is ("Whatever flaws may exist in the current social, economic, or educational system, we can fix them!") and the impossibility of what could be otherwise than ("All social, economic, or educational revolutions end in disaster so it is best to focus on what is possible within the system we have").

This is the very same hubris that, in the learning apparatus, argues that children should maximize their activity and in turn "pull themselves up by their own bootstraps" through a self-initiated entrepreneurialism, that university students should accommodate themselves to the forces of the market rather than pursue a "useless" degree in the humanities, that laborers should become "self-training" and "self-evaluating" employees, and that citizens should engage in constant data collection, thus transforming their lives into resources for willful self-control and reinvention. Such theories impoverish politics and education precisely in the moment they estrange us from im-potentiality, cleaving potentiality from impotentiality, subjectification from desubjectification, possibility from impossibility. These theories of entrepreneurial optimism in the capacity to self-realize, self-generate, and self-manage our potential so as to manifest it in the form of an economically viable commodity (human capital) are not empowering so much as disempowering theories that deny the very real freedom of im-potentiality—our *capability* to be otherwise, to think otherwise, to live otherwise. This does not mean that learners are reduced to a pure lack or gap, but rather that they become a generic potentiality subjected to relentless actualization according to the necessities of market control and institutional capture. In their constant quest for actualization of latent potentiality, markets strangle the im-potentiality of the student and thus leave the student without a sense of freedom.

Although policies such as No Child Left Behind, Race to the Top, 21st Century Skills, and a host of for-profit, technical universities all seek inclusion through equal access to a broad array of learning tools, impotentiality does not simply disappear when it is cleaved from its primordial relation to potentiality. Rather than recognize the failures of the market and the limitations of neoliberal democratic government as internal manifestations of a constitutive impotence, impotentiality is projected outward onto the radical other. For Faulkner, this means that third-world children in particular become the screen onto which developed countries project their own internal anxieties. Faulkner writes, "Children in the developing world—whose material circumstances

10   Introduction

cannot support our fantasies of childhood innocence—are ignored, a source of embarrassment to our prosperity" (2010: 208). Thus if the learning society submits a child's im-potential to the rule of actualization, then the disavowed impotential is subsequently projected outward onto the vulnerable other whose fate remains forever a source of humanitarian paternalism and deferred anxiety over the contingencies of our own fragile economic and political systems. The obscene logic at work in such cases is not one of investment into the potentialities of entrepreneurial selves, but rather systematic, educational abandonment (also see Lewis 2006).

If Faulkner focuses on the global South, we could just as easily turn to poor minority children in inner-city schools in the United States in order to witness a similar phenomenon. In such schools, the dominant logic is not one of investment into the potentialities of entrepreneurial selves, but rather systematic abandonment that attempts to drain life of its educational supplement (Lewis 2006). Pedro Noguera (2009) argues that social, economic, and political forces have resulted in diminishing educational returns for poor African American boys in particular. According to Noguera, African American boys are now more likely than other groups to (a) be suspended or expelled from school, (b) classified as "mentally retarded" and placed in special education classes, and (c) absent from honors courses. In turn, Black males tend to internalize low expectations and thus identify with and enact behaviors that reinforce their academic "failure." In short, neoliberal society effectively manages anxieties concerning its own impotence by projecting it onto the internally excluded other: African American boys. But what is important to note is that this is not simply the projection of a lack or gap. High-stakes testing, zero-tolerance policies, and teachers and administrators who lack commitments to the multicultural, low-income communities they serve constantly demand that African American boys *actualize their impotence* through policies and procedures that create a self-fulfilling prophesy. In other words, "the trouble with Black boys" (as Noguera argues) is not that they are simply reduced to a lack or gap and thus made dependent on the schoolmaster, but rather that they are burdened with the responsibility to compensate for the anxieties of the learning society by self-actualizing the system's own internal impotence. Rather than correct their potentialities by maximizing outputs, schools impose an impossible mandate: to maximize one's own failure. They become the most radical actualization of impossibility ("these kids can't be saved") and of necessity ("there are no viable options remaining besides dropping out") within the learning apparatus. As Michelle Fine calls them, such students join the anonymous rank and file of the "disappeared" (1991: 24) or, in Agamben's language, *desubjectified* others who are sacrificed by a learning apparatus that can only operate through their internal exclusion. The result is an *ontological* educational division between those who are burdened with the task of carrying the social system's disavowed impotence and those who are burdened with the task of realizing the very same system's over-inflated hubris. For those included and excluded, freedom is no longer an educational possibility, for only in the moment of "I can, I cannot" does the student recognize the contingency of a life to be *rather than* what it is or will become. This fundamental ontological splitting through a bifurcated educational system is therefore nothing less than evil.

In response to these conditions, the goal should not be to "fulfill one's true potentiality" for fulfillment itself is part of the lie of capitalist hubris that always sacrifices impotentiality, contingency, and thus possibility. In fact, Agamben argues that freedom has little to do with fulfillment. The moment of redemption "means that the unfulfilled is what remains" (2007b: 34). Instead of projecting the remnant of the unfulfilled onto the educational other (those labeled as failing or at risk), or temporally displacing fulfillment into a utopian future, education should recognize in the unfulfilled a new kind of freedom, a new kind of student, and a new practice. As such, the remnant of the unfulfilled rudely interrupts the narratives of progressive development that inform economic as well as educational plans—plans that force potentiality into recognizable forms and functions thus denying the ontological indeterminacy of the human. For Agamben, the obstinate refusal of the unfulfilled to participate in either evolution or progress

> is why we do not want new works of art or thought; we don't want another epoch of culture and society: what we want is to save the epoch and society from their wandering in tradition, to grasp the *good*—undeferrable and non-epochal—which was contained in them.
>
> (1995: 88)

This book will be a rethinking of potentiality, and thus an attempt to reconnect im-potentiality with a practice of education beyond the logic of biocapitalism. While Agamben draws our attention to the centrality of im-potentiality within politics, ontology, and literary theory, he only makes a passing gesture toward the theme of education. Yet this does not mean that education is unimportant for Agamben. Indeed, we could think of education as the *unthought* potentiality of his own thinking. Returning to Agamben's oeuvre with a certain sensitivity to educational themes, we immediately recognize the veiled problem of education in many places. For instance, in *Infancy and History: On the Destruction of Experience* (2007a) as well as *The Man Without Content* (1999b), Agamben concerns himself largely with the issue of cultural transmissibility, and in particular, the role of the child in this process. If transmission of cultural values was once a clear task, especially for the arts, then in the modern era such transmission is no longer guaranteed, and we are faced with the accumulation of meaningless data, objects, and things that compile without significance. Such a condition seems to be indicative of the vast databases of information collected by Google just as much as the seemingly arbitrary nature of information to be learned for standardized testing in schools—knowledge students are forced to learn even though it has lost all meaning or significance. Could we not make the argument that the crisis in transmissibility highlighted by Agamben is symptomatic of a society obsessed with learning and testing? The desperate

12   *Introduction*

attempt to ensure transmission through high-stakes testing merely conceals the inability to actually transmit any sense of *what should matter* to us. The question of transmission, which preoccupied much of Agamben's early literary writings, is thus just as much educational as it is aesthetic.

A tentative answer to the question of transmissibility can be found in Agamben's marginal comments on the experience of *studying*. Briefly summarized, studying is an "interminable" and "rhythmic" activity that not only loses a sense of its own end but, more importantly, "does not even desire one" (Agamben 1995: 64). The studier seems suspended in a state of oscillation between sadness and inspiration, of moving forward and withdrawing from certain aims, subjectification and desubjectification. Thus, studying emerges as a kind of im-potential state of educational being that interrupts any notion of educational "growth" or educational "realization" of latent potentialities found in either learning discourses or progressive responses to learning. If we think of learning as oriented towards the measurability of determinate, reliable skill sets, studying suddenly appears to be a "useless" activity, devoid of quantifiable significance in the life of the student. And if we think of progressive education as a kind of willful pursuit of one's interests and desires in the name of self-determined subjectification, then studying, which does not desire ends and thus appears to be indifferent, seems rather odd, if not anti-educational. Studying is a paradoxical state between education for subjectification and learning for desubjectification, between possibility and impossibility, between contingency and necessity. Studying is most properly understood as a *remnant of education* that exists between these possibilities, and the life of the studier is a *precarious* life of one who is neither the learner nor the student. As I will explore in detail throughout the chapters of this book, studying for Agamben is not reducible to education broadly conceived or learning more specifically. Indeed, studying is not simply one of many, but, in my extrapolation of Agamben's comments, becomes the zero-point for critically examining both the logic of necessity that characterizes the current age of biotechnological control and the proposed alternatives. It does so by returning the studier to a pure experience of im-potentiality, which offers a radically different notion of educational freedom. This paradoxical freedom (a freedom of indetermination) is a challenge to conceptualize precisely because it interrupts educational expectations, suspending definable outcomes indefinitely. Indeed, to think of studying is to think beyond not only learning but also limitations in the various educational alternatives that are incapable of meeting the radical demands of freedom in the face of current threats. The uniqueness of the subject, the activity, and the methods of study all demand treatment of their own. It is to this end that I have enlisted Agamben's assistance—even if this assistance is, in the last instance, impotent.

In this manner, Agamben can be placed within a broader genealogy of the theme of study that has had an underground presence in educational philosophy for years and is now emerging as a concern for interdisciplinary humanities more generally. In his classic essay "Toward a place for study in a world of instruction" (1971), Robert McClintock provided a genealogical warning against the educational trends that have culminated in policy such as 21st Century Skills. From philosophers including Socrates, Montaigne, Erasmus, and others, McClintock undermines what he sees as the dominant threat to education in the modern era: learning. He laments:

> Rarely does one hear that study is the *raison d'etre* of an educational institution; teaching and learning is now what it is all about, and with this change, has come a change in the meaning of the venerable word "learning." Once it described what a man acquired as a result of serious study, but now it signifies what one received as a result of good teaching.
>
> (1971: 179)

In other words, learning becomes the activity of submitting one's potentiality to the "paternal instruction" (ibid.: 180) of the teacher. The key question for the instructor becomes "what *ought* to be learned" so as to achieve x outcomes rather than "what opportunities for study *ought* to be offered?" (ibid.: 187). Without this second line of questioning, the relation between education and freedom is effectively severed, and the question of education becomes reduced to the mere tallying up of a student's powers in relation to pressing economic and social realities.

As students in Germany recently proclaimed "We are no human capital!", we can begin to understand the political and economic dimensions of learning. Masschelein and Simons argue

> the term "students" has become synonymous with the resources to be exploited, the talents to be mobilized, the object of investment, the guarantee of a country's competitiveness or, when addressing the possible disobedient component of human capital, the customers to be seduced.
>
> (2011: 165)

Against this backdrop, students are protesting the collapse of education into the educational logic of biocapitalism, and proclaiming that they are not merely vocational potentialitites. For Masschelein and Simons, this means a recuperation of studying as "free time" (ibid.: 167) within the public space of the university. As opposed to the student as "not yet" (the employee, the citizen) who "must be" (this or that subject with x, y, and z skills), the student should be rethought of as the one who studies without determinate ends, without identifiable interests, and thus one who is open, exposed, and attentive to the world (Masschelein and Simons 2009). In a world of quotas, bottom lines, and instrumental calculations, the student is the political figure par excellence: the one who suspends the underlying educational logic of the system of biocapitalism.

In a special issue of *Polygraph* dedicated to the question of the fate of the university and of the student in contemporary society, editors Luka Arsenjuk and Michelle Koerner further argue against the categorization of the student as a depoliticized educational consumer and/or indentured servant who is

14 Introduction

submitted to a host of administrative and managerial discourses and practices. If the protests of May 1968 have taught us a political lesson, it is that the figure of the student is not simply a sociological category to be managed, but the name of a political dissensus. Drawing on a host of contemporary theorists concerned with the "student crisis" in the United States, Arsenjuk and Koerner ponder the emergence of a new form of educational logic that harkens back to McClintock's genealogy of study. They write,

> Study . . . would not be reducible to the accumulation of information, to the current organization of knowledge, or to the logic of professionalization that governs so many of our activities in the University. Study would instead name those "unprofessional activities" of thought and experimentation that leave one intoxicated, those moments of encountering in a text or conversation that blow one's mind, driven by curiosities that are closer to pleasure, to play, to wandering, to leaving work. From here it becomes possible to further disengage the figure of the student from the docile consumer or the inert product of the University and provide an additional definition of a "student": a student is not only an exploited and invisible worker, a person in debt, but also someone who *struggles to study*. Or even, as our favorite dictionary definition of the student has it: a student as someone "addicted to study" . . . [and] study [is] an activity of sabotage and refusal of . . . the dominant form of capitalist production today: governance.
>
> (2009: 8–9)

To struggle to study is to struggle to regain the freedom of im–potentiality as a capability to be *and* not to be any one kind of subject. It is to reject the fundamental logic of necessity (economic, educational, or otherwise) for the political expression of contingency—an expression that undermines learning at all levels of the educational apparatus of biocapitalism from primary school to higher education and beyond.

If we simply remain mired in the discourse and practice of learning, studying remains a burden, and the goal becomes an attempt to overcome this latency period as quickly as possible through the constituting act. Thus there is a rush to meet national standards through testing ("we have to meet standards *now* so that you can become productive citizens!") or there is a rush to close the gap between education and political praxis ("we have to act *now* in order to change the world!") or there is the rush to finish the dissertation ("the only good dissertation is a done dissertation!") or there is a rush to transform self-study into a quantifiable stream of data ("the only way to maximize my happiness is to build a statistical model of my daily practices!") or there is the need to become revolutionary vanguards ("now is the time for action, not studying!"). In these perspectives, studying is an obstacle, an irritant, an infuriating reality whose only utility is its instrumental value for reaching another end. This apparent urgency erases the equally urgent need to study in order to rekindle inspiration out of its rhythms and its sadness. Inspiration is a state of suspension that has "joyously forgotten its goal" (Agamben 2007b: 86) to become this or that in order to sustain a relation of immanence with its own im-potentiality. It is in this sense that Agamben should be recognized along with McClintock and others as a central figure in the ongoing struggle to define the im-political politics of studying.

In the chapters that follow, I will further explore the implicit potentiality of studying as a radical alternative to the educational logic of biocapitalism. To accomplish this task, I will continue to situate Agamben within educational theory and practice. Although Agamben's notes on study are sparse, his emphasis on the connections between study, im-potentiality, messianic time and space and freedom are provocative precisely because they offer an invitation to think through the ontological, temporal, spatial, aesthetic, and political dimensions of study. Through a comparison with other philosophers and theorists of education, I will demonstrate how educational philosophy has reproduced the very logic of learning, leaving little space for the practice of studying to emerge with any degree of clarity or precision. At stake here is the need to carve out of the super-saturated learning landscape of biocapitalism the various locations and temporalities of study as they appear when children tinker with trash, when friends dialogue, when lone individuals suddenly become lost in reverie, when students gather in public spaces to experience collective becoming without definitive end. In this sense, I hope to expand the notion of study beyond the university scholar and his or her scholastic activities to include a host of studiers and variations of study. These are the liminal practices of study that open to a *coming education*, one that refuses to submit to the command of biocapitalism: "Learn!" or "Be all that you can be!"

In the pages that follow, I argue that studying redeems desubjectivation, opening up to a new notion of an educational community that does not define itself in terms of interests, skills, or capability but rather a form of life that remains between necessity and contingency, impossibility and possibility, I can and I cannot. To study is ultimately to study the appearance of an im-potentiality that refuses to be managed, optimized, commodified, controlled or captured, and ultimately fulfilled through a social orthopedic or economic or institutional imperative. To study is to undo the knot tying learning to the aims of instruction and the modalities of measure that transform our potentiality into abstract data recognizable only to the apparatuses of standardization and learning. In its profanation, the dispersed and decentered apparatuses of learning are left to idle, and thus opened to unforeseen usages beyond measure and beyond identification with this or that utility within a market driven by entrepreneurial self-management. In this sense, to study is to live an educationally profane life without end.

1 From being willful to being more willing

There is a persistent theme in modern, Western educational philosophy: the centrality of the will for overcoming inequality and alienation. From Rousseau onward, the will becomes a central issue for educational philosophy and practice. It is both a problem (how to direct the will) and a solution to multiple problems, including the problem of self-determination, attention, and so on. In this chapter, I first attempt to provide a very brief genealogy of the will that illustrates its pervasiveness. In order to historicize the will—and in particular the educational variants of willful thought and action—I will turn to Heidegger and his critical distinction between willfulness and willingness. For Heidegger, being-in-the-world is radically historical, thus different epochs of being open up new understandings, meanings, roles, and practices that define a culture and a civilization. Throughout many of his later writings, Heidegger repeatedly emphasizes that the rise in importance in the will is a symptom of certain transformations in the nature of being-in-the-world related to the nihilistic effects of technological enframing. When educational philosophy insists on the priority of the will as a psychological ground, it fails to take into account how the insistence on the will is itself a *metaphysical commitment* to the very logic of the technological (or biotechnological) age. What is most important to note is that this metaphysical dimension is not restricted to any one field of educational philosophy, any one school of thought, or any one particular political agenda. Rather, we find its residue in the most progressive forms of pragmatism and the most critical of radical pedagogies (that is, we can think of everyone from Kant to Nietzsche as theorizing the relationship between education, will, freedom, and power). As such, the will becomes a kind of global logic that, even as it stands before us, remains unable to account for its own historical specificity, and is therefore ignorant of its complacency with a current tendency toward nihilism.

After tracing this genealogy of the will through various canonical figures in the history of educational philosophy and theory—including Rousseau, William James, and Jacques Rancière (an incomplete list, but a representative one)—I will turn to possible alternatives to education as "willful production" (of the self, of the world, of social relations, and so on). There are those, such as Hubert Dreyfus and Sean Dorrance Kelly (2011), who suggest that in the face of nihilism, we must reassert a sense of the sacred. From this perspective, what is needed is a return to the classics of Western philosophy and culture to sensitize the reader to the existence of residual sacredness on the margins of these texts. Instead of reducing education to a meaningless resource to be consumed, education in this model becomes a human activity for (a) cultivating sensitivities to meaning-rich affordances and (b) offering thanks for these affordances. In terms of educational philosophy, Dreyfus and Kelly would suggest reading beyond the theme of the will (a negative project of critique) in order to listen for traces of the sacred that lie below the level of subjective powers of personal invention and meaning-making (a positive project of rehabilitation). Yet, as I will argue below, this strategy is lacking in one significant respect: the current technological epoch is not simply an obstacle to be overcome but is also an opening to im-potentiality. Here, I gesture toward the theme of study which is perhaps best articulated in the work of Agamben. As stated in the introduction, studying is an "interminable" activity that not only loses a sense of its own end but, more importantly, "does not even desire one" (Agamben 1995: 64). The studier seems suspended in a state of oscillation between sadness and inspiration, of moving forward and withdrawing from certain aims. Thus, studying emerges as a kind of im-potential state of educational being that interrupts any notion of educational "growth" or educational "realization" of willful self-production and does not rely on any notion of the sacred to redeem Western culture. If we think of progressive education as a kind of willful pursuit of one's interests and desires in the name of growth and personal transformation, then studying, which does not desire ends and thus appears to be indifferent, seems rather odd, if not anti-educational. Yet in an age of what Heidegger refers to as "ontological leveling" where meanings have been suspended and the world does not call human beings to take up significant practices that precede the entrepreneurial will, it is through studying that this pervasive darkness can be turned into a kind of infancy or new beginning *without* recourse to the practice of willful production or existential care for that which shines. At stake here is what Heidegger sees as a distinction between willful pursuit and willing receptivity to im-potentiality. The care exhibited in study through this receptivity is not for this or that result but for im-potentiality as such. It is my wager that studying is a significant educational practice that can attune us to the *significance of a loss of significance* in our technological age, for only with the loss of significance can we care for im-potentiality in and for itself, freed from any particular end.

Genealogy of the will

What follows is not an exhaustive genealogy of the will in educational philosophy, nor does my analysis of individual philosophers have great depth. The function of this genealogy is very simple and straightforward: it is meant to illustrate a certain continuity of theme across progressive and critical philosophies of education. This coherence is not the result of any ontological reality of the will as a biological fact or universal existential structure. Rather, as I will show in the next section, coherency is produced in the wake of epochal shifts in the nature of being-in-the-world, and as such, is fully historical. The meaning and nature of willing for the following educational philosophers cannot be taken as a neutral starting point, but as a heavily invested, and thus contestable claim concerning the nature of being arising out of a given set of circumstances and assumptions that, in the end, are connected directly to the rise of technology and capitalist production. But before examining the larger phenomenological background out of which the problematic of willful production emerges, I would like to provide a glimpse at the consistent priority granted to the will in multiple educational philosophies spanning several centuries.

The will as the ground of education is perhaps first described in Rousseau's *Emile: Or, On Education*. In fact, the pedagogical problematic of *Emile* is nothing less than the problem of will and willful action. Although Rousseau argues that we are all born "devoid of knowledge and of will" (1979: 61), it is the relation between the two that forms the fulcrum of early childhood education. Thus the first lessons the child learns concern willful action and freedom. Rousseau writes of the infant,

> Prepare from afar the reign of his freedom and the use of his forces by leaving natural habit to his body, by putting him in the conditions always to be master of himself and in all things to do his will, as soon as he has one.
> (ibid.: 63)

The exercise of the will is absolutely essential for maintaining nature's true path: that humans be free and self-determinating. It is key that in the above quotation, the authority of the tutor is never exerted over the child in any immediate way. Rather it must always prepare experiences for the child "from afar" so that the appearance of freedom remains absolute from the first-person, engaged perspective of the child. But as the will grows, the power of the will must be constantly circumscribed so as never to command anyone or anything except the voluntary actions of the child as he or she learns to master the world. For instance, Rousseau warns that when the child cries for an object, the tutor must be careful not to carry the object to the child but rather to carry the child to the object.

> It is important to accustom him early not to give orders either to men, for he is not their master, or to things, for they do not hear him. Thus when a child desires something that he sees and one wants to give it to him, it is better to carry the child to the object than to bring the object to the child.
> (ibid.: 66)

Two important points are raised in this example. First, carrying the child to the object empowers the sense of the child's will to reach out and grasp the world, to bring the world into focus/nearness through his or her embodied actions.

Second, the will of the child must be cultivated yet at the same time it cannot over-reach its prescribed boundaries. If the will is overextended to ordering things and people then the lesson of freedom will be lost on the child. Instead of an active, self-regulating, self-realizing subject, the tyrannical child will simply order others to do his bidding. The lesson learned here contradicts the self-sufficiency of nature. If the free man for Rousseau "wants only what he can do and does what he pleases" (ibid.: 84) then the tyrannical man imposes his will on others in order to do what he cannot yet do for himself, creating chains of inappropriate dependencies that break the laws of natural man. Stated differently, the free man knows how to extend the will without over-extending desires. Without this equilibrium between the power of the will and desire, the child will be perpetually unhappy. Rousseau writes, "He is a despot. He is at once the most vile of slaves and the most miserable of creatures" (ibid.: 87). Although superficially the master of his surroundings, the overly willful child actually is a slave to his abundant desires and to the work of others to satiate these desires. The result of an over-extension of desire and an accompanying misdirection of the will is thus slavery and sadness rather than freedom and happiness.

The authority of the tutor, as hinted at above, can never be imposed on the child directly. If the problematic for the child is the relation between will, desire, and freedom, then the problematic for the tutor concerns will and authority. The will of the tutor must remain absolute without ever taking on the guise of authority over the child. Rousseau warns,

> Command him nothing, whatever in the world it might be, absolutely nothing. Do not even allow him to imagine that you might pretend to have any authority over him. Let him know only that he is weak and you are strong, that by his condition and yours he is necessarily at your mercy.
>
> (1979: 91)

In this sense, lessons come from the experience of necessity rather than from the command of the tutor. The battle of wills must remain exactly as it is: a battle of forces rather than of intellectual persuasions or machinations of political power/negotiations. By hiding authority, the tutor is able to perfect the appearance of freedom which conceals a deeper set of temporary dependencies. In a rather Machiavellian move, Rousseau urges tutors to "let him always believe he is the master, and let it always be you who are. There is no subjection so perfect as that which keeps the appearance of freedom. Thus the will itself is made captive" (ibid.: 120). Authority must remain absolutely invisible to the student in order to safeguard the appearance of freedom. If freedom is conforming to what one *ought* to do rather than merely what one *desires* to do, this distinction must be safeguarded by the tutor who "from afar" dictates the nature and order of the student's experiences according to the ultimate authority of nature itself. In conclusion, hiding authority ensures that "leaving him thus master of his will, you will not be fomenting his caprices" (ibid.: 120). When force between tutor and student is the only operating factor, there is no strict hierarchy between the two, no inequality based on the authority of the one over the other. Indeed, Rousseau describes his relation to Emile as one of friendship—granted a friendship that does not erase the operations of the will but rather recognizes them as natural and necessary outcomes of one's developmental stage. In this manner, Emile will be free from all inequalities, all forms of oppression, and all forms of hierarchy. The key to social reconstruction hinges of the correct relationship between wills in the educational relationship.

The centrality of the will is, in essence, an educational embodiment of Rousseau's larger metaphysical claims. As discussed in Book IV of *Emile* in the dialogue with the Savoy Vicar, Rousseau argues that

> The more I observe the action and the reaction of the forces of nature acting on one another, the more I find that one must always go back from effects to some will as first cause; for to suppose an infinite regress of causes is to suppose no cause at all. In a word, every motion not produced by another can come only from a spontaneous, voluntary action. Inanimate bodies act only by motion, and there is no true action without will. This is my first principle. I believe therefore that a will moves the universe and animates nature. This is my first dogma, or my first article of faith.
>
> (1979: 273)

Although Rousseau cannot explain how a free, voluntary, spontaneous will comes to produce a physical action, the experience of volition is enough to give his materialist metaphysics all the "proof" necessary to transform speculation into a dogma. And it is this dogma that, in retrospect, informed much of Rousseau's theory of early childhood education. In both cases, freedom can only be secured through a benevolent will. If Rousseau argues that "the world is governed by a powerful and wise will" (ibid.: 276) it appears as though his educational philosophy follows the same fundamental principle: the tutor must also be such a powerful and wise will—a will that binds the will of the student to nature's path "from afar" in order for the student to ultimately come to see freedom as a first principle or irrefutable law of nature. Thus for Rousseau, the relationship of humanity to God is identical to the relationship between the student and the tutor. In both cases a benevolent will intervenes from the outside to gently guide the individual toward natural autonomy and freedom that would otherwise be sacrificed. The question of the relationship of wills between men and women (which concludes *Emile*) as well as the question of the general will in Rousseau's political writings fall under a similar problematic. Indeed, Rousseau's metaphysical commitments reach a certain plateau in his formulation of the "general will" that transcends and stands above the "will of all." In all cases, the will is the unquestioned metaphysics of educational, social, political, and theological relationships.

Like Rousseau, William James speaks of the fundamental centrality of the will to education, and, like Rousseau, transforms a materialist, psychological

From being willful to being more willing 21

perspective into a metaphysical principle that cannot be justified through either science or rational argumentation. For James, the will

> designates our entire capacity for impulsive and active life, including our instinctive reactions and those forms of behavior that have become secondarily autonomic and semi-unconscious through frequent repetition. In the narrower sense, acts of will are such acts only as cannot be inattentively performed.
>
> (1992: 808)

In order to give specificity to the will and its various functions, James proceeds to designate two modalities of the will: the precipitate and obstructed wills. When sundered, the precipitate will results in the immediate and unchecked actions of the maniac. And if the obstructed will is never accompanied by the attending capacity for impulsive actions, then the result is equally undesirable: the lethargy of the melancholic. It then follows that for James, the "highest form of character" is indeed "full of scruples and inhibitions" while at the same time "far from being paralyzed, will succeed in energetically keeping on its way, sometimes overpowering the resistances, sometimes steering along the line where they lie thinnest" (ibid.: 813).

The application of these basic observations to teaching is of the utmost importance for James. The teacher, he speculates, often comes into contact with what he refers to as the "balky will" (James 1992: 814) of the student. Such students lack the precipitate will to remain on task because interest is lacking in a given subject or because their initiate efforts were met with failure rather than success. Rather than act to "break the will" of the child and make him or her submit to a willful command, the teacher should instead divert the mind temporarily, leading the student gently back to the task at hand, only this time through an indirect rout. The duty of the teacher becomes clear. Not only must teachers supply students with a plethora of ideas in order to build mental associations, but also to deftly manage the precarious relation between modalities of the will: paralysis must never overly inhibit action, and action must never completely discharge itself without first referencing the stock of inhibitions by which social norms function and maintain civil relations. But what is perhaps most unique and challenging in James's description of the will and its central importance for educators is what follows. It is not simply that the will is linked to action, but that willing *is* the ethical quality of thought itself. Because the mind does not desire to look directly at evidence which contradicts held beliefs or reigning moods, moral effort must be exerted in order to hold steady to reasonable ideas. James thus summarizes, "Our moral effort, properly so called, terminates in our holding fast to the appropriate idea" (ibid.: 817). A moral act in its essence is, in turn, "the effort of attention by which we hold fast to an idea which but for that effort of attention would be driven out of the mind by the other psychological tendencies that are there" (ibid.). The secret of thinking is inextricably linked with willful production of *voluntary mental attention* focused on the "right ideas." In the end, James can finally state his thesis: "In all this the power of voluntarily attending is the point of the whole procedure [of education]" (ibid.: 818). Although moments of voluntary attention are brief and infrequent, they are essential for deciding the "higher or lower destinies" (ibid.: 818) of students. Because of the gravity of such moments, the skilled teacher will provide many opportunities for students to practice voluntary attention and, accordingly, develop a moral character.

But this argument is more than simply a pedagogical plea for teachers to (a) focus on the training of the will as a form of moral education, and (b) provide educational situations in which students can practice voluntary attention. Indeed, without the "natural termination of the cycle of his activities" in an external expression of his or her will, the child will suffer from "the sense of incompleteness and uncertainty" (James 1992: 735) that accompanies an inattentive—and thus *morally* deficient—character. In the last instance, James uses his discourse on the will to make a rather sketchy argument for the metaphysics of freedom in an otherwise mechanical and physical description of the relation between the mind and the body. At the end of his discourse, James turns—somewhat abruptly—to a purely metaphysical argument for saving free will within a conception of the body and mind as a kind of organic machine. "But after what we have just seen—namely, the part played by voluntary attention in volition—a belief in free will and purely spiritual causation is still open to us" (ibid.: 819). In this sense, James leaps from psychology to pedagogy to metaphysics, all of which are united by an underlying understanding of the human being as a willful being capable of realizing its own freedom through voluntary attention to reasonable ideas. Like Rousseau's intuitive sensing of the ontological priority of the free will in *Emile*, so does James intuitively sense the need for a concept of free will in order to stave off reductive materialism that might characterize his scientific study of psychological mechanisms. Yet his intuition is nothing more than this: an unsupported intuition hastily inserted into his argument so as to leave room for freedom within an otherwise mechanical model of mind. The insertion, far from allowing an escape from the corner into which James paints himself, merely heightens a sense of argumentative inadequacy, and reveals the metaphysical commitments that James has to the will for explaining the *how* and the *what* of educational psychology.

If Rousseau and James to various degrees represent "progressive" schools of thought, then radical/critical education is also focused primarily on the will. Perhaps the clearest example of the priority of the problematic of the will is found in Jacques Rancière's *The Ignorant Schoolmaster: Five Lessons in Intellectual Emancipation*. As Jan Masschelein and Maarten Simons have argued (2010), "pedagogic subjectivation" in Rancière's work concerns the verification of an "ability to" or the "will to." Indeed, the whole of Rancière's educational polemic against both schooling and critical sociological "alternatives" rests on the nature of this pedagogic subjectivation of the will. Rancière's main aim is to challenge the dominance of "stultifying pedagogy" that posits a fundamental inequality between the student (who is ignorant) and the teacher-as-explicator.

Drawing inspiration from the nineteenth-century teacher and philosopher Joseph Jacotot, Rancière argues that an educational revolution can only happen when these hierarchies between intelligences are overcome. In the explication model, the teacher's central job is to "transmit his knowledge to his students so as to bring them, by degrees, to his own level of expertise" (1991: 3). The problem is that such equality is never achieved because a certain pedagogical dependency renders the students perpetually ignorant, always relying on the explicator for the correct answer. In other words, the secret of explication is that it never shores up the gap between student and teacher. Indeed, it actually constitutes and sustains the very distance that it is meant to bridge! The result, according to Rancière, is nothing less than "*enforced stultification*" (ibid.: 7). The resulting stultification from explication is a fiction: rather than the incapable needing the explicator, it is the explicator who continually must fabricate the incapable. Rancière summarizes,

> Before being the act of the pedagogues, explication is the myth of pedagogy, the parable of a world divided into knowing minds and ignorant ones, ripe minds and immature ones, the capable and the incapable, the intelligent and the stupid.
>
> (ibid.: 6)

The net result of this myth is the division of educational labor between the stupid, who must defer to the explicator, and the intelligent who must "bear the burden" of educating the masses in order to overcome their stupidity.

Opposed to pedagogies of explication and stultification, Jacotot broke with the myth through a simple realization: that anyone can teach anything regardless of their expertise. The intellectual inequalities between ignorant student and master explicator are overturned through a displacement of the problematic of intelligence by the problematic of the will. As Rancière clearly states, "The method of equality was above all a method of the will" (1991: 12). Rather than assume a hierarchy of intelligence, Jacotot simply verified the students' will to learn. Thus without being able to read or understand Flemish, Jacotot found that he was able to teach in French to Flemish students by pointing their attention toward a bilingual translation of *Télémaque*. He was the ignorant schoolmaster, and his ignorance emancipated students from stultification. Rancière summarizes as follows:

> A pure relationship of will to will had been established between master and student: a relationship wherein the master's domination resulted in an entirely liberated relationship between the intelligence of the student and that of the book—the intelligence of the book that was also the thing in common, the egalitarian intellectual link between master and student.
>
> (1991: 13)

24 *From being willful to being more willing*

The work of the emancipated master was therefore not to give explanations so much as to command the will of the student to learn. "His mastery," writes Rancière, "lay in the command that had enclosed the students in a closed circle from which they alone could break out" (ibid.). Rather than keep hidden authority—and the secrets of learning—the emancipated master has nothing up his or her proverbial sleeve to hide from the student. Rather than hide, this new form of ignorant schoolmaster verifies a student's attempt to prove the equality of intelligences through his or her authority to command the will. Inequalities are thus not expressions of intellectual divisions or intellectual incapabilities. Rather, inequalities are symptoms of a lack of willful attention to the problem at hand. "Laziness itself," as Rancière warns, "isn't the torpor of the flesh; it is the act of the mind underestimating its own power" (ibid.: 79). The emancipated master must continue to verify the will, commanding it to pay attention and overcome the myth of laziness that continually attempts to reinforce stereotypes of intellectual inferiority over and against the power of the will to prove otherwise. The command is a command for equality to actualize itself, and the will is the ultimate power to demonstrate that such equality exists before all distinctions are drawn.

Underlying the maxim of equal intelligences is Jacotot's fundamental metaphysical claim: "Man is a *will served by an intelligence*" (Rancière 1991: 52). The will emerges, yet again, as a kind of hero in educational growth and emancipation. It is the ultimate ground (and ultimate problem) that all education must face if it is to be more than mere rote learning. In fact, it is not intelligence that indicates one's personal genius but rather the will. According to Rancière, "I can't" is nothing less than a "sentence of self-forgetfulness" (ibid.: 58) that denies how intelligence serves the will and not the other way around. Indeed, genius, for Rancière, is nothing less than

> the relentless work [of the will] to bend the body to necessary habits, to compel the intelligence to new ideas, to new ways of expressing them; to redo on purpose what chance once produced, and to reverse unhappy circumstances into occasions for success.
>
> (ibid.: 56)

In other words, genius is the *power of the will to command the intelligence*. It is a kind of sovereign injunction to do, to redo, and to produce, to make manifest the maxim of equality.

Given this brief genealogy of the will, there are several major continuities that I would like to point out. First, the will is almost unanimously given priority as *the initial and central human faculty*—a key point that can never be proven or argued but must merely be *asserted* as the most basic building block of education. The will is *what* concerns educational theory and practice. Second, this initial metaphysical claim then demands that education concern itself first and foremost with the training of the will through willful production. Without such training, disasters will happen (for Rousseau, this means tyranny or servitude, for James this means either mania or melancholia, for Rancière this means the reproduction of stultification and inequality). The will is not only what is to be trained but also the faculty that enables such training to occur in the first place. In sum, as a metaphysical ground, the will provides education with a *what* and a *how*. The training of the will for willful self-production is, in short, the *essence* of real education. Third, in all cases, the problem of the will is never with the appearance of the will itself but rather with the relation between will and freedom, will and attention, will and equality. Below, I will argue that such common-sense considerations remain mired in metaphysical commitments that can only be theorized when placed within a broader context of the history of being-in-the-world. As such, while the first half of this chapter has been descriptive, the second half will be critical. I will then end with a third move that is largely reconstructive.

The will and technology: Heidegger's intervention

The three authors discussed above fail to address the relationship between the metaphysics of the will and the logic of the technological age. Instead of a historically specific manifestation of a particular metaphysical outlook, the will becomes a transhistorical, psychological ground—the *what* and the *how* of educational theory and practice is therefore secured. Yet, as I will now explore in detail, the will is a symptom of the metaphysical commitments underlying technological enframing. Technological enframing, according to Heidegger, reduces meaningful and significant entities into mere resources to be used at will to achieve instrumental ends. For Heidegger, enframing "is the way in which the real reveals itself as [a] standing-reserve" (1984: 23) of raw materials to be controlled by humans. One particularly important mode of such control is scientific research wherein research "has disposal over anything that is when it can either calculate it in its future course in advance or verify a calculation about it as past" (ibid.: 127). Only that which can be calculated, assessed, and thus controlled counts as an entity. In this sense, scientific or technological research stands over and above things as mere objects to be manipulated through calculation. Instead of being receptive to and thankful for the world as it has been given as a meaning-rich set of background practices and solicitations, the researcher is in control of the world reduced to a standing reserve.

There are explicit connections between the rise of technology and an understanding of the human as a willful subject. Heidegger writes, "willing determines the nature of modern man" who conceives the world as "given over to, commended to, and thus subjected to the command of self-assertive production" through "purposeful self-assertion" (2001: 109). Or stated differently, "As a way of objectifying beings in a calculative manner, modern science is a condition posited by the will to will itself, through which the will to will secures the dominance of its essence" (Heidegger 2009: 231). In Heidegger's view, the

26 *From being willful to being more willing*

ultimate project of scientific calculation is the appropriation of resources by a will whose only interest is the manifestation of its own willfulness. "Self-assertive man," warns Heidegger, "whether or not he knows and wills it as an individual, is the functionary of technology" (2001: 113). In other words, instead of standing and waiting, listening, sensing the arrival of affordances granted to it by the world, modern technologically defined humanity impatiently stands against the world as mere meaningless, raw material that can only be animated through a kind of willful action. The result is that the world becomes a kind of mute resource that only has meaning and purpose in relation to the will's own striving and self-enhancement. Freedom is the freedom to actively express one's capabilities in order to remake the world in one's (free) self-image. Freedom is freedom that is willed. Theories of entrepreneurial optimism in the capacity to self-realize, self-generate, and self-manage our potentials are not empowering so much as symptoms of an overall enframing of human potentiality within a means-end logic that denies the freedom to prefer *not to will*.

Drawing heavily from Heidegger and other existentialist sources, Hubert Dreyfus and Sean Dorrance Kelly argue that the leveling caused by the technological age and the attending belief in the powers of individual self-production have caused a crisis in Western culture. "The nihilism of our secular age," they warn, "leaves us with an awful sense that nothing matters in the world at all. If nothing matters then there is no basis for doing any one thing over any other, and the contemporary burden of choice weighs heavily" (2011: 71). The sense of the sacred is not something we have power or control over. Indeed, to experience the sacred—the possibility of meaning-rich lives defined by focal practices that orient our actions and decisions—is precisely to experience that which supersedes the will. A Nietzschean metaphysics of the will that places the burden of meaning-making (or shine) on the shoulders of the individual and his or her powers presents us all with an impossible task, one that is destined to fail and plunge us into nihilism. The sacred cannot come from within but must come from without, or even better, it can only come from the indeterminate zone that lies below the subject/object split that the will rests upon.

Perhaps the perfect example of technological enframing is found in current practices of standardized, high-stakes testing, and, more broadly, in the economic restructuring of education as such. Throughout the educational sector of the economy, calculation of scores and the assessment of potentialities dominate over and above personally meaningful educational experiences. Education becomes a calculable resource for developing competitive human capital in a global market. In this scenario, the student is reduced to the status of the "learner," who, for Gert Biesta (2006), is akin to a consumer of a mass-produced product. Within a Heideggerian frame of reference, the key here is that learning as the educational logic of biocapitalism subsumes educational relations under economic relations of production and consumption, reducing meaning-rich, personal experience to the repetition of standardized ritual and the calculability of testing. Drawing from and extending Heidegger's own analysis of the university, Iain D. Thomson argues that in the technological age, we are witnessing the

> ubiquitous quantification of education, which preconceives of students as *Bestand*, not as human beings with intrinsic talents and capacities to be identified and cultivated, but rather as educational "outcomes" to be "optimized" in uniformly quantifiable terms, shackling educators to systems of standardized testing to which they must conform or else be deprived further of their already severely limited material resources.
>
> (2005: 158)

Agreeing with both Biesta and Thomson, I would like to extend their analyses by connecting the enframement of education as mere resource (learning) with the sustained (if not expanding) emphasis on the will as a faculty responsible for the optimization of outcomes.

Without a clear critique of enframing *and* the will, reconstructions of educational freedom *beyond* the metaphysics of the technological epoch of biocapitalism might very well remain locked within a highly suspect understanding of education as *Bildung*. As Heidegger warns, *Bildung* has become nothing more than a kind of educational equivalent to the metaphysics of the will to power—a kind of intellectual manifestation of Promethian hubris capable of perpetual improvement of self and culture according to subjective powers that presuppose more than they can ever hope to take account of by their own principles (thus Rousseau's reliance on intuitive feeling or James' sudden and unjustifiable turn to spiritual volunteerism at a crucial step in his argument or even Rancière's axioms). Highlighting the ambiguity within the concept of *Bildung* that enables it to be absorbed into a technological framework, Heidegger reminds us that *bilden* means to form or cultivate, while *Vor-bild* means to set up a preestablished rule (*Vor-schrift*). Self-cultivation comes to regulate individual behavior according to an internalized, prototype or idea of "the educated person" that must be made manifest via willful action. The root for this concept of *Bildung* as forming someone in accordance with a predefined paradigm can be found in Plato's allegory of the cave. For Heidegger, the allegory of the cave is pivotal for understanding not only Plato's thoughts but for understanding a monumental shift in Western philosophy as a whole. With the cave, Heidegger pinpoints the arrival of three equally dominant themes in modern Western thought: *Bildung*, humanism, and truth as correctness. The interconnectedness between these themes cannot be underestimated. Turning away from shadows toward the light of the sun is, for Heidegger, the moment when the experience of truth transforms itself from unhiddenness or presencing of being to correctness of intellectual representation and assertion according to abstracted forms. Thinking comes to define the essence of human being, and *Dasein* turns away from entities that are experienced toward transcendental ideas. Because reason is the only faculty capable of communing with ideas, humans gain a new, privileged position within the order of being. And from this fundamental, metaphysically established hierarchy of beings, humans emerge as rational animals capable of their own self-production and self-improvement through rational calculation. The result is a form of education whose sole purpose is

> [the] shaping of their "moral" behavior, as the salvation of their immortal souls, as the unfolding of their creative powers, as the development of their reason, as the nourishing of their personalities, as the awakening of their civic sense, as the cultivation of their bodies, or as an appropriate combination of some or all of these "humanisms."
>
> (Heidegger 2009: 181)

Bildung emerges as an educational manifestation of a metaphysically determined system that manifests the essence of the human being and its capability for continual self-improvement through rational self-reflection. The danger here is that *Bildung* is reduced to the "invincible power of an immutable reason and its principles" (Heidegger 1984: 180) that denies the phenomenological possibility of sensitivity to that which is beyond our control, beyond our rational self-interest, beyond willful determination by our creative powers. For Heidegger, this is a perversion of *Bildung*, whose true nature must be rigorously separated from the Platonic tradition of humanism and rationalism which culminate today in the "rational self-interest" of the entrepreneurial student. Educational scholars Biesta (2006) and Thomson (2005) take up Heidegger's project and attempt a rehabilitation of *Bildung*, not so much as a subjective power but as a kind of sensitivity to what is called for by a situation. In particular, for Biesta, what is called for is more often than not a kind of radical interruption that disturbs the internally regulative ideal of the humanist, rational subject and his or her pursuit of personal perfection. Yet in both Biesta and Thomson, what is missing in their respective calls for education beyond the discourses and practices of learning is precisely the move Heidegger repeatedly emphasizes: an explicit problematization of the will. Heidegger summarizes: "The essence of freedom is *originally* not connected with the will or even with the causality of human willing" (1984: 25). The essence of *Bildung* must be sought in an alternative notion of education beyond willful self-cultivation of a human essence.

Agamben's analysis of the epochal shift from Greek poiesis to technological praxis furthers Heidegger's argument and enables us to theoretically flesh out a more originary sense of *Bildung*. Throughout his early literary works such as *Idea of Prose* (1995), *The Man Without Content* (1999b), and *The End of the Poem* (1999a), Agamben picks up on Heidegger's critique of the metaphysics of the will and stresses that poiesis is not the result of a commanding and self-asserting subject who gives meaning and significance to the world through creative production. The notion of praxis as self-construction has come to dominate the modern world as the last vestige of a metaphysical principle in a biotechnological age of learning. Instead, poiesis is an exposure of the self to the open affordances of the world—to the possibility of letting objects shine forth as meaning-rich. In other words, poiesis is beyond the individual, subjective, intentionally guided will. Heidegger writes that poets who are more venturesome than the most adventurous of willful subjects "will more strongly in that they are more willing" (2001: 116). "More willing" in this citation must be read with caution. More willing does not mean more commanding. Rather than more *willful*, Heidegger passes beyond the metaphysics of willing to a mode of being that is more willing to be responsive, sensitive, and thankful for what is offered up by the world. In the illuminating essay "On the Essence of Truth," Heidegger makes a similar claim, arguing that the essence of truth is found in freedom to "to let be" (2009: 144). Being more willing is, in my argument, being open to letting beings be the beings that they are. It is not simply more willing or willing differently that get us out of the metaphysics of the will that permeate today's educational landscape, but rather a letting loose of the Promethean thesis. In other words, letting beings be is to remain open and receptive to what presents itself without the interference of willful self-production. While technology, according to Heidegger, gives the impression that "everything man encounters exists only insofar as it is his construct" and in turn that "man everywhere and always encounters only himself," then poetic willingness (as letting be) enables "presences [to] come forth into appearance" (1984: 27) above and beyond the intentional volition of the subject-as-producer. If the more willful subject transforms the world into an object to be imbued with meaning by willful productivity and spirited command, then the more willing subject turns to the world in order to listen, receive grace, and *let* things shine. Dreyfus summarizes this best with the following distinction: poiesis is not some form of creative willing so much as "*letting worlds disclose themselves*" (2005: 149).

Like Heidegger, Agamben fears that humans have lost this poetic receptivity. This loss is due to the overwhelming dominance of praxis over and above poiesis in the biocapitalist age. Agamben observes, "According to current opinion, all of man's doing—that of the artist and the craftsman as well as that of the workman and the politician—is praxis, that is, manifestation of a will that produces a concrete effect" (1999b: 68). We can see the prodigious emphasis on praxis in the aesthetic theory of Nietzsche, where the artist is a Will to Power, or even in Marx, where the essence of the human is productive labor. Summarizing a long trajectory in Western culture that has eclipsed poiesis with a biological notion of willful action, Agamben writes

> The point of arrival of Western aesthetics is a metaphysics of the will, that is, of life understood as energy and creative impulse . . . And yet what the Greeks meant with the distinction between poiesis and praxis was precisely that the essence of poiesis has nothing to do with the expression of a will (with respect to which art is in no way necessary): this essence is found instead in the production of truth and in the subsequent opening of a world for man's existence and action.
>
> (1999b: 72)

30 *From being willful to being more willing*

The outcome of willful action is nothing more than the will reaching its own limit and reflecting itself in that limit, whereas the outcome of willing openness is receptivity to the world in its truth. In terms of the art world, the artist as pure will becomes the "man without content" (ibid.: 55) who has lost the sense of dwelling in a shared world precisely because his or her creations can only *reflect* his or her aesthetic subjectivity as absolute essence. And in terms of political praxis, Agamben argues that Marx reduces productive activity to nothing more than "vital *force*, drive and energetic tension, passion" (ibid.: 85). In the end, "The essence of praxis, the genetic characteristic of man as a *human* and historical being, has thus retreated into a naturalistic connotation of man as *natural* being" (ibid.). The structure of the world within the paradigm of praxis is teleological and progressive: there is a certain forward march, or at least an everyday, common-sense notion of a forward march towards increasing levels of mastery and control over the environment and its resources, not to mention the self and its potentialities. Lost here is a sense of the world as *predating* willful production (the clearing that is necessary for willful production to take place), and the only meaning possible for the man of praxis becomes the meaning *he produces*—a kind of radical constructivism which, in educational terms, means perpetual self-(re)generation through verification of the powers of the will.

If we live in a biocapitalist age of technological enframing, then things no longer call to us as meaningful or significant, and education ceases to be about personal and social transformation and is reduced to mere calculation of outputs in the name of instrumental quotas. For Heidegger, this means that *Dasein* exists in a state of inauthentic conformity to *das Man*, for Dreyfus and Kelly this means living in a nihilistic world that lacks a sense of the sacred, and for Agamben, this means that humanity no longer has a sense of its own impotentiality. In such circumstances, there can be no intuitive sense of anything as anything at all. Rather, all that appears are mute resources waiting to be animated by a will (and thus reflect back to humankind its own self-image as "man the producer"). Again, Heidegger summarizes this condition when he states that calculative thinking "compels itself into a compulsion to master everything on the basis of the consequential correctness of its procedure" (2009: 235) and neglects to *care for the being of beings*. In this dire set of circumstances, it would appear that educational philosophy can do little to help. Indeed, the emphasis on willful self-production found in progressive and radical educational theories does not seem to promote freedom so much as reproduce the metaphysical preconditions for technological enframing and ontological leveling.

But is all lost? Perhaps not—recalling an early clarion call by Heidegger, Dreyfus and Kelly argue that the task of the philosopher is to help in the project of "rediscovering the practices that reveal the sacred enchantments of the world" (2011: 89). In this sense, we can once again return to Rousseau, James, and Rancière in order to grasp those moments in their writing that point toward alternative paradigms beyond the willful subject. In marginal comments, asides, or tangents we can find certain moments wherein *Dasein* is released from the metaphysical constraints of the will in order to become open to the

From being willful to being more willing   31

possibility of the sacred. For instance, we might be apt to read in Rousseau's interpretation of divinity as found in nature a call for *Dasein* to be open and receptive to what has been given to it and receive it with gratitude. In this sense, to will for Rousseau is to be open to the will of nature that, on an intuitive level, gives *Dasein* access to a divine principle it can neither rationally fathom nor control. Throughout Rousseau's work such miraculous appearances occur with some frequency, including the savoy vicar in *On Education*, the mysterious legislator in the *Social Contract*, and so on. The problem here is that for Rousseau, the dependency upon that which is outside the will remains trapped in the discourse of the will, creating an infinite regression from will to will to will, and so on. Behind what is given remains *a will* that in turn must be given something that is, again, the product of another will. Nothing, in other words, is ever truly given but always produced by a willful subject. *Willingness always seems to necessitate willfulness*. Thus, even in our attempt to salvage the sacred in Rousseau's work, we reach the obstacle of the will. As such, it is not clear that the retrieval of willing openness that Dreyfus and Kelly search for is of any real help. In fact, this reading strategy merely reconstitutes the centrality of the will. The sacred escapes us even when we attempt to retrieve it through open receptivity to the divinity in nature. In the end, the problem of the rise of technological enframing *goes all the way down*. Given this, Dreyfus and Kelly's hermeneutical practice seems overly optimistic.

In his talks to teachers, James places emphasis on the psychological principles of willful production and voluntary attention, yet in the talks to students, focus shifts dramatically to the aesthetic question of receptivity to the meaningfulness of the world. As with Heidegger, James worries that students now suffer from "stone-blindness" (1992: 857) to the world around them. Indeed, the world has, for James, withdrawn and become increasingly inaccessible. In light of this pressing and urgent problem, James argues that students need to cultivate a "responsive sensitivity" (ibid.: 856) that is below the level of conscious thought, and in this sense is a kind of intuitive openness. In fact, James points out that artists and poets have repeatedly demonstrated that "Divinity lies all about us" (ibid.: 867), but that we only need to become sensitive to its shadowy presence. The sacred is not in another, transcendental world beyond the flesh and blood world of lived social relations but is being-in-the-world itself! Still problematic here is the contradiction between the what and the how of the two talks: one focusing on will and the other on poetic sensitivity. It is unclear how willfulness and sensitivity correlate, nor is it clear how teachers have a role to play in cultivating such sensitivity. Indeed, for Heidegger, Dreyfus and Kelly and Agamben, the two projects might very well *be at odds* with one another. It is precisely the emphasis on will that is the fundamental roadblock to cultivating responsive sensitivity to what exists on the pre-subjective, pre-volitional level of worldly affordances. The goals of teachers and of students therefore will not correspond, creating an unstable dissonance in James' talks. It is my argument that this fundamental dissonance is a symptom of an underlying loss of meaning within biotechnological enframing.

32   *From being willful to being more willing*

The same symptom is repeated in Rancière's work. Rancière's emancipated and ignorant schoolmaster commands the will of the student to manifest itself thus verifying the equality of intelligences. In this model, the relationship is not intellectual but rather a battle between the forces of two wills. Interest, desire and meaning are not part of Rancière's educational problematic. Viewed in light of the leveling of meaningful affordances in the age of a reified standing reserve, the fact that meaning drops out of Rancière's description of "universal teaching" is important to note. If the world still offered up affordances to which the receptive subject could respond with an intuitive sense of meaningful practice, then such command would not be necessary. Simply placing the book before the student would be enough for the student to hear, see, or be touched by the call of the world. Yet in a world were nothing shines more meaningfully than anything else and all ontological differences have been leveled, the teacher must not simply place before or point at but also must *command* the will of the student.

Because of this condition, Rancière cannot find a way to combine his interest in the aesthetics of curiosity and the educational verification of the will. According to Rancière's reflections on aesthetics, to be curious is to stumble upon something, some clue that draws one into a mystery. It is a peculiar capacity that indicates a faltering in our understanding, a location where the eye "does not know in advance what it sees and thought does not know what it should make of it" (2009: 109). In this sense, curiosity is the passive sensual *affliction* of an anomalous detail that resists identification (and thus classification as this type of object, subject, or action) yet calls us, solicits us to remain open to its appearance. The "labor of attention" that the curious gaze produces is not a willful action so much as a more willing "encircling."

Rancière's vivid description of Irene's psychological state in Roberto Rossellini's film *Europa '51* (1952) clearly maps onto his later theorization of curiosity:

> The moment arrives when the call of the void has an effect but no longer makes sense. The time to connect, explain, and heal has passed. Now something else is at stake: to repeat the event, go look somewhere else, see for oneself. This is how one falls into the unrepresentable, into a universe that is no longer the society sociologists and politicians talk about.
>
> (2003: 117)

Curiosity is a moment when we fall into that which we do not understand and thus gaze at the void that exists in surplus of the categories, narratives, and principles of experts and professionals. The void here is not a lack but rather a gap or fissure between common sense and sensation, opened by a strange call that reminds us that the world is meaningful even if this meaning remains obscure to us. The subsequent fall is beyond the time to explain (to make sense), and instead is the exploratory time of going to "see for oneself" what can be done in the absence of grounds, names, and representational content. The fall of curiosity is

From being willful to being more willing   33

always a rupture of sense by the anomalous detail—in Irene's case, the question involving her son's last testimonial before his death—that offers something new and unexpected, a new path or space that is not reducible to the given order of things nor reducible to individual desires, intentions, or willful capabilities. For Irene, the work of curiosity pulls her away from easy answers about her son's suicide toward an unknown that nevertheless appears more authentic than the choices afforded her by society. She must leave the professional interpretations of the doctor and the socialist convictions of her cousin, Andrea, in order to allow the call to pull her curiosity this way and that. Indeed, Irene *falls* into her predicament not through willful action so much as through unintentional stumbling. Thus curiosity, for Rancière, seems to be a pre-subjective, receptive response that sets Irene in motion, moving her beyond the frame of medical science or social critique into the atopic world of grace/madness that she finally discovers only by letting it discover her.

Although the description above seems to have some bearing on the question of education, Rancière completely separates his aesthetic theory of affective curiosity from his educational reflections, thus separating curiosity from willfulness. As for James, for Rancière only artists and poets have the possibility of being gripped by the "divinity" of the world—a divinity that is in short supply if you are not trained to see with an artist's eye. When the will is left naked before the empty world, without the responsiveness and sensitivity of curiosity to the affordances of this world, the only educational recourse is indeed a *pragmatic one*: the teacher must command the will of the student to produce. If Rousseau focused on hiding authority of the teacher in order to safeguard freedom of the student, then here we see an almost complete reversal of course. Rousseau could only advise tutors not to command students as long as the world could shine forth as meaningful, as long as things could call to students to care for them in particular ways. In such cases, the world—although out of sorts, monstrous, and upside down according to Rousseau—is still *a world* composed of things, practices, and roles that hold certain forms of significance in themselves. Letting nature be the first teacher (indeed the first education is always an education of and through things without the mediation of signs) means letting things shine and thus pull the student in certain directions rather than others. Yet for Rancière, the world grants no such affordances. In a world that has gone dark, as Heidegger claims, there is a distinct sense of loss of meaning; curiosity cannot be relied upon as a kind of taken-for-granted, pre-conscious, pre-thematic grip. Things no longer have the ability to present themselves as the kinds of things that they are, and in such a circumstance, the body cannot respond with thankfulness or respect for what has been offered. Meaning withdraws into art, which becomes the only source for igniting curiosity. Without a world, the teacher can only train the will (James) or issue commands (Rancière). In both cases, the results are paradoxical: (a) the goals of the teacher stand in the way of the goals of the student (to be responsive to meaning), and (b) freedom must be sacrificed to the command in order to ensure equality of intelligences. Because of the world collapse

34 *From being willful to being more willing*

caused by technological enframing, neither James nor Rancière *can connect education and worldly sensitivity*. As such, they both stand as symptoms of the enframing that they both desire to overcome. Neither can see that it is not willful production but rather being more willing that offers a way out of the paradox.

For Dreyfus and Kelly, the task at hand is a difficult but straightforward one: sensitize ourselves to the traces left by the gods in the margins of the Western classics in order to prepare for their return. In other words, read figures like Rousseau, James, and Rancière in order to discover moments when education can be disconnected from the metaphysics of the will in order to return to a notion of the sacred. The paradox is clear: to get to being more willing, Dreyfus and Kelly have to embody a kind of hermeneutical will-to-power or supreme act of willfulness to read the classics against the grain and uncover fleeting moments of the sacred. The resulting performative contradiction does not sit well with their repeated emphasis that trying more or trying harder *blocks* the sacred from shining forth. While praising willingness, their method exhibits nothing less than willfulness. On my reading, this is not merely a regrettable oversight on the part of the authors but rather a necessary outcome of their project. In a world that has gone dark, willingness is not enough to make things and signs shine—there must be a supplement of willfulness (even if this willfulness is disavowed). But perhaps there is another "solution" to the problem of ontological leveling that does not rest on recovery of the sacred and, in turn, a replaying of the logic of the will. A solution that does not see such leveling as an immediate evil leading to nihilism but as a window opening up onto the primordial experience of im-potentiality. I would like to conclude with a final turn back to Agamben and his theory of study. It is my contention that study presents us with a different relationship to the classics than that proposed by Dreyfus and Kelly and thus opens up to a new educational paradigm that has yet to be fully thought through, let alone appreciated: a profane educational practice.

From calculative learning to studying: Agamben's alternative

Although the will "solves" the problem of inequality (for Rousseau and Rancière) as well as voluntary attention (for James), it nevertheless fails to recognize its own historicity, and therefore its complacency with technological calculation. When placed within the history of being, the solution becomes a symptom. Dreyfus and Kelly thus propose to read these authors against the grain of the will in order to rekindle a sense of the sacred. Yet this return to the theme of the sacred in order to solve the problems of a secular age is, I argue, unsatisfactory precisely because it misrecognizes an *opportunity* unique to ontological leveling: the exposure of pure im-potentiality as the precondition for meaning-making. Instead of defining our lives according to a rehabilitation of the sacred, Agamben and his theory of study open *Dasein* up to the possibility

From being willful to being more willing   35

of a *profane* solution—one that is no longer within the logic of technological enframing and yet not outside of it either.

The studier stands before all possibilities with a certain detached indifference to personal gains, outcomes, and ends. As Agamben argues,

> Those who are acquainted with long hours spent roaming among books, when every fragment, every codex, every initial encounter seems to open a new path, immediately left aside at the next encounter, or who have experienced the labyrinthine allusiveness of that "law of good neighbors" whereby Warburg arranged his library, know that not only can study have no rightful end, but does not even desire one.
>
> (1995: 64)

The studier stands before a world where fragments open new paths, yet these paths are immediately left idle as further paths open. In other words, no path, codex, or encounter shines forth as any more meaningful or significant than any other. Because the grip of meaningful solicitations have waned, the studier is freed to wander, achieving a kind of maximal flexibility to explore whatever remains in the wake of nihilistic world collapse. This is precisely why study is interminable, and can have no end. For the studier who is lost in the interminable rhythms of study, there cannot be (a) a desire to realize certain latent potentials, (b) a will to guide one's studies toward educational growth, (c) a command to verify the equality of intelligences, or (d) a shining light to guide him or her toward definitive projects. Like Heidegger's description of the venturesome poet, the studier "is turned away from all purposeful self-assertion" and therefore does not engage in "willing in the sense of desire" (2001: 135). Rather than the will taking up the fragments of world left by enframing and building a new world in one's self-image or expressing sacred gratitude toward the gods for having given the gift of meaning, the studier remains quiet, listening to this collapsed world that no longer affords meaning, rule, or measure for what counts. To study is to undergo a certain inoperativity where we are, to appropriate a phrase from Thomas Carl Wall's insightful study of Agamben, "exposed to *all* its [thought's] possibilities (all its predicates)" and yet are "undestined to any one or any set of them" (1999: 152). Without either the pull of worldly, engaged solicitations or the command from the emancipated master, the hubris of Promethean production grinds to a halt and the sacredness of things becomes a kind of profane abandon.

The state of leveling experienced in study becomes an *opportunity* as much as a crisis for opening up and sustaining a new notion of freedom. When studying, the studier experiences a willing openness to the potentiality of the world to be *and* not to be simultaneously. The im-potentiality of a world enables the world to be experienced *rather than* what it has become, without forcing any particular actualization of this im-potentiality. When all ontological differences disappear, all that is left is a potentiality without a project or focal practice. This state of suspended ends and willful calculation is reminiscent of Heidegger's description of originary thinking, which "does not effect any results, because it has no need of effect" (2009: 237). Instead of obsessing on ends, evaluations, and measurements, the kind of thinking experienced through study suspends the very logic of means and ends altogether, enabling the studier to stand before an im-potential world that is no longer sacred but rather profane.

The result is not simply nihilism (as a lack of potentiality for meaning). Through study, the retreat of the sacred becomes infancy: a state that, for Agamben (2007a), rests between "no longer" simply being paralyzed by the loss of a meaning-rich world and "not yet" gripped by new projects that give the studier a definitive orientation. The studier lacks either willful pursuit or command to guide him or her; thus, from the outside, the studier appears to be melancholic (in James' pessimistic sense), lacking any sense of the sacred to give a purpose and directedness. Yet what James misses is precisely the efficacy of melancholia as an educational rather than pathological response to the leveling of meaning in the world—a state that returns humanity to its origin in infancy—a state of stupification. In the state of arrested development that is infancy, the studier does not simply wait for future solicitations but rather receives the lack of solicitations as a solicitation to study im-potentiality as such—a kind of demand placed upon the studier that has no content and thus is perpetually open. In short, the studier does not let a world disclose itself, as Dreyfus and Kelly call for, but lets the im-potentiality of a world disclose itself. Citing Hölderlin, Heidegger argues "But where there is danger, there grows also what saves" (2001: 115). The destruction of education by the collapse of the sacredness of the world under biocapitalist enframing is not to be lamented but rather strategically employed as a new anchoring point for an education beyond either nihilism or sacred reverence. *To study is to care for the indeterminate potentiality of potentiality itself.* It is to let shine not this or that practice, thing, or sign but rather the potentiality of this or that *to* shine. Studying is therefore not a decision to opt for the nothing of nihilism or the willful production of the self or the shine of the sacred but rather a discovery of the conditions for the world, its primordial im-potentiality. To study the lack of signification as significant is to dwell in an im-potential realm where potentiality appears in its withdrawing from any actualization of this potentiality. In their desperate attempts to save the things, signs, and practices that shine, Rousseau, James, and Dreyfus and Kelly all miss how the study of nihilism uncovers the very im-potentiality of shining. And this is the most profane gesture of studying. In a state of infancy we find the one who studies—the one who would prefer not to continue the production of willful self-creating or to be moved by a sacred project to take up this or that stance, and instead remains quietly attuned with willing openness to the only thing that remains when the gods have fled and the world stands in darkness: the silent call of im-potentiality.

2 Im-potentiality
The ontology of study

A central question, often overlooked in educational theory, concerns the implicit or explicit ontological commitments embedded in the social practices of the classroom. If ontology was once seen as a dead-end for philosophy (especially in analytic circles which simply dismissed ontological questions as unintelligible), it is in the wake of Heidegger's notion of being that philosophers such as Deleuze, Negri, and Agamben have returned to ontology as *the* terrain for rethinking politics, ethics, and I would add, education. In terms of education, the notion of ontology has not had its renaissance. In fact, one could say that if educational philosophy is the backwaters of educational practice, then educational ontology is even further removed from important (or even relevant) debates and concerns. Yet ontological statements concerning the being of the student abound in common, everyday practices and beliefs of teachers, administrators, parents, and students. Many of these ontological claims concern the nature of actuality and potentiality (what is and what can be). As pointed out in the introduction to this volume, the normative framework for understanding potentiality in classrooms organized according to the basic logic of learning looks something like this: teachers should identify what potentialities a student has in order to maximize future outputs, and tests should measure the student's capability to actualize these potentials. When potentialities fail to actualize themselves in terms of measurable outcomes, then education fails.

In this chapter, I want to problematize the ontological underpinnings of this logic further, only this time, I would like to do so by turning away from a critique of learning toward the alternative offered by progressive educators. As such, I will be moving from the psychological discourse of the will to the ontological discourse of potentiality. In this sense, the argument outlined in this chapter will present a more basic, more primordial articulation of the critique of willful production. As an entry point into this project, it is important to return to the work of Israel Scheffler, whose *Of Human Potential: An Essay in the Philosophy of Education* (1985) helps clarify the issue of potentiality in relation to education. Right off, Scheffler is critical of several common myths of potentiality—myths often articulated in my undergraduate philosophy of education courses. Scheffler writes, "In no case is potential a metaphysical essence governing the predetermined direction of the subject's development, nor is it a durable feature intrinsic to the subject" (1985: 63). In other words, potential is not a special nature that is fixed and predetermined. Potentiality can develop into alternative potentials, change directions, or simply multiply depending on environment, context, and experiences. Another important myth that Scheffler rebukes is that *all* of one's potentials should be fulfilled. Lacking here is the need to evaluate between different kinds of potentials that, at best, may lack the coherent harmony of a unified set of potentialities or, at worst, might lead to outright contradictions. Finally, Scheffler is leery of the myth of "uniformly valuable potentials" (ibid.: 15), which denies the simple observation that, according to specific contexts, all humans have the potentiality both for "good" and "evil."

Once the ground has been cleared, Scheffler proceeds to present three interrelated yet relatively autonomous forms of potentiality: capacity, propensity, and capability. Scheffler's reconstructive analysis provides a rich insight into the relation between potentiality and education, nevertheless, his argument is lacking in one important respect. A key assumption of the book is an underlying ontology of action that is teleological. Subjects organize their activities according to intentional content in order to achieve specific goals. In other words, representations of success conditions enable the subjects to accomplish their purposes. In short, Scheffler argues that "human nature" involves "desire, intention, purpose" (1985: 34). Potentiality within this threefold structure is potentiality to become or to do according to the consciously held intentions and desires of a willing subject.

I want to complicate this picture somewhat by turning attention to Giorgio Agamben's theory of potentiality. For Agamben, potentiality is not simply a positive capacity, propensity, or capability to achieve specific goals through specific courses of action. Rather, potentiality is always already accompanied by an equally primordial impotentiality. When thought together, potentiality to be and the impotentiality not to be form a paradoxical tautology: the impotentiality to be and not to be simultaneously. Below I flesh out my cursory introduction to Scheffler's work highlighting its importance to Agamben, and in turn, Agamben's importance to Scheffler. Indeed, Scheffler's taxonomy of the forms of potentiality is invaluable because it helps to clarify where exactly Agamben's treatment of the im-potential is to be situated. At the same time, retreating from the question of the educational ramification of incapabilities limits Scheffler's own insights. In fact, Scheffler seems to deny the existence of the very idea of incapability precisely because capability, for him, is a reliable measure of one's (a) conscious intentionality, (b) internalized criteria for success conditions, and (c) propensity for determinate action. What is missed here is the place of study in education through which we experience a capability as an incapability in a moment that suspends our intentionality (through desubjectification), thus postponing the arrival of any determining assessment of our actions. For Agamben, without an emphasis on the peculiar features of study, we miss an opportunity to experience freedom within education. In conclusion, I will end with a philosophical analysis of the character of Bartleby the Scrivener, who provides an excellent literary analysis of Agamben's characterization of study.

Potential and impotential: from Scheffler to Agamben

As mentioned above, Scheffler divides potential into three mutually supportive dimensions. First, Scheffler distinguishes potentiality as *capacity* to acquire x, y, or z. The study of potentiality as capacity in turn takes on a very specific significance. Instead of a search for a fixed capacity, the analysis of potentiality turns toward those factors that block progressive acquisition. Stated differently, one has a capacity when one does not face certain impediments obstructing learning. As Scheffler summarizes, the study of potentiality concerns "conditions that block learning, prevent development, [and] necessitate failure to attain some designated outcome" (1985: 49). The educator's role in turn is the negation of the negation—i.e. the strategic removal of obstacles. For Scheffler, educators play this decisive role during "critical periods" of development in a child's life where blockages to certain stimuli prevent the development of language acquisition, motor skills, and so on. Although an important dimension of potentiality, all of human potential cannot be reduced or confused with capacity.

Next, Scheffler argues for potentiality as propensity. Attributing someone a capacity simply means that the acquisition of x, y, or z cannot be ruled out. Given the right circumstances we all have an equal capacity to learn to speak, to think, and to act. Yet sometimes the attribution of potentiality is stronger than mere capacity. To have a propensity means that a subject *will* acquire some trait, skill, or disposition given the right circumstances. Scheffler refers to propensity as a kind of "conditional prediction: *if* he has the chance *and* his choice is not constrained, he is likely to swim" (1985: 52). Stated differently, a propensity is not a certainty but rather a *likelihood*, assuming, of course, that there are no external contingencies that interrupt the choice of the individual.

Finally, Scheffler turns his attention to potentiality as capability. A capability is even stronger than a propensity for x, y, or z. When someone has a capability, he or she "can be generally *relied on* to perform properly under these conditions, *if* he chooses to" (1985: 58). The subject can be relied on because the proper skills and knowledge have been acquired to perform a specific task. Furthermore, the subject's skill acquisition is accompanied by "the internalization of standards of a certain sort of performance" (ibid.: 84) that enables the subject to become self-regulating and directing. Capability is conceptualized as the "capability *to become*" (ibid.: 85). As such, the agent embodies freedom through the choice to become x, y, or z subject according to a specific desire, intention, or purpose. The role of the educator here is to "empower him [the student] to perform" (ibid.). If the student has a capability, then empowerment includes enabling the student to choose to perform the capability by promoting permissive conditions. The skillful artist, the chess player, the surgeon—all have a capability that enables them to be who they are and to freely make the choice

40 *The ontology of study*

to exhibit their skillful being in the world without reserve. And we can count on their general success because they have internalized a normative representation constituting success conditions. Thus, the second part of the proposed definition emphasizes choice. Here the educator should encourage the student to value his or her capability and thus create the optimal conditions necessary for the student to *want* to realize his or her potential in the form of an action. This step is crucial for Scheffler, because choice bridges capacity with the "freedom of action" (ibid.: 59). The picture that emerges is one of a free subjectivity that decides and thus has confidence in the "growing sense of what *he* can do and the proper conditions presupposed by such doing" (ibid.: 84).

In sum, Scheffler argues that these three dimensions of potentiality are not only compatible but also mutually supportive. Synthesizing the three into one coherent model, potentiality as whole becomes the interrelation between "the *enabling* of learning [capacity], the *development* of learning [propensity], and *self-development*, or the *empowering* of learning [capability]" (1985: 65). Working together both diachronically and synchronically, the three dimensions of potentiality ideally lead to increased freedom, which for Scheffler is the self-aware and self-reflective control over the direction of one's future experiences. Potentiality as capability is both the desire and the power to act. It is explicitly a "growing sense of what he [the student] can do" (ibid.: 84) and the passion to enact this growing sense *with confidence*. In this model, freedom is realized through action, which enables the progressive ability to master one's capabilities according to internalized, regulative principles. Such mastery manifests itself in willful action directed toward actualizing certain effects in the world. As such, Scheffler connects capability less with the question of "I can, I cannot" and more with the affirmative experience of "I will" or "I must" as a sovereign desire/power that commands capabilities actualize themselves. In other words, we are purposeful, willful subjects with intentions and desires that command our capabilities and orient them toward action.

It is at this point in the analysis that I want to turn to Agamben and, in particular, his theory of the cooriginary relationship between potentiality and impotentiality. While Scheffler provides an excellent overview of the question of potentiality, he neglects the constituting role of impotentiality in his model which is beyond what a subject wants to do or must do. In turn, he seems to leave little space for the practice of study to emerge outside of a pragmatist notion of intentional, goal-driven activity (that achieves further mastery, growth, or cultivation of the self). Yet at the same time, Scheffler enables us to specify the exact dimension of expressive potentiality that Agamben is interested in: capability. Indeed, Agamben's theory of expressive potentiality as a potentiality that can conserve itself or give itself to itself presupposes precisely the definition of capability Scheffler offers us. As stated in the introduction, "I cannot" is a possibility only as long as one remains in relation to "I can." To demonstrate this point, Agamben focuses on those who have already acquired a certain skill set and thus are, to use Scheffler's terminology, capable. Capable individuals who have knowledge are *in potential*, meaning that they equally have the

The ontology of study   41

capability to bring knowledge into actuality and *not* bring knowledge into actuality. Agamben gives the example of an architect who "is in potential insofar as he has the potential to not-build, the poet the potential to not-write poems" (1999c: 179). By conserving itself, potential remains impotential, and it is this reserve of im-potentiality that maintains the freedom to choose otherwise than. Stated differently, the master is not defined by his or her capability to become (as in Scheffler's model) but rather by the in-capability to express "I can, I cannot" in a single gesture. Such in-capability enables the studier to remain indeterminate and thus free.

The central reason why Scheffler fails to recognize the mutually interconnected relation between "I can" and "I cannot" is because of an impoverished notion of human ontology, which obscures or represses the aporia of "I can, I cannot" with the affirmative power of "I will." In this sense, Scheffler misrecognizes that capability is not simply defined in terms of what can be willed, but also by the capability's capability for not being exerted (its incapability). It is the precarious and somewhat paradoxical nature of human im-potentiality that Agamben attempts to theorize as the unique ontological condition of the human. Throughout his various essays and books, Agamben refers to this state of potentiality to be and, simultaneously, not to be as "whatever" (*qualunque*) or "special being." Commenting on the ontological status of whatever, Agamben argues "The being that is properly whatever is able to not-be; it is capable of its own impotence" (1993a: 35). This whatever being becomes special and delightful when "without resembling *any* other, it resembles *all* others" (2007b: 59) as a generic form-of-life. In letting life be special, we undo "the original sin of our culture" that consists precisely in "the transformation of the *species* into a principle of identity and classification" (ibid.). Whatever being is special in that it can never be attributed to a subject (of rights, of knowledge, of interests, of understanding) or to an identity (of this or that kind person) and as such is a *desubjectification* that renders impossible the demarcation of all hierarchies, divisions, and ordinals that separate, demarcate, and classify potentiality into this or that form of labor, learning, or political affiliation. A whatever-being is special, or a pure singularity, because it does not belong to any set or class. It does not have one particular property or set of exclusive predicates but rather contains within itself all properties without strict divisions. In other words to be special is to remain indistinct and unrepresentable, and free of any determination to be or not to be set in advance. Stated differently, whatever being is being *rather*. Commenting on section nine of Heidegger's *Being and Time* as well as proposition 6.44 of Ludwig Wittgenstein's *Tractatus*, Agamben writes, "In the principle of reason ('There is a reason why there is something rather than nothing'), what is essential is neither *that something is* (being) nor *that something is not* (nothingness, but that something is *rather* than nothingness)" (1993a: 104). Im-potentiality is the fundamental ontology of whatever, and exists prior to an either/or logic that sets being and not being against one another in a kind of dialectical contestation. Not-not being is not simply a redundancy but rather an intrinsic indeterminacy of whatever. As Agamben argues, the im-potentiality of

42   *The ontology of study*

whatever (as opposed to the *potentiality* of *something or someone*) is an "ambiguity" or an "undifferentiated chaos" (1999c: 254) that resists any clear distinction between wanting and not wanting, affirmation and negation, occurrence and non-occurrence that keeps open the "luminous spiral of the possible" (ibid.: 257): our freedom to be *rather* than that which we have become or are destined to become. Stated differently, whatever is an ontological tautology, or what I would call an *ontotautology*, wherein each side of the equation (Agamben gives the example "it-will-occur-or-it-will-not-occur" ibid.: 264) remains an open possibility. Whatever as a tautological structure holds within itself both being and not being *without choosing either*, and therefore remains within a luminous spiral of contingency as a necessary ontological un-grounding.

As an example of whatever being, Agamben turns to the strange creature known as the axolotl, or albino salamander. This creature has the peculiar appearance of a larval amphibian, even when it has reached full maturity as an adult. Oddly enough, the human creature shares this same characteristic. Unlike other adult great apes, the adult human remains largely hairless, thus retaining the appearance of a fetus. "Characteristics which in primates are transitory become final in man," observes Agamben, "thereby in some way giving rise, in flesh and blood, to a kind of eternal child" (1995: 96). What is therefore uniquely human is our permanent state of infancy, and this state is not a purely negative, helpless state but rather a kind of protean *openness* to the world, to the "luminous spiral of the possible" that defines our whatever being. The eternal child is the appearance within the adult of an im-potentiality, of a radical indeterminacy that rejects any notion of a destiny or vocation. Like the salamander, *the human adult is not the actualization of an infantile potentiality but rather the potentiality of a suspended actualization*. The eternal child within is thus the remnant of whatever that preserves itself in the adult. What we hand down from generation to generation then is, in the end, not a set of laws or traditions that tell us who we are supposed to be or how we are supposed to act when we finally become mature adults, but rather this open space that is ontologically prior to and necessary for tradition to appear in the first place. This means that education can no longer be concerned with self-mastery in order to realize some sort of latent potentiality for socially useful ends, and must be rethought of as exposure to the (un)mastery of specialness, our whatever being, which is always de-completed and therefore open to different modes of being.

What makes the human unique, then, is precisely its capability for incapability! As Agamben (2004b) describes in Heideggarian terminology, the zone of indetermination through which the animal and the human are both conjoined and separated is the relation between captivity and boredom. Unlike the human world with its potentiality for uniqueness and authentic responses to particular situations, the animal environment is closed to the openness of being, producing a state of captivation or predetermined behavioral reflexes to fixed stimuli. In the state of captivation, the being of being cannot be unconcealed. But, according to Agamben's interpretation of Heidegger, this closedness to being is complex, indicating "a more spellbinding and intense openness than any kind

The ontology of study   43

of human knowledge" (ibid.: 59). The very poverty of world the animal suffers is the zone of indistinction leading from the animal to the human—not as a supplement to the animal, but as an "operation enacted upon the not-open of the animal world" (ibid.: 62). Boredom is the place of this operation where "human openness in a world and animal openness toward its disinhibitor seem for a moment to meet" (ibid.). If boredom speaks to the closeness of the human to the animal, it also reveals a unique difference between the two. Anthropology often describes the human as the negation of the animal, as a supplementary being whose greatness lies in reason and language. Yet, an analysis of boredom reveals a surprising twist on this narrative. Quoting Agamben in full:

> In captivation the animal was in an immediate relation with its disinhibitor, exposed to and stunned by it, yet in such a way that the disinhibitor could never be revealed as such. What the animal is precisely unable to do is suspend and deactive its relationship with the ring of its specific disinhibitors. That animal environment is constituted in such a way that something like a pure possibility can never become manifest within it. Profound boredom then appears as the metaphysical operator in which the passage from poverty in world to world, from animal environment to human world is realized . . . The jewel set at the center of the human world and its *Lichtung* [clearing] is nothing but animal captivation.
>
> (2004b: 68)

In this complicated passage, Agamben argues that in a state of captivation, the animal is only capable of action in response to the particular disinhibitors or stimuli of its environment. The animal can only exist as a potential-to-be given a set environment. What distinguishes the human is, paradoxically enough, the potential-not-to-be, a profound impotence or deactivation of specific possibilities. Summarizing, Agamben writes,

> Other living beings are capable only of their specific potentiality; they can only do this or that. But human beings are the animals who are capable of their own impotentiality. The greatness of human potentiality is measured by the abyss of human impotentiality.
>
> (1999c: 182)

In direct opposition to the hierarchies of value found in anthropocentric anthropology, here the human emerges not as additive but as subtractive. It is the animal that enables our potential-to-be, and it is the human that enables our potential-not-to-be: thus the site of indistinction between the two is precisely the location of potentiality itself (as both the capability to be *and* not to be simultaneously). If the animal is open to the stimuli of its environment and the human open to the world, then the monstrous between opens up to a pure potentiality, a whatever being that is not simply lazy but rather bored. In other words, boredom is not strictly human or animal but rather is the *inoperative*

44   *The ontology of study*

open that exists between the two through which capability and incapability become indistinguishable.

If there is no concept of im-potentiality in Scheffler's work, then there is equally no space or time for the work of studying. In a short aphorism from his book *The Idea of Prose*, Agamben argues that studying, the freedom of redemption, and messianic time are deeply interconnected and mutually constituting. Instead of the linear, forward march toward actualization or realization of potentiality in terms of skill acquisition and measurable outcomes, Agamben argues that studying is an educational suspension. Studying resists concretizing potentiality in terms of definitive ends that can be measured according to predetermined success conditions. Instead, the studier undergoes the infinite "rhythm of study," which oscillates between "passive potentiality, passivity, a pure and virtually infinite undergoing, and on the other hand, an active potential, an unstoppable drive to undertake, an urge to act" (ibid.). In essence, studying has a recursive structure where undergoing (the impotential experience of passivity) folds into undertaking (the potentiality for action). The result is a *suspension* of recognizable outcomes, an *interruption* of measurable outputs, a *neutralization* of learning imperatives, an *idling* of determinate actions. The studier is directly exposed to his or her im-potentiality, and *forgets* any preexisting, determinate aims, forgets that he or she can be relied upon to perform such and such an action according to expectations. In the moment when capabilities supposedly can be relied upon to actualize certain effects according to predetermined success conditions, they withdraw, and through the withdrawal process remain in-capable of this *and* that action. To study is precisely to bear witness to the remnant of the unfulfilled. In this sense the master is always the best studier precisely because he or she rhythmically turns back to the aporia of im-potentiality as a reserve for the freedom to be "rather than."

While Agamben has defined politics as the "exposition of humankind's creative semi-indifference to any task" (2000: 141), such a definition is perhaps even more applicable to studying wherein the studier becomes semi-indifferent to any judgment, conclusion, or evaluation that transforms studying into a means to achieve a certain goal. In other words, semi-indifference to criteria defining the proper versus the improper is the unique educational terrain of studying something without end, of becoming lost in an archive, set of texts, and so on. Semi-indifference holds the studier in a state of perpetual rhythmic oscillation between passive and active potentialities without sacrificing one for the other. Semi-indifference is not, after all, simply indifference. In such a state of suspension, the co-constitutive relation between capability and incapability, which has been systematically repressed by Scheffler, emerges once again as a critical educational issue.

In sum, the studier is not defined in terms of specific skills sets that are reliable, measurable, quantifiable, and reproducible, nor is he or she defined in terms of subjective desires, nor can the one who studies be relied on to realize any particular definition of a success condition. Study is the *capability for incapability* or the experiencing of a having (a capability) as a not having (an incapability), an "I can" as an "I cannot," a potentiality as an impotentiality, an impossibility as a possibility (for new uses). And it is in this paradoxical state that the student finds his or her freedom to prefer not to be measured, calculated, or evaluated. Such freedom is not the freedom of choice as defined by the capable subject, but rather the freedom of im-potentiality as an ontological opening to new possibilities. This is a freedom to remain in the "luminous spiral of the possible" that defies whatever. To experience study is to experience the moment *before* either instrumental or existential meaning orients us in the world, helps us realize desires, directs us on this or that path rather than another. It is the experience of a power released from any determinate project, a projectless potentiality.

In conclusion, Scheffler enables us to locate the specific valence of potentiality that Agamben is concerned with: the valence of capabilities. In a sense, Agamben takes for granted the existence of in-capabilities and propensities as the necessary background for the appearance of capabilities. He assumes that one *can*. The importance of Scheffler's taxonomy is absolutely necessary in this sense for locating the precise valence of potentiality to which studying corresponds. This insight is missed when educational philosophers such as Joris Vlieghe (2012) all too quickly move from studying to practicing. Vlieghe's characterization of educational practices such as reciting the alphabet or multiplication tables is rather insightful in terms of Agamben's theory of im-potentiality and both quite ingenious but also somewhat misleading. Through repetition of the alphabet or of multiplication tables, the student experiences letters or numbers freed from distinct uses (to form words that communicate or to solve mathematical problems). The words or numbers, for Vlieghe, become pure means. Practices suspend the forward march toward self-development and self-improvement. But what is missed in this description is that when one practices reciting the alphabet or multiplication tables, one does not yet have a capability. Thus unlike Vlieghe, I would propose that practices are much more an experience of "I can" than "I can, I cannot." As I will explore in Chapter 3, the rhythmic oscillation of study is not reducible to the repetition of practice as Vlieghe argues. Here Scheffler's analytic of potentiality seems to intervene at the right moment to remind us that Agamben's theory of im-potentiality is uniquely related to the in-capable studier.

Yet, without Agamben, what Scheffler misses is that capabilities are not simply intentional states of mind that organize our actions in order to accomplish certain goals. For instance, capabilities, precisely because they are capabilities, can hold within themselves the capability to do *and* not to do simultaneously. In other words, the one who studies is *trying not to try* or *preferring not to prefer* or *desiring not to desire* in order to remain open to the experience of possibility as such. And when one tries not to try, trying and not trying become indistinguishable. And when one prefers not to prefer this or that, then this *and* that are held together in a moment of inoperability or suspension. Only with the development of capabilities can these capabilities undergo such a privation or withdrawing from actualization, and this is the moment of a most precarious kind of freedom—freedom from the capability to.

46   *The ontology of study*

The studier: a case study

As strange as it might first appear, Bartleby the Scrivener is Agamben's prime example of study. The short story by Melville concerns a scrivener who one day "would prefer not" to actualize his potentiality for being a copyist yet nevertheless refuses to leave his desk. Every day, Bartleby does less and less work around the Wall Street office, and when the narrator attempts to dialogue with him about his actions, Bartleby refuses to explain himself. Finally, Bartleby stops working all together yet remains within the office, dwelling in the space as a kind of inoperative remainder, frustrating his former boss and fellow employees. In this sense, he no longer conforms to the notion of a capable subject—halting the productive capabilities of willful action, ceasing to be self-assertive, rejecting the logic of "reliability." Often mentioned as the embodiment of Agamben's theory of im-potentiality, it would be a mistake to assume that Bartleby, for all his melancholy, is simply passive, inert, and inactive. Indeed, Agamben writes that at the moment when Bartleby stops writing, he becomes the "most exemplary embodiment of study in our culture" (1995: 65). As the quintessential example, Bartleby does not belong to any class of "educational subjects." In suspending such classifications, he exemplifies how the studies is always paradoxically included in the class of educational subjects by being excluded from this class.

Importantly the first example offered in the story of Bartleby's "preferring not" is his refusal to check the accuracy of his work. Melville describes the scene as follows:

> It is, of course, an indispensable part of a scrivener's business to verify the accuracy of his copy, word by word. Where there are two or more scriveners in an office, they assist each other in this examination, one reading from the copy, the other holding the original. It is a very dull, wearisome, and lethargic affair. I can readily imagine that to some sanguine temperaments it would be altogether intolerable. For example, I cannot credit that the mettlesome poet Byron would have contentedly sat down with Bartleby to examine a law document of, say five hundred pages, closely written in a crimpy hand. . . .
>
> In my haste and natural expectancy of instant compliance, I sat with my head bent over the original on my desk, and my right hand sideways, and somewhat nervously extended with the copy, so that immediately upon emerging from his retreat, Bartleby might snatch it and proceed to business without the least delay.
>
> In this very attitude did I sit when I called to him, rapidly stating what it was I wanted him to do—namely, to examine a small paper with me. Imagine my surprise, nay, my consternation, when without moving from his privacy, Bartleby in a singularly mild, firm voice, replied, "I would prefer not to."

(Melville 2002: 10)

The ontology of study   47

In this shocking turn of events, the narrator is left dumbfounded by Bartleby's "I would prefer not to." What is important to note is that Bartleby's refusal is an *interruption of testing and examination*. Up to this point in the narrative, he continues to work—indeed he is the most productive of employees, the most reliable—yet he prefers not to be compliant with a system of evaluation. If such work must be submitted to external review by a jury of expert scriveners, then Bartleby excuses himself from any notion of self-evaluation. He will not test or be tested, he will simply work. He has the capabilities (to use Scheffler's terminology) to perform his assigned work, and, thus far, can be relied upon to actualize these capabilities. But, importantly, these capabilities for Bartleby must become a pure means (*un mezzo puro*) and thus never be submitted to any test or measure.

"To prefer not to" becomes a kind of mantra that Bartleby repeats throughout the story. Here is but one example of the strange function that this formulation of refusal plays:

> "Bartleby," said I, "Ginger Nut is away; just step round to the Post Office, won't you? (it was but a three minute walk) and see if there is any thing for me."
> "I would prefer not to."
> "You *will* not?"
> "I *prefer* not."
>
> (Melville 2002: 14–15)

Instead of completing the assigned task, Bartleby, once again, prefers not. As the story progresses, Bartleby prefers not to work, to run errands, to leave the office, and even to eat. Thus there is a slow and steady withdrawal from not only the logic of examination but also the logic of actualization. If, at first, Bartleby recalled Scheffler's capable student who had cultivated the necessary capabilities to be successful and could be counted on to actualize these capabilities, here there is a full suspension of the logic of actualization, leaving only the nude appearance of im-potentiality as a kind of zero-degree of Bartleby's existence. No longer can he be relied upon to be this or that kind of subject with these or those kinds of capabilities. Instead what is left is a remnant that is radically inoperative. At the moment of maximum exertion, suddenly Bartleby withholds his capabilities, keeps them to himself.

Crucially, "I prefer not to" is distinct from "I will not." Colby Dickinson aptly summarizes this distinction as follows,

> Rather than "I will not" being the declarative phrase of resistance uttered to his boss, Bartleby's "I prefer not to" is an emphatic distancing of himself from the entire machinery of actuality and its formulation of a decisive will, which is to be seen here as little more than a slightly veiled attempt to obtain power.
>
> (2011: 43)

48 *The ontology of study*

Agamben argues as much when he states, "Bartleby calls into question precisely this supremacy of the will over potentiality" (1999c: 254). To will is always an attempt to gain power over something, to impose one's internal force onto the other. By withdrawing from the will, his resistance remains obscure, eliciting empathy rather than violence from his boss. Stated differently "to prefer not to" is a resistantless form of resistance, a powerless power. Because preferring not to is affectless, devoid of anger, passion, or spite, it catches the employer completely off guard, defenseless before the polite, seemingly impotent conditional. "To prefer not to" is radically passive, so passive that it manages to interrupt the law without *offending* the law. As Julian Patrick rightly points out, Bartleby "does not insist on his resistance, merely persists in it" (2002: 731). While insistence produces a violent battle between two wills, persistence avoids such violence and yet remains absolutely militant. Indeed, "preferring not to" quickly reorients criticism away from Bartleby back toward the employer himself who becomes increasingly self-reflective over the nature of his own power. In fact, the inaction that is the ultimate action of in-decision (preferring not) results in a withdrawing of the power of the employer. Ironically, it is the sovereignty of the boss that in the end is rendered impotent, for the only recourse before Bartleby's militant "preferring not to" is to pack up and move the business elsewhere! Exacerbated, the employer concludes:

> Since he will not quit me, I must quit him. I will change my offices; I will move elsewhere; and give him fair notice, that if I find him on my new premises I will then proceed against him as a common trespasser.
>
> (Melville 2002: 28)

The most threatening gesture to the power of the law is that which is most polite, most inconspicuous, most inoffensive. Without a will to battle against, sovereignty quietly retreats from the scene, ashamed of its own powers. In this sense, Bartleby can stand before the law of the employer's command with indifference and impunity without incurring the violence of what Agamben elsewhere refers to as the sovereign's ban, or the sovereign's unmitigated violence over and against a bare life. Bartleby is not simply bare life (abandoned life) but a *studious life* that stands before the law, suspending it through the act of refusal to be complacent with its commands. In this sense, he remains in proximity to the law in order to study exactly what happens when it is left idle.

To "prefer not to" opens up a new notion of living that (a) stands before the law of production, utility, and examination yet (b) suspends the efficacy of this law in order to (c) study the im-potentiality that shines forth. This is an educational life of *ease* without any desire for mastery, without any desire to reach an end beyond ease itself. To live a life of ease, writes Agamben, is a life "which contemplates its (own) power to act" while rendering "itself inoperative in all its operations, and lives only (its) livability" (2011a: 251). By rendering inoperative the specific work and labor of *a* life, life itself begins to experience a potentiality untethered by predetermined, economic ends. This is precisely what is so mysterious about Bartleby to his employer. After experiencing the *impotent force* of "I prefer not to," the employer reflects: "But there was something about Bartleby that not only strangely disarmed me, but in a wonderful manner touched and disconcerted me" (Melville 2002: 12). This strange mystery that resides in Bartleby's behavior is precisely the ease at which he prefers not to—an ease that indicates a life beyond the performance principle, a life of pure potentiality that shines forth in the most im-potential of gestures. What is disconcerting is the im-potential withdrawal of productivity upon which Wall Street—and its internal logic of learning—functions, leaving only a sense of "wonderful" ease wherein humanity can appear as it is: nude in its pure livability, vulnerable, silent, and at the same time powerfully disarming. The only preference that seems to interrupt the continual flow of goods and services defining the economy is in the end the preference not to prefer.

In this state of ease, the law is suspended but also the work of producing and maintaining a subject before the law. The indifference to subjectivity is captured by Melville in the following dialogue between an impassioned boss desperately trying to understand *who* Bartleby is, and a semi-indifferent Bartleby.

> "Will you tell me, Bartleby, where you were born?"
> "I would prefer not to."
> "Will you tell me *any thing* about yourself?"
> "I would prefer not to."
> "But what reasonable objection can you have to speak to me? I feel friendly towards you."
> He did not look at me while I spoke, but kept his glance fixed upon my bust of Cicero, which as I then sat, was directly behind me, some six inches above my head.
> "What is your answer, Bartleby?" said I, after waiting a considerable time for a reply, during which his countenance remained immovable, only there was the faintest conceivable tremor of the white attenuated mouth.
> "At present I prefer to give no answer," he said, and retired into his hermitage.
>
> (2002: 19–20)

Bartleby is indeed *no one*. He has no past and no future. Only his present actions are known. When studying before the suspended law, the subject undergoes a suspension: a no-body who does not seem to have a definitive destination or occupation. Indeed to study is to undergo a kind of loosening of the grip that ends have over means—hence Bartleby's first act of refusal is precisely to prefer not to examine his work. Although disagreeing with Eric Santner's overall reading of Bartleby, I would like to highlight his description of the protagonist as a kind of "unmistakably singular yet also utterly generic" (2011: 251) character. In other words, Bartleby is, along with various characters in Beckett's plays, "strangely abstract; they no longer belong to a recognizable world or form of life. And yet they never cease to be utterly, even excessively concrete; everything has been

50   *The ontology of study*

brought irremediably down to earth" (ibid.). Stated differently, Bartleby withdraws from any recognizable social role or form of life that would be admissible as a *bios*. If the educational life for Scheffler is one of increasing confidence to act on one's capabilities in order to realize goals that can be recognized as personal growth and betterment, then Bartleby presents a radical reversal of these terms. The studious life that Bartleby leads does not culminate in actualizing his potentiality in determinate forms. Rather he maintains a relationship to his indistinguishing im-potentiality. It is this relationship to im-potentiality that renders him absolutely singular (no one can take his place) yet generic at the same time (he lacks any of the individuating characteristics that define a person as *this* person). While the educational life advocated by Scheffler *distinguishes* individuals in terms of the concrete manifestations of willful capabilities to perform as expected, the studious life advocated by Agamben *indistinguishes* life. When Bartleby prefers not to work as a scrivener, he lives the life of a scrivener *as not* a scrivener, thus introducing a surplus into the order of things. The result is the impossibility of describing the radically generic and seemingly empty life of Bartleby while also managing to convey its radical singularity and its uniqueness. This is a singularity beyond any notion of the capable subject and beyond the willful pursuits of a constituting will to power. What Santner has missed in his analysis is that Bartleby's existence as a generic singularity is not simply the result of his preferring not to but rather because this preferring not to is the negative inscription of study: for only when one prefers not to engage with the trials and tribulations of everyday coping and dealing can one then open a space of ease where one can study.

Generic singularity—neither desubjectified nor subjectified—is depicted in another brief exchange between employer and "employee," this time a dialogue concerning Bartleby's "preferences." At wit's end, the desperate boss attempts to pique Bartleby's interest in alternative forms of work:

> "There is too much confinement about that. No, I would not like a clerkship; but I am not particular."
>
> "Too much confinement," I cried, "why you keep yourself confined all the time!"
>
> "I would prefer not to take a clerkship," he rejoined, as if to settle that little item at once.
>
> "How would a bar-tender's business suit you? There is no trying of the eyesight in that."
>
> "I would not like it at all; though, as I said before, I am not particular."
>
> (Melville 2002: 30)

Although preferring not to be this or that, Bartleby nevertheless insists that he is "not particular." He has no preferences, no particularity, no desires to become x, y, or z. At the same time he equally prefers not to become a clerk or a bartender. The logic here seems paradoxical but becomes clear when we realize that *to be open to all professions without reserve is equally to prefer not to partake in any one profession*. Thus Bartleby's semi-indifference to all the suggestions given to him does not indicate a simple laziness or lassitude or lack of aptitude but rather a manifestation of his im-potential freedom from all determinations. He holds the potentiality for all these various occupations inside himself in a kind of suspended animation in the precise moment when he withdraws from actualizing his capabilities for any particular one of them. The result is a life that studies (an occupation that is not an occupation) without conclusions, without ends, and thus open to a world that no longer submits the subject to any normative call or commanding pressure to perform and be evaluated. At this point it is important to remember that for Agamben, the ethical experience of freedom is precisely "the experience of being (one's own) potentiality, of being (one's own) possibility—exposing, that is, in every form of one's own amorphousness and in every act one's own inactuality" (1993a: 44). The more singular Bartleby becomes, the more he (as a particular subject with reliable skills and dispositions) seems to disappear; his actions enact his amorphous inactuality, exposing the nudity of his im-potentiality. He becomes amphibian.

Bartleby's inaction is a kind of action that interrupts the flow of signs and the exchange of things in order to expose the underlying backdrop—the incessant paradigm of productive work and willful pursuit—upon which meaningful relations draw their efficacy. In this sense, Bartleby could not work and could not leave, not because he was doing nothing but because he was *studying* and, in the moment of study, he lost his occupation and his identity as this or that kind of person with this or that set of capabilities, desires, or interests. He had nothing to say for himself, no clear project that he could possibly articulate beyond "preferring not to." Crucially, only after having acquired the skills and dispositions to be a scrivener is he able to study. Thus, it is not simply that he is incapable of performing the required tasks assigned to him, but rather that he is in-capable, withholding his capabilities from actualizing themselves according to the commands imposed upon him or even his desire to "live up to expectations." In this sense, the studier is always a profanity, a blight on the efficiency and necessity of *the way things are and the way people are supposed to act*. Indeed, the studier appears to be radically un-educated, or, perhaps even worse, radically un-educable—recalcitrant to any call to assert anything beyond his or her preference not to do, not to say, and thus postpone evaluation of his or her "success" and "failure." Yet for Agamben, it is only in such a state of suspension that *whatever* can be studied, that a modicum of freedom can suddenly appear in a society that has become obsessed with maximizing capabilities *to do, to be, to will*.

As Gilles Deleuze once wrote,

> The problem is no longer getting people to express themselves but providing little gaps of solitude and silence in which they might eventually find something to say. Repressive forces don't stop people from expressing themselves, but rather, force them to express themselves. What a relief to have nothing to say, the right to say nothing, because only then is there a chance of framing the rare, and even rarer, the thing that might be worth saying.
>
> (1997: 129)

52 *The ontology of study*

Repression for Deleuze is a kind of imperative or sovereign command to *produce evidence* of one's potentiality through the form of the examination, the test, or the evaluation. To submit one's potentiality to measure is to engage in a form of servitude that separates the human from his or her im-potentiality. Deleuzian freedom asserts itself by withdrawing from the actualization of latent potentiality and remaining in the darkness of silence and solitude. In my reading, Bartleby can be seen as an expression of such freedom, which inappropriately interrupts the law, its force, and its destination opening up a kind of ease that is unique to the studious life.

In sum, capabilities—as Scheffler describes them—allow us to be and to do in a world and have success within its parameters, yet it does not allow us to *study* this world. To study is to move beyond any pragmatic notion of capabilities oriented toward particular projects with definitive success conditions as an educational ideal. Like Bartleby, the one who studies seems to be inactive, lazy or simply apathetic. Yet this apparent inactivity of "preferring not to" is, in the end, an im-potential rejoinder to the power of command. In the face of the imperative to work, to learn, to be relied upon, to maximize one's outputs so as to be judged, tested, and evaluated, the studier simply "prefers not to" and in turn retains a little bit of freedom before the man of the law. So what do we gain from studying Bartleby, a scribe who prefers not to write? For educators, the example is a profound one: Bartleby does not teach us *what* to write, or *how* to write, but rather that we *can/cannot* write. And this is perhaps the most difficult thing to study precisely because it cannot be submitted to evaluation. We can only bear witness to its peculiar and perplexing appearance.

3   The aesthetics of study
Poetic rhythm, mood, and the melancholic angel

Although Alfred North Whitehead is not a name that appears with great frequency in contemporary philosophy of education, his notion of the rhythm of learning has garnered a modest amount of interest since its initial appearance in his classic text *The Aims of Education* (1967). For instance, Howard Woodhouse (1999) has argued for a reconceptualization of the university in relation to Whitehead's theory of the cyclic or spiral relationship between freedom and discipline in order to rekindle student interest, administrative vision, and professorial scholarship. Most importantly, Hannu Soini and Mark Flynn's empirical research has demonstrated the ongoing relevancy of Whitehead's notion of the "rhythm of mental growth" for capturing the aesthetic aspects of learning. In an attempt to understand the "aesthetic experience of learning more concretely" (2005: 73) Soini and Flynn have discovered the correlation between students' reflections on educational events in their lives and Whitehead's philosophical analysis of cycles of discipline and freedom. In this chapter, I will further extend Soini and Flynn's revitalization of Whitehead's work in order to define (a) the poetics of learning, (b) the temporality of rhythm, and (c) the structure of human potentiality conserved through the rhythmic temporality of learning. To accomplish this threefold goal, I will turn to the literary theories of Giorgio Agamben, who argues that rhythm redeems potentiality in the messianic break with linear chronology. If Agamben enables us to fully appreciate the poetics of the rhythm of mental growth as a window into the nature of potentiality, then in turn Whitehead enables us to fully appreciate the implicit connections between the literary Agamben and Agamben's passing remarks on learning or, more accurately, studying. In this sense, I am calling for a dialectic between Agamben and Whitehead in order to enrich both Agamben's literary criticism and Whitehead's educational theory.

Rhythm and the cycles of potentiality

In his seminal work *The Aims of Education*, Whitehead argues that learning is composed of cycles of freedom, discipline, and freedom nested within cycles of romance, precision, and generalization. On the most basic level, romance is the earliest stage of mental development where students are emotionally engaged

54   *The aesthetics of study*

with the "vividness of novelty" (Whitehead 1967: 17) at the world. Here we find experience is unmediated by a particular *logos* and instead proceeds according to sensual discovery and wonder. The stage of precision follows with its emphasis on discipline and "exactness of formulation" (ibid.: 18). More often than not, it is this stage that occupies formal education at the expense of romantic freedom. Modern schooling, for Whitehead, reifies learning into the mere retention and memorization of facts and performance of allotted tasks. Finally, the stage of generalization is in a sense a return to the initial freedom of romance only now with the added reflective tools gained through precise analysis and the acquisition of relevant processes and techniques. Education, according to Whitehead, should concern itself with the "continual repetition of such cycles" (ibid.: 19). Thus while university life concerns itself mainly with the state of generalization, there is no reason why it cannot, through its internal development, lead back to a new period of romance. Whitehead argues as much. When describing the university student, Whitehead states, "He relapses into the discursive adventures of the romantic stage, with the advantage his mind is now a disciplined regiment instead of a rabble. In this sense, education should begin in research and end in research" (ibid.: 37). Each successive stage thus simultaneously gestures toward its own future overcoming by the next stage (romance necessarily forces the student onward to precision in order to refine wonder with analytic tools) while at the same time gesturing backwards toward its own past (generalization, in its final moment of perfection, suddenly returns to the romantic moment of open wonder). In this sense, there is a continual loop between cycles that press forward and backward simultaneously—a continual loop between desubjectification, where the subject is struck by the novelty of the world, and subjectification, where the subject disciplines the self through attentiveness necessary to further analyze this novelty. Simply stated, each stage emerges out of an internal contraction of past and future stages. Whitehead puts it best when he argues, "there is not one unique threefold cycle of freedom, discipline, and freedom; but that all mental development is composed of such cycles, and of cycles of such cycles" (ibid.: 31). If modern learning relies solely on the stage of precision, then the result is an "unrhythmic collection of distracting scraps" (ibid.: 21). Schools and universities operating under this banner are not actually concerned with education but with something else entirely.

Key to Whitehead's theory of mental development are the rhythms that exist both across stages (leading from romance to precision to generalization) and within stages (nesting the wonder and freedom of romance within the wisdom and precision of generalization). Rather than a linear, chronologically uniform, and sequential model of learning, Whitehead argues for a spiraling/cyclic model that involves a continual loop between past and present, emotion and reason, freedom and discipline. The rhythmic nature of learning is, in short, "the conveyance of difference within a framework of repetition" (ibid.: 17). For Whitehead, the life of a child is essentially periodic, composed of cycles of growth between romance, discipline, and generalization. At the outset it is of the utmost importance to recognize that "there are also subtler periods of mental growth, with their cyclic recurrences, yet always different as we pass from cycle to cycle, though the subordinate stages are reproduced in each cycle" (ibid.). In other words, there are cycles within cycles, and while each stage of development might be dominated by a particular inflection of freedom or discipline, there are constantly recurring elements from past cycles that are drawn up and maintained within each stage. As Whitehead summarizes, "romance, precision, generalization, are all present throughout. But there is an alternation of dominance, and it is this alternation which constitutes the cycles" (ibid.: 28). Or, stated differently,

> During the state of precision, romance is the background. The stage is dominated by the inescapable fact that there are right ways and wrong ways, and definite truths to be known. But romance is not dead, and it is the art of teaching to foster it amidst definite application to appointed task.
> (ibid.: 34)

Having outlined Whitehead's general theory of the rhythmic development of thought, I will now argue that we must further develop Whitehead's initial insights through Agamben's reflections on poiesis. While humankind cannot simply return to a poietic relationship with the world, nevertheless, the trace of poiesis remains within the work of study. To see this connection, it is crucial to highlight the rhythmic nature of poiesis. We can use Agamben's analysis of the rhythms of poiesis to unravel the strange formulation offered by Whitehead that rhythm is both a cycle and a cycle within cycles. I will use Agamben to push this claim further than Whitehead, and suggest that the cycles within cycles that he describes actually suspend the residual influences of developmentalism informing Whitehead's overarching psychological framework. Through an enhanced notion of the poetics of study, cycles within cycles can emerge as a kind of rhythm that is neither simply educational stasis/paralysis nor teleological self-mastery and self-actualization. Instead, what can be glimpsed from within the indistinction of cyclic folding is a form of education that makes explicit one's im-potentiality, leased from the command and capture of determinate measurement or quantification.

According to Agamben's formulation, rhythm is a process where "in the work of art the continuum of linear time is broken, and man recovers, between past and future his present space" (1999b: 102). In other words, rhythm, as best exemplified in the structure of the poem, negates any notion of linear, chronological unfolding. The rhythm of poiesis is simultaneously projective and recursive, a suspension of movement *and* its resumption, a continual oscillation of forward and backward momentum. Agamben argues "rhythm grants men both the ecstatic dwelling in a more original dimension and the fall into the flight of measurable time" (ibid.: 100). In other words, rhythm is not outside chronological time but rather is a disruption of linear time from inside its own chronological unfolding. Rhythm, which presses forward as much as it gestures backward, produces a cyclic space of what William Watkin refers to a

56 *The aesthetics of study*

"developmental reiteration" (2010: 155)—rhythm is thus simultaneously a backward and forward movement in time. Counter to common-sense understandings of rhythm, Agamben highlights how it is the complex interplay between interruption and endless, unperturbed flow. In fact, it is precisely the rupture of flow that inaugurates a return to flow (or rather announces its cyclic return). Agamben argues, "Rather than defining a problem and then seeking to solve it conclusively, let's say the problem of being, it [poetic thinking] is always already within the problem ... If traditional thought advances, poetic thought turns" (cited in Watkin 2010: 201). In other words, poetic thinking is the rhythmic turning that in its propulsion toward conclusion turns in on itself, perpetuating the paradox of its finite infinity.

For Agamben, this aporia is captured best in the rhythmic structure of verse, which is a space of "memory and repetition" (1991: 78). The rhythm of poetry anticipates what will be only as it recalls what has come before it. In this sense the overall rhythmic structure that unites the individual lines in a poem is a "unity that intersects and unites a plurality and a repetition" (ibid.: 79). If, as Agamben writes, "The poem is therefore an organism or a temporal machine that, from the very start, strains toward its end" (2005b: 79) then the end of the poem strains backward recursively to its own beginning through the tension between the unit of the sentence and the unit of the line. This description of the poem as a cyclic structure of forward momentum and recursive folding illustrates the intimate relationship between poiesis and learning as described by Whitehead. For Whitehead learning is the complex of relationships of cycles within cycles where every stage of freedom both propels the learner forward while simultaneously suspending or interrupting that propulsion through what he refers to as "the conveyance of difference within a framework of repetition" (1967: 17).

The greater import of this observation is conveyed by Agamben's further analysis of poiesis in relation to messianic time. If, in the moment of rhythmic poiesis, "we perceive a stop in time ... an interruption in the incessant flow in instants that, coming from the future, sinks into the past" (1999b: 99) then poiesis opens up a time that is neither the end of time or the chronology of everyday learning. Rather it presents a time of disjunction—the messianic kernel of time that remains between the progression of linear events and the final moment of judgment. This disjunction is not outside of chronology, but rather is offered as its remnant where the future folds into the present and the past explodes into the future. Again, the structure of messianic time is revealed through the poem's rhythm. For Agamben, every poem is a "sotoriological device which, through the sophisticated *mechane* of the announcement and retrieval of rhyming end words (which correspond to typological relations between past and present), transforms chronological time into messianic time" (2005b: 82–3). The time of the poem is the "metamorphosis that time undergoes insofar as it is the time of the end, *the time that the poem takes to come to an end*" (ibid.: 83). In other words, the developmental/recursive model of the poem illustrates the nature of messianic time as a time between chronological linearity and the end of time. In fact the poem, especially the lyric, is always an attempt to delay its own end and thus remain within the space of its own radical de-completion. Stated differently, the end of the poem conserves the potential of its beginning. "The poem," writes Agamben,

> is like the *katechon* in Paul's Second Epistle to the Thessalonians (2:7–8): something that slows and delays the advent of the Messiah, that is, of him who, fulfilling the time of poetry and uniting its two eons, would destroy the poetic machine by hurling it into silence.
>
> (1999a: 114)

If the poem is an attempt to delay its own end, then Agamben argues that the end of every poem always seems abrupt or forced "as if the poem as a formal structure would not and could not end, as if the possibility of the end were radically withdrawn from it, since the end would imply a poetic impossibility" (ibid.: 113). In fact, the only way for the poem to prolong the time of its becoming is to suddenly end with what Agamben refers to as a "catastrophe and loss of identity" (ibid.: 112). If the structure of a poem is defined by certain features including the possibility of enjambment or rhyming couplets, then the end of the poem is a loss of this identity and thus the last verse of a poem is not a verse at all but rather the transformation of verse into prose. The only way to ensure its own de-completion is for the poem to undergo a radical desubjectification as a poem and to become something else entirely: prose. The sudden transformation at the end of the poem maintains the potentiality through an enactment of an impotentiality to come to an end. Thus the moment when the poem turns into prose is the also the sudden proclamation "I would prefer not" to end. In short, the end of the poem is only achieved through the paradoxical *suspension of the end of the poem*.

Agamben again returns to the question of the rhythm of messianic time in a short essay dedicated to an analysis of the relationship between creation and salvation. If the two have been effectively separated from one another in the contemporary Western world, this need not be the case. While the function of the angel is to create, produce, and look ahead, and the function of the prophet is to retrieve, undo, and arrest development, we can find in the messianic moment a "rhythm according to which creation precedes redemption but in relation follows it, as redemption follows creation but in truth precedes it" (Agamben 2011b: 4). Salvation redeems the past by suspending or de-completing the work of creation, which is rendered inoperative. This relation between creation and decreation is not a dialectical sublation of the former into the latter and vice versa into a completed whole. Rather it is a "tenacious, amorous conflict" (ibid.: 7)—a kind of maximal intensification of the two actions captured in a single rhythmic sway on the *threshold* of indistinction.

Applying this same analysis to studying, we can argue that mental development as a "rhythmic sway" (Whitehead 1967: 35) is not simply a forward progression marked by increased test scores or graduate degrees that signify the

58 *The aesthetics of study*

full actualization of the learner through measured progress but is a complex cycle of freedom, discipline, and freedom in a never-ending rhythm of flow and punctuation. The educational danger in missing this fundamental insight is that studying would be submitted to the artificial constraints of linear chronologie with fixed deadlines and learning quotas at the expense of the complex and rather enigmatic interpenetration of suspension and resumption captured in the messianic time of poiesis. Like the poem, studying resists its own end, its actualization as a measurable quantity fully mastered by the "subject who knows" and commodified into manageable and marketable skill sets. In Whitehead's analysis, this means a turn from generalization (as the certainty of a willing subject guided by intentional content of the mind) to romantic intensity—a radical desubjectivation that is not simply a repetition, but, as Whitehead emphasizes, a conservation of the romantic potentiality within the generalization itself. In this sense, romance *de-completes* any discipline defining a generalized subject introducing a momentary sway backward toward the beginning at the very moment when studying has reached an "end." Romance is akin to redemption (an undoing) and discipline to creation (a doing). The rhythmic sway between the two is thus simultaneously an undoing that is a doing and a doing that is an undoing. In other words, the cycles within cycles that Whitehead mentions create a threshold wherein romance, discipline, and generalization become indistinct, issuing forth a kind of *educational state of exception*.

Read with new messianic eyes, the rhythmic development described by Whitehead is not for subjective development (the actualization of subjective willpower through the production of a biography composed of public acts) but rather for the continual desubjectification initiated by poetic conservation of romantic potentiality within the rhythmic sway of study. The studier properly resides in the most improper of locations: the space and time between subjectification and desubjectification, oscillating between poles to the point of indistinction. According to Agamben's theory, the fundamental experience in poiesis is precisely sway between these two operations. The subject of poiesis is the subject of its own de-completion—the suspension of the subject as defined by measurable mental mastery, definitive judgments, reliable capabilities, or professional accreditation. For Whitehead this would amount to the repetition of romance within generalization that interrupts mastery at the precise moment when mastery is called upon to fully actualize itself. The rhythm of research is the destabilizing factor in Whitehead's model that continually presses discipline back to the necessary freedom to explore the im-potentiality of thought and thus return necessity to contingency. In other words, the experience of rhythm (of the poem for Agamben or of learning for Whitehead) is an ontological reexperiencing of our potential to be *and* not to be. It is this in-capacity that, for Agamben, forms the backbone of freedom. Agamben's politics of poetic rhythm coupled with Whitehead's educational theory suggest that freedom is, on the other hand, a sort of hesitation or suspension between a pure potentiality and a specific action in the moment of romantic wonder. Simply put, rather than education as the exclamation of "I will *x*" the rhythm of study returns us to the more primordial experience of "I can, I cannot." If the former rushes to the fulfillment of potentiality in the moment of actualization of *this* subject with *these* beliefs and *these* skills, then the latter sustains poetic freedom that vibrates between no-longer and not-yet, between accepting and rejecting, between nothing and being captured in the phrase "I can, I cannot."

It is my conclusion that Whitehead, when read through Agamben's extended notion of rhythm, is gesturing toward an appreciation of study as an activity that sustains the experience of the indeterminate zone between subjectification and desubjectification. This is an education that resists subordinating potentiality to actuality, possibility to necessity, impotentiality to will, or contingency to necessity. In Whitehead's language, we see that every freedom (to be and not to be) creates the conditions of discipline (to be) which in turn only produce the cyclic folding back into the moment of indistinction between the two (to be and not to be). Stated differently, every act conserves within itself a certain potentiality not to be and thus retains the trace of freedom. It is this trace that rhythmically pushes learning forward to new cycles through the recursive repetition of past cycles. In short, learning as rhythmic poiesis is the redemption of the potentiality for further romance within every generalization, and as such stands in stark contrast to learning conceptualized as praxis.

If Agamben's analysis of poiesis enables us to fully appreciate the aesthetic dimension of Whitehead's rhythmic model of mental development then, in turn, Whitehead helps clarify a rather dense passage in Agamben's work concerning the relation between poetry and study. In regards to St. Thomas's interpretation of Dante, Agamben argues that studying can be defined as a "double disjunction between the intellect and speech in which language exceeds the intellect (speaking without understanding) and the intellect transcends language (understanding without speaking)" (1999a: 39). Stated differently, studying is the internal tension that exists between romance (as the freedom to speak without understanding) and generalization (as the intellectual mastery that suddenly lacks language and thus inaugurates a turn back to romance). Dante's genius, writes Agamben, was

> his having transformed the two into a double but nevertheless synchronous movement traversing the poetic act, in which invention is inverted into discipline (into listening) and the discipline is inverted into invention, so to speak by virtue of its own insufficiency.
>
> (ibid.: 39)

Rephrasing Agamben's eclectic observation using Whitehead's language, the philosopher is suggesting that Dante folds the two movements of studying into a single, synchronically poetic structure—a structure that is cyclically captured between discipline and freedom, romance and generalization, creation and redemption, without end.

The movement between speaking without understanding and understanding without speaking that defines the poetic structure of studying is repeated on

60   *The aesthetics of study*

the macro level in the dichotomous gap between the poet and the philosopher that forms the overarching theme of Agamben's work as a whole. As Watkin argues, Agamben's writing embodies a form of logopoiesis, or writing that exists in the indistinction between poetry and philosophy. Long standing in Agamben's work is the insight that the disciplines of poetry and philosophy have "lost all memory of the relationship that had previously linked them so intimately to one another" resulting in an "almost schizophrenic character that seems to make this relationship" (2010: 5). In *Nudities* Agamben begins with the observation that critics have lost the ability to create while poets have lost the ability to redeem their poems. This is basically a restatement of the beginning of his book *Stanzas* (1993b), where Agamben argues that while philosophy has the ability to know (redemption), it has lost its object, and while poetry retains a relation to its object (creation), it has lost the ability to know this object. Logopoiesis is an attempt to dwell in the gap that both unites and separates poetry and philosophy in order to enter into a threshold between the two. This peculiar threshold is precisely the location of Agamben's critical work that "neither represents nor knows, but knows the representation" (Agamben 1993b xvii). Is this not, in the end, the perfect location for study? The studier is neither the philosopher (who has knowledge and no object) nor the poet (who has an object without knowledge). Rather the one who studies finds him or herself in the gap between these poles. Thus Agamben himself is neither a philosopher nor a poet but rather a perpetual studier who is confronting the question of what it means to study.

The mood of rhythmic study

Without Agamben's emphasis on poetic rhythm as the aesthetic dimension of educational im-potentiality, Whitehead's insight into educational rhythm could be appropriated as another form of (complex) developmentalism. As with my previous analysis of Scheffler, Agamben adds to educational discourse a renewed emphasis on the relation between potentiality and impotentiality, this time on the aesthetic level of rhythm. He is also helpful in defining the mood the studier is gripped by when undergoing this oscillation between freedom and discipline, passivity and activity. This moodiness is completely lacking in Whitehead's description of educational cycles, which is impoverished as long as it reduces aesthetics to mere educational formalism without the supplement of educational affectation. In particular, the mood of study is not so much an internal emotion of the studier as the atmosphere produced by and through engaged studying. To get at this mood, I will first argue that the rhythmic sway of the poem is phenomenologically equivalent to hesitation. When hesitating, one is neither not doing something nor doing something. Indeed, it is a paradoxical state of not-not doing something. As hesitation prolongs—as its temporality extends—the moment of hesitation becomes a form of boredom, which, for Heidegger is one of the basic attunements (*Gundstimmungen*) of *Dasein*. The boredom of prolonged hesitation (hesitation

The aesthetics of study 61

without end, that has forgotten its end) is what, paradoxically, offers an opportunity to open studying up to a new form of educational inspiration.

According to Alexander García Düttmann in the foreword to *Idea of Prose*,

> Hesitation does not abandon itself to the sphere of "pure potentiality": however, it does not exclude potentiality either. Even if it seems to perpetuate the possible, even if it seems to perpetuate it in its multiplicity ... hesitation begins to thwart the opposition between possibility and reality, between act and potentiality, between existence and essence ... a potentiality actualized as such.
>
> (Agamben 1995: 12)

Hesitation is between chronological time and the end of time, a moment of distillation and condensation where time seems at an end while that end equally remains distant and inaccessible, ultimately fading from view altogether. Hesitation is therefore not simply pure potentiality divorced from the mediating passage to the act but rather offers the slightest of shifts that signal potentiality reaching its limit without yet having passed into determinate form. In other words, hesitation is a particular phenomenological temporal state betwixt and between potentiality and activity that signals the beginning of the end of time without passing into that end. It is a gap that separates and joins potentiality and actuality without collapsing the two. In Agamben's words, potentiality is the "possibility suspended between occurrence and nonoccurrence" (1999c: 267), not unlike hesitation. Indeed, hesitation is akin to the moment at the end of the poem where enjambment is no longer possible and poetry and prose seem to intermingle. This moment is the moment of exception where the tension between metrical limit and syntactical limit is most acutely felt. Citing Valéry's definition of poetry, Agamben asserts "The poem: a prolonged hesitation between sound and sense" (1999a: 109). Stated differently, withdrawing/progressing and sound/sense become indistinguishable in the mood of hesitation crystalized at the end of the poem—or better yet, at the end*ing* of the poem (as a movement that never reaches its conclusion).

At this point we might turn to one of Agamben's favorite images, Dürer's etching *Melancholia I* (1514). The question of the angel is itself a perpetual interest for Agamben, appearing at important moments throughout his many books. I would argue that this reappearance of the angel in a secular age is itself what Jorge Luis Borges refers to as the "near miracle" of the "survival of the angel" (2000: 18). Borges points out that while the human imagination has, over the centuries, given birth to innumerable monsters, "all have disappeared, except angels" (ibid.: 19). Indeed, poetry in particular seems to continually return to the figure of the angel as if the angel were somehow necessarily connected on an ontological level to the very form of poetry. Thus Borges writes "no poetry, however modern, is unhappy to be a nest of angels and to shine brightly with them" (ibid.). The importance of this marginal observation cannot be overestimated, for poetry *shelters* angels, and in turn, angels provide the last

62 *The aesthetics of study*

remaining icons of study. While Agamben does not connect Dürer's melancholic angel directly with the idea of education, we can argue that the angel is lost in the hesitation of study. Describing the relics of the past that fall at this angel's feet, Agamben writes, "these objects have captured forever a gleam of that which can be possessed only with the provision that it be lost forever" (1993b: 26). The melancholic figure studies the world indefinitely precisely by suspending the law of the world—rupturing the chronological time of event and the production of things—and transforming its sacred objects into discarded relics that nevertheless still "gleam." The melancholic angel is, for Agamben, the angel of modern aesthetics, who represents "a culture that is losing its transmissibility" as the "sole guarantee of its truth" and is thus "threatened by the incessant accumulation of its nonsense" (1999b: 110) without the ability to find a clear direction, path, or project. This description sounds shockingly similar to Borges' own imagistic description of the angel in a destitute time:

> I always imagine them at nightfall, in the dusk of a slum or a vacant lot, in that long, quiet moment when things are gradually left alone, with their backs to the sunset, and when colors are like memories or premonitions of other colors.

> (2000: 19)

The angel does not appear at dawn but at sunset, in back allies, slums vacant lots, and so on. In other words, the angel appears in a world that has become empty.

Connecting this description of the angel with the theme of education Dürer's etching becomes a phenomenological rendition of "brown study." "Brown" in this phrase indicates a focused concentration on something opaque or dark, thus something with a brownish complexion. Originally associated with deep melancholic brooding, brown study later became associated with absorbed thoughtfulness and contemplation. Brown study is a kind of withdrawal into shadows only to discover a strange illumination. The angel of brown study is perhaps best represented in literary work by none other than Bartleby the Scrivener, whom I discussed in Chapter 2. Like Dürer's angel, Bartleby stares anemically out at the world—a world that does not call or solicit this or that kind of action. All that is left is a resolute experience of impotentiality stripped of any constructive project of selfcultivation or self-renewal. Both figures offer a weak withdrawal into a state of perpetual study through their gestures of "I would prefer not to."

The mood of study expressed through the in-actions of the angel and Bartleby is very similar to Heidegger's description of profound boredom. According to Heidegger's argument, the problem with the contemporary world is that the distractions of consumerism, idle talk, curiosity, and frantic activity (busyness) deny us a fundamental attunement to ontological differences. Through "profound boredom," we can once again gain access into being and thus understand latent potentiality within the world freed from any determination of these potentialities by *das Man*. Revealed through the simple phrase "It is boring for one" (Heidegger 1995: 143) profound boredom disrupts the coordinates of self and world beyond the given status quo. "It" indicates an indeterminate world where specific solicitations are suddenly stripped away, and "one" indicates an impersonal self beyond the definition of a particular "me" with certain identifiable predicates (a whatever being without determinate ends, a generic singularity). Heidegger writes that the attunement of profound boredom "*brings* the *self* in all its nakedness *to itself*" (ibid.) as a being that exists in its own im-potentiality without specific destiny. Elsewhere Heidegger refers to the state of boredom as a kind of "entranced calm" (ibid.: 90) that emerges when the affordances of the world are suspended. Stated simply, when we are busy continually producing or learning specific things to achieve specific goals in accordance with the expectations of *this* world, we miss the insight that profound boredom brings into the possibilities of *a* world beyond the current order of things. It is only when things and signs do not call us in their particularity that the world as such appears before us, and it is this appearance of the world stripped bare that induces a state of calmness or profound boredom captured graphically in the languid, slumped pose of the angel in Dürer's etching. The emptiness that surrounds the angel is therefore not simply the negation of entities but rather their im-potentiality to be and not to be. The "gleam" that, as Agamben points out, remains when things and signs stop soliciting *Dasein* is precisely this im-potential trace. In fact Agamben argues the same, writing "What, for example, is boredom, if not the experience of the potentiality-not-to-act?" (1999c: 181). There is nothing left to become competent in, no action to which *Dasein* can comport its being, no skillful way to cope. To study the gleam that remains is to study without pressing into possibilities. It is to let idle the moment of resolution or the *Augenblick* that Heidegger refers to for the indefinite suspension of hesitation. To sum up, *profound boredom is the mood of study as an educational hesitation*—a study of the possibilities of new possibilities that emerges when the will is suspended before the strange and uncanny glow of the shadows of a world.

Yet profound boredom is not simply inertia. It is a *hesitation*, which is a state betwixt and between inaction and action, potentiality and actuality. In this sense, hesitation is an oscillation, a movement that withdraws in its progression and progresses in its withdrawal. Agamben can argue that Bartleby "neither accepts nor refuses, stepping forward and stepping backward at the same time" (1999c: 255). The hesitation of study is not simply active or passive, freedom or discipline, potentiality or impotentiality, but rather their rhythmic sway that culminates in a kind of indistinction or indetermination between the vibrating poles. Agamben describes studying as a kind of dialectic at a standstill between "bewilderment and lucidity, discovery and loss, between agent and patient" (1995: 64). It is a rhythm that moves from withdrawing to pursuing and back again without resolve. The cycles within cycles described by Whitehead are not simply descriptive of the particular work of study. Indeed, they reveal the dynamic ontology of freedom to be *and* not to be held in suspension of one another. These cycles within cycles resist any notion of linear developmentalism or simple apathy and lethargy. Rather they offer a recursive model for explaining the simultaneous push and pull between undertaking and undergoing that define the human being as a being whose freedom is bound to im-potentiality.

Holding these seeming opposites together, studying is a kind of impossible synthesis or barrier between opposites that is also their articulation. Both the structure of the poem and the structure of study offer a kind of "laceration that is also a suture" (Agamben 1993b: 157) or new sense of logopoietic *harmonia*. In other words, the poetry of study and the studiousness of the poem are concretizations of im-potentiality, and thus are like inoperative machines that only complete themselves through the gesture of de-completion. De-completion brings both melancholia (a sense of infinite and impossible undergoing) and boredom (as a perpetual projecting without a project) into an erotic entanglement. Indeed, the vibration of study results in a unique sense of inspiration all its own. Inspiration is, as Agamben points out in his aphorism on study, the "self-nourishment of the soul" (1995: 65) that stands in opposition to the infinite sadness of mere nihilism. To be precise, when emptiness is suddenly apprehended as im-potentiality, then boredom becomes inspiration and the soul is nourished. The nourishment does not come from the transmission of this or that message or way of being (which secures *Dasein*'s grip on the world) but rather in the much more precarious transmission of transmissibility (the faint glow left when affordances suddenly stop calling *Dasein* to action and im-potentiality is divorced from any definitive project). We can therefore conclude that study is the poetic phantasm that haunts learning as its angelic, inspirational supplement.

On melancholic relief

In this chapter, I have demonstrated that the rhythm of poetry, the temporality of messianic hesitation, the mood of melancholia, and the in-activity of study are linked together. Whitehead and Agamben, when read as good neighbors, offer us a more complete appreciation for this set of internal relationships than when they are read separately. Yet it is only through the poetry of Adrienne Rich that a true synthesis of form, affect, time, and study merge as an integrated whole. In particular, I would like to turn briefly to Rich's poem "The Burning of Paper Instead of Children" as a kind of poetic study or studious poetry.

The poem centers on burning. The first section of the poem (a long poem with both prose and lineated sections) introduces the burning of a mathematics book, which, as the speaker describes, recalls "memories of Hitler" (Rich 1975: 40). The scene then shifts abruptly from an act of violence over and against a book to the violence described in various books, in particular, the burning of Jeanne d'Arc. The book is, in the first case, physically burned, becoming a martyr for freedom of speech. The book plays the role of the "oppressed" being silenced by a chilling reiteration of totalitarian censorship now played out between

The aesthetics of study   65

children. In the second case, the book describes an historical burning of a French peasant girl. The book transmits the pain of the past into the present, offering a kind of ethical/political message concerning power and abuse. For the narrator, "they" (the reader can easily imagine the teacher or parent who is "in charge") "take the book away/because I dream of her too often." The book not only describes a burning but also *burns* with a certain indignation at the burning of an innocent woman. The narrator identifies with this burning: "love and fear in a house/knowledge of the oppressor/I know it hurts to burn." The burning of Jeanne d'Arc becomes the indignant burning of the narrator, who finds in the book the knowledge of oppression: the methods of torture, pain, and suffering induced by the powerful over the powerless. Thus the book *ignites* an identification between the suffering of historical figures and the present suffering of the speaker. "They" take the book away because such knowledge is not meant for her (a child, a student, a woman, a minority, a Jew, a lesbian) who is reading precisely what she is not supposed to be reading (a book for *educated adults*), where she is not supposed to be reading ("back there" in the library), when she is not supposed to be reading (at night, before bed, we imagine, when the images in the book are most likely to haunt her dreams).

The third burning concerns the corporal burning of love, desire, and "sexual jealousy." While books continually attempt to describe this type of burning, "they are useless" because some loves are unwritten or written out of history. Books might "tell everything" and yet, "no one knows what may happen." The book that was burned, described burning, burned with indignation, is now cold and "useless." The potency of sexuality escapes the impotency of the book. The possible violence of sexual desire becomes, in a dialectical leap, the burning of villages and temples during the Vietnam War by American soldiers (who themselves were, as a repetition of the first burning in the poem, nothing more than children). In the state of exception marked by war, the book becomes a witness to atrocities, yet is incapable of taking action to prevent further bloodshed. The book, which once could outrage, now only records, passively, the oppressor's version of what has happened. The power of the book has *burned out*. Rich cites Artaud at this point in the poem: "*burn the texts*." The burning of desire, the burning of war, and finally, we return to the burning of books: not as a reactionary return to totalitarian oppression, but as a politically revolutionary statement concerning the ineffectiveness of books to *change the world*, of an impatience with the language of the book to challenge oppression. No longer are books oppressed, no longer do they convey oppressive actions over the innocent; they have become tools of the oppressors, transmitting/normalizing/universalizing their language. In other words, the book is "knowledge of the oppressor/this is the oppressor's language." When the book legitimizes who can speak and how language is to be spoken, a division between proper and improper opens up—a division that is projected outward onto the division between the educated and the uneducated. Potentiality and impotentiality are cleaved in half by the book. To "burn the texts" as Artaud implores is to divide the division, to render the texts inoperative.

66   *The aesthetics of study*

But Rich's strategy to burn texts is peculiar. It is not the destruction of texts, as would at first be implied by Artaud's clarion call, but rather *their suspension* that she demands. There are three modes of suspension in the poem: three ways of separating language from the act of separation. The result is a paradoxical burning that is not burning, and this inoperative operation is a *freeing of the text for new uses* beyond burning or being burned. The first suspension comes in the form of an interjection or interruption of the book by those voices deemed impotent: the uneducated, illiterate students in Rich's own New York City English class. Rich records these voices marked by italics as a voice outside of the speaker's in the third section:

> 3. *People suffer highly in poverty and it takes dignity and intelligence to overcome this suffering. Some of the suffering are: a child did not had dinner last night: a child steal because he did not have money to buy it: to hear a mother say she do not have money to buy food for her children and to see a child without cloth it will make tears in your eyes.*
> (the fracture of order
> the repair of speech
> to overcome this suffering)

Here the excluded, abandoned voices of the illiterate suddenly appear precisely where they are most unwanted and unwelcomed: next to the words of the book (of the oppressors). This language is not merely an alternative to the language of the oppressors; it is scared by this very oppression, marked as a remnant of the exclusion that it testifies to. Thus, the poem does not create a dichotomy between langauges, but rather demonstrates how the language of the oppressed is a "fracture of order" but also "the repair of speech"—a laceration that is also a suture. The result is a poetic state of exception where inside (the book) and outside (the book), literate and illiterate mingle, contaminate one another, render the tools of oppression inoperative while nevertheless recognizing "this is the oppressor's language/yet I need it to talk to you." The result is a kind of im-potential language that can "overcome this suffering" of the oppressed precisely by a profanation of the act of division that divides the world in two.

The second suspension takes the form of suspended words that have been separated from both the poetic line and the sentence. Two such words in the poem are "relief" and "deliverance." They glow like embers in a fire, or ashes that have yet to be fully swept away. They are remnants that are *no longer* possible and *not yet* extinguished. These words—now inoperative, unknowable, detached from syntax—seem to offer themselves up for new uses from the silence of the empty spaces that surround them. These are the words that suspend the dialectic between oppressor and oppressed; they no longer *belong* (to anyone or anywhere). And precisely because "relief" and "deliverance" dwell in a kind of poetic limbo, they offer a moment of hesitation or withdraw from the violence of burning. The relief they offer is, in the end, neither a solution nor political platform but rather *the miracle of their appearance despite being burned, lost, destroyed.*

Rich concludes the poem with a turn to prose. She writes:

> The burning of a book arouses no sensation in me. I know it hurts to burn. There are flames of napalm in Catonsville, Maryland. I know it hurts to burn. The typewriter is overheated, my mouth is burning. I cannot touch you and this is the oppressor's language.

Rich cites the burning of selective service records from the Maryland draft board office by Vietnam war protestors. The words of the oppressor have been sacrificed, burned, in a moment of rage against an unjust war. And these cycles of burning (being burned, burning, burning out, burning again) cause the typewriter to become "overheated" and cause the poet's mouth to "burn." Burn with what? With the unending rhythmic oscillation between the burning draft records in protest (that ends the poem) and the burning of mathematics textbooks that recall totalitarian censorship (that begins the poem). As the typewriter overheats and the mouth is left burning, the conclusion of the poem is infinitely delayed. The typewriter is too hot to continue, the tongue too swollen to speak. "I cannot touch you and this is the oppressor's language." The poem ends with a touch that is deferred, with a language that is never one's own. There is then a sense that *one must hesitate* before typing, speaking, touching. To continue would be to injure the self, to send it back to the spiral of burning which propels the poem. Thus hesitation at the very end is not an act of cowardice or retreat but of relief and deliverance. Hesitation becomes a kind of ethical injunction to stop the burning and bear witness to what has been burned, the ashes that remain.

The rhythmic sway between progression and regression, burning and being burned, produces an overall melancholic affect: relief and deliverance are phantasmal things which can only be present in their absence (in their inoperative state). Indeed, whereas Agamben only gestures toward a connection between Dürer's *Melancholia I* and study, Rich makes the connection explicit. The first image in the poem after the burning of the mathematics textbook is none other than Dürer's "baffled woman" who stares at a world that has collapsed, wings grounded, pensively studying the fragments left when all has been burned. The resulting melancholia is not simply the repetition of burning, but rather, through the hesitation of study, burning is left idle. In this sense, the poem, like a linguistic salve, provides what the poem describes as a "time of silence/or few words" of "relief." Rich's thesis could thus be summarized as follows: we must be burned to study, but in study, there is a melancholic relief which, in the end, is an inspiration to listen to the crackling of the embers of im-potentiality that remain when all else has been destroyed.

Notch: Night study

The night has more often than not been dismissed by educational philosophy as a time of deception and confusion. If we return to the founding myth of educational philosophy, Plato's cave, we can see that it is the underground world of shadows that must be overcome in order to find the truth, which is analogous to the sun in the blue sky. When describing the struggle of the one who leaves the cave of ignorance, Plato writes,

> At first, he'd see shadows most easily, then images of men and other things in water, then the things themselves. Of these, he'd be able to study the things in the sky and the sky itself more easily at night, looking at the light of the stars and the moon, than during the day, looking at the sun and the light of the sun.
>
> (1992: 516b)

Shadows are a transitional prop to be left behind in the quest for truth and a brighter life, a quest that leads from night to day and ultimately to the source of light itself. The character of Socrates summarizes,

> But this is how I see it: In the knowable realm, the form of the good is the last thing to be seen, and it is reached only with difficulty. Once one has seen it, however, one must conclude that it is the cause of all that is correct and beautiful in anything, that it produces both light and its source in the visible realm.
>
> (ibid.: 517c)

The one who studies is therefore like an eye that turns from darkness to light, from obscurity of shadows to the brilliance of the sun, from blindness to vision. The question of education is, in this founding metaphor, a question of illumination, and truth is reified as a Form that changes the sky from night into day.

This basic model is replicated throughout the Reformation through the ubiquitous image of light overcoming darkness. Except for the occasional mystical practices first envisioned by figures such as Gregory of Nyssa and Denys, Christianity has associated the night with demons, witches, and the devil. As Erasmus argued in 1523, "Ignorance of the truth is night" (cited in Koslofsky 2011: 22). Craig Koslofsky demonstrates that from 1450–1650 texts such as *Macbeth* and *Doctor Faustus* perpetuated a general fear of the night and its various associations with the Devil. Altogether this dominant religious discourse effectively "diabolized" nocturnal folk beliefs through the imposition of Christian demonology. Again, Koslofsky provides a clear summary of this process: "The reformation of popular culture beginning in the sixteenth century challenged the nuanced folk view of the night with an intensified linkage of the night with infernal evil, diabolical temptation, and human sin" (ibid.: 43). And yet, despite this prejudice against the night, there was nevertheless a certain "nocturnal revolution" (ibid.: 46) that happened in the sixteenth century with movements such as the Anabaptists, who explicitly turned toward the image of Nicodemus who sought out Jesus's teachings in the night. Darkness, shadows, and the night might lead to melancholic, brown study but for various mystical traditions, such brooding could lead to the highest level of the Divine. Furthermore, in the sixteenth and seventeenth centuries, the Catholic church attempted to either limit the night life of villages (and in particular those activities that were associated with local rituals, youthful courtship, social gatherings, etc.) or undermine folk practices by sanctifying the night. In both cases, as Koslofsky demonstrates, there was wide resistance to the colonization of the night, and the lack of implementation of Catholic regulations demonstrated the limits of religious disciplinary power over the unruly nature of night practices and night knowledge.

If the Reformation historically diabolized the night, then Marxist philosophers have likewise colonized the night, imposing on its darkness the veil of "dialectical science." Hence in *The German Ideology*, Marx juxtaposes the darkened, upside-down representation of the *camera obscura* (ideological mystification) with the clear, sun-filled landscape outside the lens of the camera (ideological critique). We see not only Marx's Enlightenment opposition between the darkness and the light but also religious inheritances: both fuse into a certain suspicion of darkness, its practices, and its epistemological claims. Jacques Rancière's book *Proletarian Nights: The Workers' Dream in Nineteenth-Century France* (2012) demonstrates that—counter to dominant Marxist narratives—nights for the proletariat were not for sleeping and replenishing labor-power that would be expropriated the following day. Rather, nights were full of study, play, and thought. As opposed to the scholarly sciences that submitted the days and nights of the proletariat to expert interpretation, Rancière returned to the workers' archives in order to uncover what various laborers had to say about their own conditions. What he saw radically disrupted the authoritative image of the worker found in the abstractions of Marxist philosophers and social scientists. Summarizing his methodological principle, Rancière writes,

> I had the urge to make an about-face and go back in the company of those whom I had come across first: those who were traveling the road in the opposite direction, deserting what was said to be their culture and their truth to go toward our shadows. I mean those worker dreamers, prattlers, versifiers, reasoners, and indulgers in sophistry whose notebooks serve as a replacement screen in the mirror of reality granted and appearance withheld and whose falsetto voice creates dissonance in the duet of mute truth and contrite illusion. Perverted proletarians whose discourse is made up of borrowed words.
>
> (2012: 15)

In other words, Rancière returned to the "contraband intellectuals" (ibid.) whose work remains hidden from the official story of the proletariat precisely because they labor beyond the fixed dichotomy that separates day from night. For the Marxist intellectual, it is the analysis of the day that matters: the science of exploitation and of expropriation of labor-power. As such, the rogue intellectuals who borrowed words that were not theirs and who worked in the shadows of night appear to be nothing less than class traitors merely mystifying oppression through their dreams and through their melancholic reveries. Those who write between the work of the factory and the sleep of night have no place within the Marxist framework precisely because they say what they are not supposed to be capable of saying, they study what is not supposed to be of concern to them, and they work when they are supposed to be resting. To these contraband intellectuals, the secret of the commodity was no secret at all—its truth was readily available to anyone who labored under capitalism. Rather, what was at stake in their study was something more mysterious and shadowy. Reading the vast literature produced by the proletariat-who-studies-at-night, Rancière realized that "It is not day but night that is involved here, not the property of others but their 'chagrin,' their invented sorrow that contains all real sorrow" (ibid.: 20). In other words, the secret was the ability to speak and think thoughts reserved for others and in the process divide the division that separates day from night, manual from intellectual work, labor from study.

While Plato (and perhaps more indirectly, Marx) argued that blindness is the result of lack of vision or clarity, Jorge Luis Borges once argued the opposite. His own partial blindness offered him the most precious of gifts: the gift of study. In the darkness, Borges turned from the world of vision to the aural world of words. "So I began," he recalls, "my study of Anglo-Saxon, which blindness brought me" (2000: 478). While others might have seen this condition as a deficit, Borges was quick to retort,

> Being blind has its advantages. I owe to the darkness some gifts: the gift of Anglo-Saxon, my limited knowledge of Icelandic, the joy of so many lines of poetry, of so many poems, and of having written another book, entitled, with a certain falsehood, with a certain arrogance, *In Praise of Darkness*.
>
> (2000: 478)

Thus for him, blindness was not merely a transitional passage from ignorance to knowledge but was a kind of suspension of the division, opening up a world of language, of poetry, and of study. The connection between the four (language, poetry, study, and darkness) should not be underestimated here, for it was precisely when the quest for vision was left idle, when the teleological movement toward the Forms of illumination was suspended that Borges found the time and the space for studying what remains. For what is language if not a certain kind of shadow thrown on a wall by fire? Borges ended his short rumination on blindness with a citation from Goethe: "*Alles Nahe werde fern.*" "Everything near becomes far" refers not simply to the evening twilight, but also to the night of the body when it is stricken with blindness. When that which is closest to us moves away from the eye, we can, ironically enough, finally study it.

Bearing these counter narratives of the night and of blindness, we can return to Plato's original image of the cave of shadows. In the canonical interpretation of this passage presented above, the shadows are at best temporary transitional props on the path toward Truth and illumination. They are, in other words, means to another end. Yet could we not give the shadows an importance in themselves as pure means without an end? A consciously iconoclastic interpretation might emphasize the space of shadows, a space that is not transitional but rather paradoxical, an impossible synthesis of the darkness in light and the lightness in darkness. Neither in the cave of ignorance nor "illuminated" by the light of Ideas, the one who studies lives in shadows. Through the shadows, one's special nature is oddly suspended: the studier does not know if he or she is gold, silver, or bronze and thus does not know his or her destination or occupation, does not have clear knowledge of the things themselves. Like Rancière's contraband intellectuals or the voices in Rich's "The Burning of Paper Instead of Children," they speak inappropriate words from inappropriate locations, at inappropriate times.

72   *Night study*

This no man's land is a place of *freedom*. The studier is not *not* a craftsman, guardian, or philosopher king. Within the state of study, all occupations remain possibilities without these possibilities actualizing themselves.

Night knowledge is absolutely necessary for discovering the Forms, and ultimately Justice that founds his fictitious republic, yet what Plato misses is that this is not simply a means to an end—an "unfortunate" yet necessary delay that is to be overcome in order to progress toward theoretical knowledge.

Perhaps we could argue further that the shadow is the halo of the thing. A halo for Agamben is situated at the periphery "between every thing and itself" (1993a: 54). It is the tiny gap that exists between the sign and the signature (a gap that is otherwise seamlessly concealed or crossed out in our everyday coping). In this way, the halo is a kind of "indetermination of its [a sign's or a thing's] limit" (ibid.: 56). With the indetermination of the limit, the efficacy that exceeds any one manifestation in sign or thing, offers a strange glow: "the being that has reached its end, that has consumed all of its possibilities, thus receives as a gift a supplemental possibility" (ibid.: 56). In the vibration of the halo, the thing or the sign that is determinate becomes indeterminate, and in this sense returns to its whatever being.

The illumination of the halo is not so much akin to a photographic positive as that of a photographic negative wherein the *darkness* of the signature becomes its own kind of shadowy light. In study, one stands back from engaged, everyday coping, and by pulling away from the immediacy of these relations, the studier becomes attuned to the appearance of the faint halo of a dark glow that envelope signs and things. This glow which remains concealed as a transparent backdrop in our dealings with the world, is unconcealed through study—this dimness becomes its own kind of light. As Agamben argues, darkness is not simply the absence of light. Drawing on recent discoveries in neurophysiology, Agamben points out that the experience of darkness is caused by the activity of certain "off-cells" in the retina. As such, it is not a mere loss of sight, but is an actively produced state. And, in terms of the perceived darkness in the heavens above, Agamben argues that the vast darkness of the sky is not simply a lack or void, but is rather the negative presence of light from distant galaxies that will never reach the Earth. The ones who study the present are those who "do not allow themselves to be blinded by the lights of the century, and so manage to get a glimpse of the shadows in those lights, of their intimate obscurity"

(2009b: 45). Indeed, for Agamben, the one who studies the signatures of the present is "the person who perceives the darkness of his time" (ibid.). It is the seemingly impotent halo of darkness that in the end is the efficacy that makes the signs and signifiers of the world circulate. The solidity of our perceptions grows hazy by the halo-effect of the shadow that blurs out the force of the sign with a much more powerful force: darkness as a coming light, a light that is no longer absent yet has not arrived either. The halo is therefore blinding, but it is a blindness that is also an impotent kind of sight—sight of the im-potentiality of light. Hence, the Old English term "brown study" truly captures the essence of study and its relationship to shadows and darkness. Brown study is to study in the dark, in the shadow, to become lost through perpetual wondering or withdrawing from determinate ends. It is a kind of night practice where we encounter the mysteries obscured by the daylight. Studying is therefore a kind of acute sensitivity to the demand of the dark—eyes adjusting to the dim light of shadows, lingering in the brownness of night to discover what one can make out after the sun has set.

We linger in Heidegger's "destitute time of the world's night" (2001: 90). Night is no longer the phase of a rising and falling sun, or the camera obscura's reproduction, or the eye's physical blindness, but the whole world cast in shadows. Here the *whole world*—as the totality of meaningful practices, roles, and intelligible background inheritance that constitute our lives—has become dark. Nothing shines forth when all cows are black. Not only that, but, with the radical elimination of all ontological difference in a biotechnological epoch (the leveling of importance and significance under the reign of technological logic that transforms beings in mere resources), we are now on the precipice of a midnight in which "the destitution of time is the greatest" (ibid.). What makes this time most destitute is that we cannot even sense the destitute nature of destitution. In other words, destitution appears absolute and necessary rather than a contingent *problem*. Given that the present is cloaked in darkness, how are we to live? The Platonic story of education would have us turn away from the night, to fire and the shadows that dance above it, and finally to the light of Truth existing in the fullness of day. Yet Heidegger suggests something else—a new way to study. Instead of escaping, we must find within darkness and night certain resources for a new cultural, political, and social turn: "In the age of the world's night, the abyss of the world must be experienced and endured. But for this it is necessary that there be those who reach into the abyss" (ibid.: 90). Enduring and experiencing the abyss is the only way beyond the abyss. Through

74   *Night study*

study, the studier dwells in obscurity and shadow, night and darkness. He or she endures it, and experiences it. Through this enduring, the studier becomes receptive to the touch of the fugitive gods whose signatures, like the unearthly ether of the night air, float amongst the ruins.

In common, everyday language, we say that "studying clarifies something," thus "providing insight." There is some truth to this statement: studying gives us a clarification of the obscurity of things and signs. This is not enlightenment; it is en*darken*ment.

4 The method of study or collecting signatures

How is the method of study to be differentiated from the method of learning? If learning teaches the proper use and meaning of signs and things, then studying, if it is truly distinct from learning as an educational activity, must have its own domain, its own methods. Perhaps the best example of studying is Agamben's own work, which can be described as an archaeology of signatures. When reading Agamben, one feels as if lost in a dizzying labyrinth of references, clues, and traces that plunge the reader into murky and mysterious depths that are oddly familiar yet strange at the same time. Webs of relationships between disparate items emerge that simultaneously collapse distances between time, space, and meaning while opening up new distances between taken-for-granted concepts. Like a kind of imagistic monad, obscure, centuries-old texts suddenly unfold into the present as the key to contemporary crises of state, art, and culture. Likewise, the most contemporary of phenomena such as fashion are set within a constellation that throws them back into medieval iconography. Time speeds up as one anticipates the next genealogical leap while also slowing down to almost a languid pace as one passes through endless references. This experience of reading Agamben is the result of Agamben's method of study: the archeological collecting of signatures. Through an overview of this method, I will compare and contrast archaeology of signatures to the act of collecting described by two of Agamben's key inspirations: Walter Benjamin and Aby Warburg. In conclusion, I suggest that the collection of signatures through archaeology *is the method of study* that does not transmit knowledge deemed useful or essential to new generations (learning the significance of signs and things through a socialization process) so much as transmit the possibility of transmission (studying the very possibilities for transmission in the first place). In other words, the unique work of study is the appearance of transmissibility *as such* through the collecting of signatures.

The gesture of the signature: studying beneath signs and things

Discussing the ancient texts of Paracelsus, Agamben draws our attention to the role of similarities in medical science during the Renaissance and Baroque periods. For instance, pomegranate seeds as well as pine nuts were thought to cure dental ailments because of the similarity between the shapes of the seeds, nuts, and human teeth. For Agamben this chain of mimetic reasoning illustrates a *signature relationship*, where a signature creates a relation between two seemingly unrelated objects (seeds and teeth). The signature is the generative and creative relay between elements that slips, undiscovered, beneath the much more frequently cited pair of signifier and signified, *langue* and *parole*. "Signatures," writes Agamben, "which according to the theory of signs should appear as signifiers, always already slide into the position of the signified, so that *signum* and *signatum* exchange roles and seem to enter into a zone of undecidability" (2009a: 37). This fecund undecidability of the signature precedes and enables things, practices, and statements to enter into unrelated domains or networks of dispersed correspondences. Tracing the genealogy of Paracelsus's thought, Agamben then turns to Jakob Böhme's text *De signatura rerum*, in which Böhme extends the basic meaning of the signature beyond mere correspondence between domains. In Agamben's reading, Böhme reveals that the signature is "the decisive operator of all knowledge, that which makes the world, mute, and without reason in itself, intelligible" (ibid.: 41) Signatures are the background of criss-crossing resemblances that make signs intelligible as signs within a system of other signs. In other words, signs presuppose a more primordially rich set of holistic relations between signatures—a background that is "inseparable from the sign yet irreducible to it" (ibid.: 50).

What is it specifically that signs need from signatures? A theory of signs and signs alone cannot account for the *efficacy* of signs. It is the seemingly transparent and taken-for-grantedness of signatures that guarantees efficacy. Perhaps the best example offered by Agamben of the efficacious nature of the signature is astrology. In the Latin text *Picatrix*, there are depictions of strange figures that are neither constellations nor zodiac signs. The decans of *Picatrix* are, for Agamben, "neither signs nor reproductions of anything: they are operations through which the forces of celestial bodies are gathered and concentrated into a point in order to influence terrestrial bodies" (2009a: 55). The decans are operators who gather and direct the powers of the stars to signify. The decans do not signify anything in themselves (hence their strangely mysterious nature), only the potentiality of the stars to shine with meaning and significance. Likewise, constellations are not signs so much as signatures that express an efficacious relation between the terrestrial lives of individuals and heavenly bodies, producing the preconditions for astrological signification. A less esoteric example can be found in Agamben's reworking of Benveniste's original description of the gap between the semiotic (individual signs) and the semantic (discourses). For Agamben, the signature is precisely what lies between these two planes as the efficacy that makes signs speak. While Benveniste argues that the gap between signs and discourses is insurmountable, Agamben argues that the signature is what separates and binds the two together. As such, the archeology of the signature is a strange science lying somewhere between semiology and hermeneutics. Drawing on Foucault's *The Archaeology of Knowledge*, Agamben summarizes,

Statements, then, are situated on the threshold between semiology and hermeneutics where signatures take place. Neither semiotic nor semantic, not yet discourse and no longer mere sign, statements, like signatures, do not institute semiotic relations or create new meanings; instead, they mark and 'characterize' signs at the level of their existence, thus actualizing and displacing their efficacy. These are the signatures that signs receive from the sheer fact of existing and being used—namely, the indelible character that, in marking them as signifying something, orients and determines their interpretation and efficacy in a certain context. Like signatures on coins, like the figures of the constellations and the decans in the sky of astrology ... they have always already pragmatically decided the destiny and life of signs that neither semiology nor hermeneutics is able to exhaust.

(ibid.: 64)

In other words, an archaeology of signatures unveils the dense network of rules, precepts, and statements that transparently distribute the possible uses of signs, and in turn point toward the potentiality of signification in general. Signatures are like the concealed matrix of constitutive relations underlying yet withdrawing from the world. In this sense, Heidegger's notion of pure being—or what he later identified as "earth" (2001)—is similar to Agamben's formulation of the signature: both found yet exceed any given signifying system. For Agamben as well as Heidegger, if signs have a definite purpose (to express this or that content), then the signature, to borrow from Kant, is a kind of "purposiveness without a purpose" or expressive efficacy that withdraws at the precise moment of its primordial founding.

The signature is, in its full sense, a textual gesture. According to Agamben, a gesture is not an acting (of this or that performance) or a making (of this or that object/meaning). "What characterizes gesture is that in it nothing is being produced or acted, but rather something is being endured or supported" (2000: 57). Signatures are neither new knowledge nor old knowledge but rather the support upon which signifiers become signifieds—the non-knowledge that upholds the very potentiality for all knowledge. Signatures are, in other words, the gesture that lies below the level of the sign and of the signifying process as a prop or support. Supporting the signifying process means that signatures are a structure below or behind the appearance of the sign—the transparent background matrix that endures and supports communicative processes without being noticed. They are the bearers of the efficacy of signs and things which solicits solicitations. If, as Agamben argues (1999c), modern society has lost its gestures, this means that it has lost the signatures that make its signs signify. The result is a heap of signs without clear destinations—a bunch of dead letters. In this case, it is no coincidence that Bartleby was allegedly a clerk in the Office of Dead Letters in Washington, D.C.!

In the modern era, the signature is perhaps best recognized in the detective work of Sherlock Holmes or the psychoanalytic detective work of Sigmund Freud. In both cases, "the clue represents the exemplary case of a signature that

78 *The method of study or collecting signatures*

puts an insignificant or nondescript object in effective relation to an event (in this case, a crime, in Freud's case, a traumatic event)" (Agamben 2009a: 70). The hidden genealogy of the signature then culminates in Walter Benjamin's notion of the dialectical image as a constellation. It is here, in Agamben's description of Benjamin's work, that the relation between the archaeology of signatures and the peculiar nature of studying meet. "The historian," or, for our purposes, the one who studies, "does not randomly or arbitrarily choose the documents out of the inert and endless mass of the archive but follows the subtle and obscure thread of signatures that demand to be read here and now" (ibid.: 73). As such, the work of studying is not the production of new, conceptual knowledge (expressed in philosophical propositions) or of hermeneutical interpretation (the production of new meanings). If the signature is the pure potentiality for transmissibility, then studying is the *transmission of transmissibility*. In other words, *study does not guarantee the transmission of any predetermined set of knowledges or traditions but rather the pure potentiality of transmission as such.* Without conclusions and without firm judgments, studying exposes the signatures of the world (their demand), the preconceptual background that grants efficacy to the sign to signify this or that proposition.

In a world that has lost its gestures, the work of study takes on a special kind of urgency. As described at the end of Chapter 1, the contemporary studier finds him or herself in a world in which things and signs no longer shine forth. There are no longer any ontological differences that help determine what matters. One course of action here is (as Dreyfus and Kelly argue) to enliven the sacred and thus rediscover how the simple ritual practices of our lives contain a hidden meaning. Yet another approach can be found in study which, like a detective on the scene of a crime, tracks down the traces of efficacy that remain within the rubble of technological enframing. Signs, things, and efficacy have disintegrated. Their holism has been irreparably splintered through technological disaggregation, specialization, and instrumentalization. The scattered pieces cannot be put back together in order for anything to shine forth as a focal point, orienting action toward certain projects of self-construction. But this is not simply a state of nihilism. In the state of decomposition where signs and things lay idle, finally the signature (or, for Foucault, the statement) can be studied on its own. In other words, the problematic of the signature only becomes apparent when efficacy and sign are split apart, and signs appear as dead and lifeless husks circulating endlessly through information superhighways as soulless data or as meaningless information. In this state of affairs, efficacy opens up for new, profane/unintended uses (the faint *gleam* described in Chapter 3) . . . but only for the studier who carefully responds to its distant call and proceeds to sift through the ashes for clues.

The studier as collector of signatures

We might also mention here the relationship between collecting signatures, which Agamben has done time and time again throughout all his work—spiraling around certain key signatures such as *homo sacer*, profanity, state of exception, study—and Benjamin's reflections on collecting. In *The Arcades Project*, Benjamin writes of the flâneur that

> The experiences of one who attends to a trace result only very remotely from any work activity, or are cut off from such procedure altogether. (Not for nothing do we speak of "fortune hunting.") They have no sequence and no system. They are a product of chance, and have about them the essential interminability that distinguishes the preferred obligations of the idler. The fundamentally unfinishable collection of things worth knowing, whose utility depends on chance, has its prototype in study.
>
> (2002: m2, 1)

In this citation, Benjamin links together several important themes. First, the collector of traces engages in an activity that cannot be quantified as any kind of measurable work or research program. In other words, labor-power cannot be extracted from the strange habits of the collector who simply prefers not to exchange his or her work for a wage. Second, the collector is not guided by predetermined success conditions or willful pursuit so much as open willingness to receiving chance happenings that are given by a situation. Thus there is no "method" to be extracted from the idiosyncrasies of the collector. The implication here is that the more one *tries* to be a collector, the more one will fail. Only when one remains flexible and responsive to what appears does one find traces of the elusive signature. The lack of predetermined success conditions means that the work of the collector is "unfinishable" and "interminable." From the outside, these aspects of collecting, when taken as a whole, make it antithetical to the performance principle of capitalist production. The collector appears to be nothing more than an "idler" who lacks the human capital necessary to be efficient or even remotely competitive on an open labor market. And finally, these central features connect collecting up with "its prototype": study. Both are unfinishable, without utility or functionality within the order of things, and chastised as "useless." The studier is therefore a collector of traces, and the collector is a studier. As Carlo Salzani states, Benjamin's "researches in the archives and in the labyrinth of the Bibliothèque Nationale emblematize the 'dangerous' and obscure pursuit of the explorer of texts and the adventurer of libraries" (2007: 186).

But more than simply a collector of ephemera found in the city or archival texts, perhaps the quintessential activity of the collector that Salzani neglects to discuss is book collecting. Benjamin's essay "Unpacking my library: A talk about book collecting" begins as follows: "I am unpacking my library. Yes, I am. The books are not yet on the shelves, not yet touched by the mild boredom of order" (1968: 59). At the outset, we can make several observations. The emphasis in this essay is on "my library" or on ownership of a private collection of books. Indeed, the public collection can never, for Benjamin, allow objects to "get their due" (ibid.: 67). Benjamin does not really believe that a public

80   *The method of study or collecting signatures*

collection is really a collection at all. In the first several lines of his essay on unpacking his library we get the immediate sense that there is a certain connection between the privateness of a private collection (each collection *belongs* to someone and is therefore never anonymous) and a certain respect for the books (the private collection allows books to "get their due"). For the private collector, books are never simply resources to be exchanged on the market, nor anonymous objects to be consumed by the crowd, nor simply utilitarian objects that grant the reader information, rather they are unique objects that are cared for and, ultimately, studied in their material singularity by the collector.

Collecting cuts across the more or less famous divisions starkly drawn between religious ritual and mechanical reproduction found in Benjamin's essay "Art in the Age of Mechanical Reproduction." Here Benjamin draws a contrast between the aura produced through traditional display and ritual performance and the decay of such aura in the age of mechanical reproduction. As Benjamin observes, "The uniqueness of a work of art is inseparable from its being imbedded in the fabric of tradition" (1968: 223). Within the framework of tradition, the work of art served a ritual purpose "first magical" and then "religious" (ibid.). In both cases, the "cult value" (ibid.: 224) of the work of art was based on the material display of the unique, particular object through highly mediated ritual performance that kept the viewer at a discreet distance from the work of art. The combination of mediated distance and material presence gave the art object a certain authority and power over the viewer. The result is an illusion of "permanence" (ibid.: 223) that hides the historicity of the tradition itself as well as the *human* labor-power that forms the backdrop of the object's cult value. Mechanical reproduction, on the other hand, erodes aura in two ways which Benjamin summarizes as follows: "the desire of contemporary masses to bring things 'closer' spatially and humanly, which is just as ardent as their bent toward overcoming the uniqueness of every reality by accepting its reproduction" (ibid.). Whereas the religious cult cultivated a sacred relationship to unique, singular objects of worship and reverence, the object of mechanical reproduction is brought down to human-scale for close inspection, and then subjected to numerous appropriations. This process of mechanical reproduction is, for Benjamin, emancipatory. He argues,

> For the first time in world history, mechanical reproduction emancipates the work of art from its parasitical dependence on ritual … But in the instant the criterion of authenticity ceases to be applicable to artistic production, the total function of art is reversed. Instead of being based on ritual, it begins to be based on another practice—politics.
>
> (ibid.: 224)

Rather than sacred, cult value—which withdraws the object from inspection, and conceals it behind a mystical, ceremonial shield—the work of art in the age of mechanical reproduction exposes the art object to open viewing, thus granting it a secular "exhibition value" (ibid.). The problem with aura is that its

The method of study or collecting signatures   81

veil of mystery grants a certain authenticity and authority to ritual repetition and the bonds of tradition over the creativity and political insurgencies of the masses. Without being shackled to tradition and to the mystical aura of the unique and authentic, objects—especially art objects—become free for new, profane uses. The "public presentability" (ibid.: 225) of that which can be mechanically reproduced suspends ritual use, traditional meanings, and mediated encounters for the immediacy of popular appropriation and reconfiguration.

Given the radical social, economic, and political changes that are part and parcel of the age of mechanical reproduction, collecting seems to be an anachronistic activity. Benjamin states as much when he writes that to the masses, "this passion [for collecting] is behind the times" (1968: 66). The life of the collector, for Benjamin, is defined by a "relationship to objects which does not emphasize their functional, utilitarian value—that is, their usefulness—but studies and loves them as the scene, the stage, of their fate" (ibid.: 60). The fate of the object can only be admired when its social function (its cult value as well as it exhibition value) has been suspended through the peculiar work of the collector, who is a private individual. In fact, it must be taken out of circulation entirely, left idle on the shelf. Indeed, the true collector hardly ever *reads* his or her books. And this suspension of all utility through collecting gives the object "its freedom" (ibid.: 64). Freedom here is neither the freedom found in the autonomy and authority of the cult or the exhibition and exchange of public display. Rather the freedom is a freedom to simply be whatever the object is that it is in its uniqueness. Importantly being left idle is not merely leaving the book "lonely and abandoned on the market place" (ibid.: 64) where it is absolutely interchangeable with other commodities. The fate of the object that the collector studies is the singular ontology of the object:

> Everything remembered and thought, everything conscious, becomes the pedestal, the frame, the base, the lock of his property. The period, the region, the craftsmanship, the former ownership—for a true collector the whole background of an item adds up to a magic encyclopedia whose quintessence is the fate of his object.
>
> (ibid.: 60)

The collection therefore cannot be mechanically reproduced because its value is predicated on its particular being: its history, its patina, its worn surfaces, its relation to the memories of the collector, etc.

Unlike the anonymity of mechanical reproduction, the book collection is unique and largely private. Here Benjamin's description of the collection returns us to his discussion of aura. Indeed, I would argue that collecting preserves aura by saving the object from the public circulation, exhibition, and exchange. The language of aura peppers the entire essay on collecting. Benjamin writes, "The most profound enchantment for the collector is the locking of individual items within a magic circle in which they are fixed as the final thrill, the thrill of acquisition, passes over them" (1968: 60). In the end, the collection

82 *The method of study or collecting signatures*

becomes a kind of "magic encyclopedia" (ibid.) for Benjamin which recalls or draws out the period, the region, the craftsmanship, and history of particular books—all of which are effaced by mechanical processes of reproduction. The magic here is the *aura* of the collection that reasserts a kind of sacred envelope around the objects collected.

This emphasis on magic, enchantment, and on saving the unique object from being lost in the circulation and exchange of commodities or the impersonal gaze of the masses suggests that the collection stands in stark opposition to the age of mechanical reproduction. If mechanical reproduction *frees* objects for new political uses, collecting pulls back from any realization of such uses. Given its interest in conserving aura against public exhibition and or commercial circulation of objects, collecting seems apolitical, or perhaps, frightfully counter-revolutionary. Yet I would like to point out several key differences between the aura established through traditional, ritual performance and the aura uniquely produced through the art of collecting. As in Ackbar Abbas' (1988) comparison of the collector in Benjamin's work with that of the collector in modern literature, the collection itself seems to subvert dichotomies and certain assumptions that separate myth from science, the private and the public, the political and the apolitical. In my reading, Abbas' analysis can be extended and enriched through a consideration of aura and its reemergence (not simply its withering) in the age of mechanical reproduction through collecting. While traditional ritual induces the effects of aura through a distance between subject and object and the autonomy and authority of the object, the private collection emphasizes intimacy and closeness between collector and collection. Even though collecting has its own sense of magic and enchantment, as Anne Keefe has illuminated in her analysis of wonder and the aesthetics of collection in the work of Joseph Cornell and the contemporary poetry inspired by Cornell (Keefe 2012: 127–168), collecting is no mere return to a pre-mechanical age of ritual incantation. Distance between subject and object collapses in the collection, producing a sense of aura through intimacy which, in the last instance, makes the collector and the collection indistinct. In this sense, the qualification of "my collection" in the opening line of the essay is redundant: true collections are always *someone's* collection, they always *belong* to a particular person.

This intimacy is conveyed through several features of the collection. First, the collection ultimately spirals around the passion of the collector and his or her love for the fate of the objects at hand. The passion of the collector, in turn, makes the logic of the library "impenetrable and at the same time uniquely itself" (Benjamin 1968: 63). What holds the collection together is not the inherent logic of display. Such logic would be merely formal in character, a kind of cataloging of books according to a predefined system that is impersonal and (even worse) indifferent to the uniqueness and impenetrable passions of the collector. In this sense, the private collection is akin to the premodern *wunderkammer* or wonder cabinet whose strange juxtapositions of natural and artificial objects lacked the stringent divisions and calculations of the modern, scientifically organized museum (see Daston and Park 2001). "For what else is this collection but a disorder to which habit has accommodated itself to such an extent that it can appear as order?" writes Benjamin (1968: 60). In this rhetorical question, he highlights the idiosyncratic nature of the collection, the order of which is inscrutable without reference to the habits of the collector. The logic of the collection is therefore indistinguishable from the memories of the collector. The dialectical relationship between collector and collection is captured in the final sentiments offered by Benjamin when he writes,

> for a collector . . . ownership is the most intimate relationship that one can have to objects. Not that they come alive in him; it is he who lives in them. So I have erected one of his dwellings, with books as the building stones, before you, and now he is going to disappear inside, as is only fitting.
>
> (ibid.: 67)

The collector literally lives (dwells) inside his or her books, and disappears into them. The collection is an objectification of a unique human spirit, and, dialectically speaking, the human spirit is what gives the collection its form as a collection (rather than simply a pile of books). Because the collection becomes a repository for the spirit and passions of the collection, Benjamin finds it plausible that a collector could indeed be driven insane if he or she lost a collection of books. Likewise, without the collector, the collection loses its intelligibility and becomes nothing more than a chaotic and inarticulate jumble of "junk." In the end, the two become completely interwoven and mutually dependent upon one another. Subject and object become indistinct as the collector disappears into the collection. In opposition to the exaltation of the aura of the object as testimony to the authenticity of a "timeless," permanent tradition, the aura of a collection is therefore *deeply personal, historical, and situated*. Instead of ritual reenactment that returns the observant back to an unchanging (and unquestionable) authority, the aura of the collection is fragile, imbricated in a finite web of impenetrable relations between personal interests, the history of production, the history of the object, and its history of ownership. Thus the aura of the object as *this* object, with *this* history, belonging to *this* individual opens up to the vista of historical archaeology rather than shutting it down. Through aura, ritual observance is suspended and history emerges once again.

And here we reach the second important distinction. Whereas the aura of tradition is predicated on ritual reenactment (the manifestation of cult value), the aura of the collection is predicated on sustained *study*. Repeatedly, Benjamin emphasizes how the collector, the enchantment of the collection, and the work of study are related. Instead of the distance between viewer and cult object or the closeness between masses and reproduced object, study allows for what Keefe calls a "*near distance*" between collector and collection (2012: 128)—a subtle yet important spatial displacement that introduces the tiniest of gaps within the immanence of the collector and his or her collection. To study is neither to destroy aura in a political gesture of revolutionary liberation from the bonds of tradition and hierarchical authority nor to dwell unthinkingly and with conformity to the ritual reenactment of tradition. Rather to study is to care for the aura of objects *as not* aura. In other words, *study is a profanation of the sacredness of aura*, rendering its power, authority, and permanence inoperative while simultaneously *preserving* aura in this inoperative state. Such preservation enables the collector as studier to pass from unthinking conformity in ritual prescription (where authority is simply granted to the object over and above the viewer) to thinking observation in study. In this sense, a remnant is introduced into Benjamin's dichotomy between cult value and exhibition value, a value that has no value: study value.

It is this study value that separates the private collection from the public museum. Summarizing his problem with public collections, Benjamin writes,

> Public collections may be less problematical from a social point of view, and can be scientifically more useful than private ones, yet they lack the greatest possibilities of private ones. The collector's passion is his divining rod and turns him into a finder of new sources.
>
> (1982: 250)

Benjamin then favorably cites the collector and historian Eduard Fuchs, who observed that in a museum, "We see the past in its splendid festive gown and rarely encounter it in its most shabby working clothes" (ibid.). In these quotations, what emerges is a critique of museums that display the grand masters of art, the heroes of history, the universal narratives of cultural evolution, and the tastes of the cultural elite. While such public displays might be of some scientific use (they give access to the "most representative types" of objects displayed in the most scientifically rigorous fashion), at best, one can only *learn* from the museum—learn the proper respect for cultural values, refined tastes, and founding myths of the nation. Bluntly stated, museums socialize the masses into accepting the status quo and celebrating its evolution. Yet what is missing here is the *particular* passions of the collector (idiosyncratic and contingent as they might be), which act as a "divining rod" for finding "new sources" beyond the predetermined script that the museum reproduces at the exclusion of the remnant. It is precisely the gathering together of such exclusions and remnants through the passions of the collector that makes *study* (as opposed to learning) possible—a study of what remains buried by the museum. Precisely because it does not afford disinterested contemplation and therefore the pretensions of universal objectivity or reasonability, the private collection offers a space and time for the de-stabilization of dominant cultural ideologies/mythologies, the cultivation of wonder/enchantment as opposed to cool, calculating curiosity, and an intoxicating auratic experience.

The work of the collection is thus achieved through private ownership. To study, one must be possession of a collection, or have access to such a collection through friendship, inheritance, and so on. Just as the retention of aura is not simply a nostalgic plea for a return to a pre-mechanical age of artisanal production, so to this emphasis on ownership (*my* collection) is not a celebration of bourgeois ownership. Here it is important to remember Benjamin's list of tactics for acquiring new books: borrowing without returning, inheriting them, failing to read them, and finally, writing books oneself. In all cases, emphasis is placed on modes of acquisition that interrupt the buying and selling of commodities on a regulated market. Drawing on Benjamin, Abbas argues that the bourgeois owner might take objects out of circulation, but the collector "takes objects that *are* out of circulation" (1988: 231) and studies them. Stated differently, the collector concerns him or herself with remnants rather than with commodities—those objects and items that have been discarded (thought to be unimportant for display in the museum or worthless on the commodities market), and through the study of the fate of these objects, finds within them new historical insights. For Benjamin, the work of the collector *transforms* the base passion for ownership through a certain kind of magic. "The alchemist," writes Benjamin concerning the collecting practices of Fuchs,

> connects his "base" desire for making gold with a complete examination of the chemicals in which planets and elements come together in images of spiritual man. Similarly, in satisfying the "base" desire of possession, Fuchs searches through an art in whose products the productive forces and the masses come together in images of historical man.
>
> (Benjamin 1982: 252)

Ownership is more than the investment in objects in either an economic or a psychoanalytic sense: rather it becomes a springboard for an alchemical trans- formation of elements that, through the study of the collection, reveals a his- torical process of production and consumption (precisely the processes that bourgeois ownership conceals or mystifies through fetishization). But whereas the alchemical process of transubstantiation of ownership remains allegorical for Benjamin, I would press him further and suggest that it is precisely study that sets this process in motion.

The connections between collecting and study make these passions so dan- gerous. Only in relation to study can we fully appreciate Benjamin's cryptic formulation that the collector is "motivated by dangerous though domesticated passions" (1982: 241). As I have outlined, the passions that motivate the collec- tor are base and highly domesticated. It would appear that nothing of impor- tance separates the passion for ownership found in the collector from the typical bourgeoisie. Yet this passion becomes dangerous when it opens itself up to history through the near distance of study. Study becomes an alchemical process of transformation whereby aura is preserved yet suspended, and where the passion for ownership survives only in the sense that it gives itself over to the passion of study.

Reading Benjamin and Agamben together, I would argue that this aura is what Agamben would refer to as the efficacy of signatures (gleam), or better yet, it is only when the individual aura of the object is profaned (through its removal from traditional ritual *and* economic exchange) that aura *as such* shines through.

86 *The method of study or collecting signatures*

In both cases, aura and efficacy are released through the work of suspension when signs and things are left idle, then and only then can we study their fate Like Benjamin's description of the chaos of his collection—or rather its inherent disorder—so too the collection of signatures is idiosyncratic: a bricolage of traces and fragments that, at first blush, seems to leap and bound without clear reason. Thus collecting and archaeology fall outside the paradigm of modern scientific calculation and delve into a deeper, more mysterious level of aura, passions, and efficacy that crosses disciplinary boundaries, taken-for-granted divisions, and common-sense separations. The systematization of cataloguing and calculation are rejected here for a more intuitive and spontaneous sense of order that is dialectically interrelated to disorder: a zone of "undifferentiated chaos" (Agamben 1999c: 254) that opens a "luminous spiral of the possible" (ibid.: 257) to think beyond the given order of things. Thus for Benjamin and Agamben, the collection is a kind of anti-instrumental, improvisational assemblage that cares for a trace of potentiality (efficacy or aura) left in the residue, separated from signs, and thus exposed, naked and pure for the first time.

The key difference between collecting, as described by Benjamin, and Agamben's theory of study—or at least his theory as I am elaborating it here—concerns the emphasis on privateness and possession. I would argue that for Benjamin, the work of collecting contains a kernel of subversion precisely because it is a form of *private* ownership that stands in opposition to *public* exhibition. Yet in Agamben's analysis, the lure of study rests not in personal ownership but first and foremost in the "demand" of the signatures that is impersonal and *that cannot be owned by anyone*. In his discussion of St. Paul's letter to the Romans, Agamben argues that St. Paul remains open to the call (of signatures) in the sense that he never "make[s] the calling an object of ownership, only of use" (2005b: 26). In Benjamin's case, books are freed through individual passion to own objects and collect them according to one's passions. For Agamben, the studier—like St. Paul—does not collect for personal ownership but rather because of a certain call placed upon him or her by the signatures. The emphasis on the private and the personal creates certain problems for Benjamin concerning the transmission of the collection. As Benjamin writes, "the most distinguished trait of a collection will always be its transmissibility" (1968: 66). Yet how is a collection to be transmitted if the collector is absent? How will it resist toppling over into nothing more than an incomprehensible mass of resources? If the aura of the collection as a collection is predicated on the memories and passions of the collector that give it form, then without access to these memories the transmissibility of the collection is put in jeopardy and its fate can no longer be studied, only exchanged on the market or exhibited for the public. For Benjamin, transmission becomes a kind of aporia precisely because the collection is dialectically inseparable from the collector (it has no autonomous capacity to demand once the collector is removed from the scene). If Benjamin's subtle reworking of aura and ownership interrupt a series of dichotomies—generating a paradoxical space and time wherein a hint of redemption emerges from within that which is most domesticated—nevertheless, the question of transmissibility becomes a kind of limit situation up against which the collector inevitably runs. Agamben seems to solve this aporia precisely by turning a lack into a kind of resource for reimagining transmission beyond personal ownership, and thus beyond the dialectic of the public and the private. When the collector is subtracted from the collection, the collection nevertheless still has the potentiality for transmissibility, which is precisely what is transmitted. Not this or that hidden order or logic but rather transmissibility as such is passed down. Thus the possible loss of meaning that concerns Benjamin when the collection–collector immanence is ruptured is not an issue for Agamben, who views liberation from the collector and his or her personal passions and desire to own as obstacles to the real freedom of the signature.

Given this set of differences between Benjamin and Agamben, perhaps a more fitting model of collecting can be found in Aby Warburg's library—a private collection that was highly personal and idiosyncratic but nevertheless was meant to be transformed into a public, research institution. Certainly Warburg is a major—though often underappreciated—influence on Agamben. *Stanzas* is in fact a book inspired by work at Warburg's institute, and thus reproduces in textual form the extremely unique nature of the collection itself. And it is also no mistake that in Agamben's remarks on studying he mentions not only Benjamin but also Warburg and his own experiences of studying at the institute. What is important for us to remember here is that Warburg's library might very well solve the problem that Benjamin never completely resolved: how a collection can retain its study value without being reduced to either (a) a domesticated form of bourgeois private property (cultish fetishization), or (b) a museum exhibit (fueled by exhibition value). If Matthew Rampley (2001) has focused on the similarities between Warburg and Benjamin's theories of mimesis, memory, and allegory, I would like to extend this argument further by focusing on their shared (yet distinct) practices of collecting and studying. More than a shared theory, it seems that the real heart of the relationship lies on the more primordial level of method itself, which in turn gains new vitality through Agamben's work.

At this point, I would like to turn to a fragment taken from the memoir of one of Warburg's closest collaborators, Fritz Saxl. In particular, I want to pay close attention to Saxl's history of the Warburg library published in E.H. Gombrich's intellectual biography of Warburg. Saxl foregrounds his memoir of the early years of the library in its peculiar and perplexing form. Neither a small, specialized collection composed of particular specimens of books and artifacts related to a single field of study nor a universal compendium of books for general research into cultural history, Warburg's library seemed to suspend the difference between the two, introducing a kind of surplus into this dichotomous distinction. Indeed, the scope of the library as well as its perplexing style of cataloguing materials produced what Saxl calls a "bewildered"

(Gombrich 1986: 327) effect in students who approached the collection for the first time. Saxl writes:

> One the one hand he [the studier] found an excellent collection of bibliographies, most of them unknown to him and apt to shorten his labours; on the other hand very detailed collections, partly on subjects like astrology with which he was hardly familiar. The arrangement of the books was equally baffling and he may have found it most peculiar, perhaps, that Warburg never tired of shifting and re-shifting them. Every progress in his system of thought, every new idea about the inter-relation of facts made him re-group the corresponding books. The library changed with every change in his research method and with every variation in his interests. Small as the collection was, it was intensely alive, and Warburg never ceased shaping it so that it might best express his ideas about the history of man.
>
> (Gombrich 1986: 327)

As Saxl describes, the collection became "alive" through the particular and highly personal passions of Warburg, who continually modified the collection according to the contingencies of his own interests. In this sense the library was alive through Warburg's constant tinkering, which created new constellations of books that defied scientific, standardized cataloguing procedures. One could perhaps go so far as to suggest that the catalogue system employed by Warburg is a kind of inoperative bibliographic machine intentionally designed to throw one off course, destabilize a clear path toward conclusions, and thus keep open a kind of im-potential quest that rhythmically moves back and forth through mimetic relations. These relations between books push outward to new discoveries far afield from one's expectations and research protocols while all the time returning to the original questions and passions that underlay the study. As Saxl argues, Warburg had a "supreme lack of interest in library technicalities" (Gombrich 1986: 329) opting for the "law of the good neighbor" over and above any abstract cataloguing system. The law of good neighbors is a contingent law, and the relations binding a constellation of texts can always be "rather than" they are. He believed firmly that "The book of which one knew was in most cases not the book which one needed. The unknown neighbor on the shelf contained the vital information, although from its title one might not have guessed this" (Gombrich 1986: 327). In other words, the library promotes indefinite and indeterminate study precisely through its modus operandi that continually sends the studier back to the stacks, searching for clues without knowing what crime has been committed. Saxl is therefore keen to emphasize that the "Books were for Warburg more than instruments of research. Assembled and grouped, they expressed the thought of mankind in its constant and in its changing aspects" (Gombrich 1986: 327). If research has some set of predefined goals that are guided by predetermined success conditions, then Warburg's collection cannot be reduced to instrumental means. Instead, it is the very experience of the collection itself that expresses its meaning as a historical process alive and shifting rather than a reified, abstracted catalogue for sorting out resources.

What makes a "good neighbor" "good"? For Warburg, it would seem that the collection should create a kind of astrological chart (or as Benjamin might say a magical encyclopedia). Warburg wrote,

> I shall begin with astrology because nowhere does the problem of the cycle of concrete fantasy and mathematical abstraction reveal its fatal agility in moving from one pole to the other more convincingly than in the metaphor of the heavenly bodies. It effects both a quite unreflective and self-negating subjective confusion with the monstrous apparatus of the astrological bodies, and also an assured subjective certitude which, oriented toward the future, calculates from a distance and with mathematical precision the rising and the setting of the phenomena of the skies
>
> (quoted in Rampley 2001: 132)

Astrology is a dialectic at a standstill: a concrete image of modernity and its two oscillating poles. On the one hand, there is the desubjectivizing process of mimeticism where the historical dimension of human life is swallowed into the ahistorical world of the heavenly bodies through an immediate relation of identity. Here the evolution of modernity is interrupted, sending the subject spiraling back in time to its archaic and superstitious origins. On the other hand, scientific distance is introduced to mediate this mimetic turn by way of the calculation of astrological charts, subjectifying discipline, and generalization. Warburg's collection seems to hold the same tension within itself: mimetic neighbors subvert scientific rationalism while at the same time, the scientific and educational function of the collection prevent a collapse into premodern "barbarism." In other words, the collection is a kind of state of exception, or remnant that redeems the past in the present in the hopes of opening up a different future possibility unapproachable by either mimeticism or scientism. Thus a "good" neighbor *both demarks divisions between proper and improper while subverting those divisions at the same time*. Hence the bewildering confusion of the studier in the face of the collection: neither scientific protocols of research nor simple divination will suffice to navigate the winding paths of mimetic relationships assembled in the collection. Instead of the immediacy of mimetic ritual performance (cult value of the religious ceremony or pagan rite of passage) or the detached distance afforded to the scientist (exhibition value of data and information), the one who studies is located in a paradoxical near distance between the two.

While one might very well have been bewildered by the collection, it was precisely this bewilderment that was the collection's study value. When offered an opportunity to move the collection to a more fitting and convenient location that could reorganize the collection according to modern library science, Warburg insisted that it remain in its cramped, claustrophobic quarters. But this was more than simply a personal decision. "For pedagogical reasons," recalls

90 *The method of study or collecting signatures*

Saxl, "Warburg had always been against making things technically too easy for the student" (Gombrich 1986: 333). Here the direct connections between the private passions of the collector and the mission for promoting public study are clearly conjoined. But also note that study value is not the same as the exhibition value described by Benjamin. While the latter focuses on the presentation of great works for the cultural enlightenment of the masses and the evolution of cultural history, the former stresses the intimate relationship between the collection and the studier who wanders, gets lost, forgets his end goals (as well as the desire for such an end in the first place!), and in the process discovers new potentialities for thought. One must wonder, tinker, get lost, dwell in obscurity, trip over the miscellaneous or forgotten: this is the im-potential experience of studying, which confronts the remnants that lie outside the master narratives of cultural progress or enlightenment selfassurance. And in this sense, the studier discovers new friends and good neighbors amongst the stacks. In this context, Agamben's comments on study become more meaningful:

> Those who are acquainted with long hours spent roaming among books, when every fragment, every codex, every initial encountered seems to open a new path, immediately left aside at the next encounter, or who have experienced the labyrinthine allusiveness of that "law of good neighbors" whereby Warburg arranged his library, know that not only can study have no rightful end, but does not even desire one.
>
> (1995: 64)

To study under the enchantment of the law of good neighbors is to undergo a rhythmic sway between losing one's self and one's purposes in the labyrinth of mimetic relations (desubjectification) and finding new inspiration for further analysis (subjectification). In a footnote on Warburg's collection, Agamben observes, "Like a true maze, the library led the reader to his goal by leading him astray, from one 'good neighbor' to another, in a series of detours" (1999c: 284). Each movement forward is replaced by a movement *to the side*. In this sense the studier is neither the worshipper nor the scientist, and must instead adopt the position of the wanderer or tinkerer. Existing betwixt and between these dichotomies, the very existence of the intimacy between collection and studier is a profanation.

If for Benjamin the problem of transmissibility seemed unsolvable (or at least a constitutive aporia), then for Warburg, it is this very problem that becomes a kind of solution in its own right. Agamben summarizes that Warburg's many projects, including the library,

> may certainly appear to some as a mnemotechnic system for private use . . . But it is a sign of Warburg's greatness as an individual that not only his idiosyncrasies but even the remedies he found to master them correspond to the secret needs of the spirit of the age.
>
> (1999c: 96)

It would seem that Warburg's collection finds in the mystery of the law of good neighbors the faint hope that while Warburg's intentions may be scarcely determinable (thus the collection always verges on disintegration), nevertheless the transmissibility of the transmissible will be transmitted to generations of studiers to come precisely because of the mimetic quality of the collection. Stated differently, the signatures of transmissibility will shine in the constellation of books at the very point where the intentionality of the collector recedes into darkness. At this obscure point, the private and personal become indistinguishable from the spirit of the age. Stated differently, *Warburg himself becomes a signature* that no longer signifies this or that but rather the very im-potentiality of signification. Such a discovery (impotent as it is) is never easy to swallow, indeed it is "bewildering" and painful, yet also, potentially inspirational as well. It is the very withdrawing of the collector from the collection that makes the collection educational, opening up the space and time for public study to happen. When the collector disappears into the collection (as Benjamin describes), the resulting bewilderment becomes a springboard for study, for being lost, and in being lost, losing hope of ever being found (by the curator, collector, author who can no longer offer the key to escape). Warburg himself seems to have been lost in his own collection—thus undermining any notion that the collector had control, reflective power, or willful authority over the mass of books that he or she selected in the first place. Indeed, Warburg was unable to draw definitive conclusions from within the expansive network he had orchestrated. As Gombrich points out, Warburg produced little scholarship in his lifetime and remained firmly on the fringes of academic life. He was often frustrated by the inabilities of language to articulate the vast networks of relations that he had submersed himself into through study. It is at this point, where Warburg's personal passions begin to disappear into a collection, that the collection becomes alive in its own right, and collecting becomes a method for prolonged, indefinite study. Like Benjamin's *The Arcades Project*, Warburg's masterpiece, *Mnemosyne*, remains incomplete. Rendering the complexity of historical processes linguistically failed for Warburg, so he turned instead to the arrangement of pictures into a large, multilayered atlas. The *Mnemosyne* is filled with "kaleidoscopic permutations" (Gombrich 1986: 285) of symbols and "pictorial inventory of expressive movements" (ibid.: 292). With little accompanying explanation, the atlas is an inexhaustible treasure trove of connections, fragments, and relationships that leap and bound across centuries and cultures. Here Benjamin's magical encyclopedia comes alive with its own peculiar aura—an aura that is neither simply a return to premodern enchantment nor modern commodity fetishism. For both Benjamin and Warburg, the construction of auratic constellations becomes a method of study that exists between magic and science, private passions and public presentation, poetic construction and historical discovery, and mimeticism and scientism. In this respect, the atlas as a montage of auratic gestures is a kind of library-in-miniature—a space wherein collecting passes into study, and dichotomies that separate and divide are left to idle.

If Gombrich laments Warburg's premature death because it left the *Mnemosyne* unfinished and opaque, I would argue that his passing is precisely what makes the atlas come alive, or, even better, become *effective*. If a particular meaning can no longer be transmitted from Warburg to the audience, what remains is the inexhaustible efficacy of the imagistic gestures themselves—not as signifiers or signifieds so much as signatures, or as Agamben describes them, "the energetic currents that animated and continue to animate Europe's memory" (1999c: 95). The tracing of energetic spirits/signatures is the primordial experience of study opened up through the collection. The death of the collector means that the signatures underlying the rhythmic undulation of images through historical epochs *can no longer be owned* by anyone, that their efficacy can no longer mean this or that according to the intentionality of the collector, and therefore are perpetually opened for new use by the studier who stands before them. As such, collecting becomes the quintessential method of study, both for Warburg as well as for the countless studiers that have, since his passing, wandered through the collection, charting a constellation of signatures that emit a strange, dark, and uncanny luminosity all their own. If the collection is originally the method of study, in the end, it becomes the remnant of study, a kind of ruin whose efficacy as such only becomes heightened as the collector vanishes into history. The collection becomes his or her final signature.

Here we might recall Agamben's own book *Stanzas*, which was researched in part at the Warburg Institute in London. An odd little book, it is a kind of tracing of the signatures of desire, erotics, phantasms, and so on through history. And like the Warburg library writ large, the composition of the text is not one of logical proofs or philosophical argument so much as spatial mimesis that follows Warburg's own law of good neighbors. Perhaps the best description of *Stanzas* is that it is the incomplete travel diary of a studier who wanders through various chambers, corridors, notches, rooms, stumbling into traces of narratives that, at the very moment of their arrival, seem to trail off into further obscurity. In the end, what is conveyed through this enigmatic travel log of the studier is not any sense of definitive completion or historical accuracy (at least in the sense defined by the discipline of history) but rather a sensitivity to the miracle and mystery of transmissibility as such, the auratic glow of efficacy that shines through the trace and the fragment and thus always offers itself up to free use. In other words, the mystery of *Stanzas* is that no meaning is conveyed, only the perpetual im-potentiality of meaning. It is, as one of Heidegger's most important collections of essays and lectures was once titled, a *Holzwege*, or path that leads nowhere (except of course to its own im-potentiality for leading somewhere).

And since Agamben's quintessential literary example of studying is none other than Bartleby the scrivener, we have to ask, did Bartleby collect anything? As outlined in Chapter 2, Bartleby is not defined by any form of action, identity, or even property. Indeed, he interrupts any notion of private ownership of goods or services through his seemingly impotent form of "preferring not." And yet, as Julian Patrick argues, Bartleby *himself* embodies certain aspects of the archive, or the collection. Patrick writes, without a biography, a past, or even psychological depth,

> the reader, however, soon becomes fascinated with Bartleby himself as his own best archive, precisely because he, having nothing and being, in some sense, nothing, nonetheless retains negatively so much of what makes up an archive, including an important determinant of archival space: that some of what is in an archive is already lost there because its address is defective.
>
> (2002: 726)

In other words, Bartleby *is* a dead letter, a remnant, a positive having of that which is absent, an im-potentiality that is semi-indifferent to all passionate attachments and attractions. The passions of the collector, as in Benjamin's description, are left idle, and the collector collects nothing but his own naked im-potentiality. Both Agamben and Bartleby are studiers in the sense that they "prefer not to" leave the indeterminate space and time of study in order to build arguments, raise demands, insist on action, or complete an assignment.

For anyone who has been lost in a collection, sketching vague sets of relationships between seemingly disparate and unrelated elements, intuitively grasping through volumes of literature in fields that seem far flung from one's discipline, bumping into seemingly tangential clues that spark new questions and new avenues for exploration, sensing a simultaneous capability to forge ahead and incapability to formulate clear arguments, feeling the pressure of the euphoria of mastery that quickly turns into a sadness at the vast volumes of materials yet to be discovered (let alone read!), then the quest for signatures is not unfamiliar territory, nor is the quasi-mystical nature of study that suspends judgment and neutralizes the forward propulsion to fulfill one's potentiality through willful production, leaving one abandoned to the demand of signatures that know no destination. Throughout my own life as a studier, I have often felt the strange mood of hesitation come over me when the faint glow of signatures derails my projects, sending me in new directions that lack predetermined destinations. And as a teacher, I have often seen the mix of melancholy and inspiration that haunt my students when they fall silent, retreating into stacks of books and articles that pile up on desks, doodling endless outlines and permutations of possible relationships between concepts, all of which end in the postponement of deadlines for extended incubation periods. To study is to dwell in the darkness and obscurity of this im-potentiality where we have lost our occupations and destinations, where we can no longer be relied upon to produce x, y, or z. Thus there is something phenomenologically true when the studier says, "I lost my way" or "I lost myself in what I was doing" or "I was sidetracked." The signature is, in the end, not a demand for this or that type of action, conclusion, or knowledge but rather a demand to explore the freedom of this obscurity, which has no destiny of its own. Responding to the demand placed on the studier is not a kind of servitude but rather—as with Kant's categorical imperative—a kind of freedom—not freedom as the total creative potentiality of the will to actualize its capabilities and desires but rather as the openness to receive the presence of an efficacy that remains after the affordances of signs and things have been peeled away—a readiness to be entranced by the efficacy of signatures as pure gestures. Unlike solicitations that produce a sense of flow between world and actions, and unlike commands that produce verifiable results, the demand of the signature has no content, no end, and no determination. Its content is its contentlessness. Its law is a law that is immanent to the form of life that is study. The studier is therefore neither a willful, calculating being nor a worshiper of sacred symbols but is a being willing to stand naked, exposed, and open to this enigmatic demand of signatures that can only stupify. And at this point we can finally clarify the difference between the learner and the studier. The method of the learner is to collect signs and things in order to reproduce them (always in measurable amounts) as evidence of the potentiality to be or do, whereas the method of the studier is to collect signatures in order to get lost, wander, and thus experience the im-potentiality to be and not to be, do and not do simultaneously.

5 The time and space of study
Weak utopianism and im-potentiality

When and where do we study? How does study necessitate a different set of spatial and temporal coordinates outside and beyond the space and time of learning, and in turn, how does study open up these alternative dimensions? I would like to venture an answer to these questions by rethinking the peculiar position of utopia in Agamben's work. For critics such as Dominik LaCapra, Agamben's political and social theories have been rejected precisely because they embody an unrealistic "anarchistic Utopia" (2007: 155). At the same time, supporters such as Carlo Salzani argue that Agamben's theory of the coming community and his emphasis on "a *messianic* notion of politics, which renounces representation and upsets the temporality of political imaginary" (2012: 214) is decisively anti-utopian. For Salzani, Agamben undermines the very idea of the utopian imagination that is predicated on the construction of images of the future. In this chapter, I will argue that both LaCapra and Salzani fail to properly understand the relationship between messianic space and time and Utopia. Rather than utopian or anti-utopian, I suggest a third category, an impossible suture between the two. Key to this impossible suture is what I will refer to as weak utopianism. As opposed to Keith Booker's reading of weak utopianism as a mode of "anti-utopianism" (2002: 29), I suggest that it is a form of utopian thought informed by messianic temporality and spatiality that is situated between everyday chronology and the end of time. In this sense, Agamben's utopianism is, like *pensiero debole* as such, a weak imagination, or a utopianism as not utopianism. If strong utopianism builds blueprints in order to actualize or concretize the potentiality of the utopian imagination, then weak utopianism resists constructing such blueprints in order to live within the im-potentiality of present possibilities. This notion of a weak utopianism is missed in LaCapra and Salzani's work precisely because both theorists neglect the central role of study in Agamben's overarching theory of potentiality.

In the first half of this chapter, I will outline Agamben's unique understanding of time as the full time of the now or *cairos*. In order to explain the distinction between full time and empty time, I will juxtapose the messianic with three other temporalities—all of which are dominate strains in contemporary educational practice and theory: bureaucratic, prophetic, and eschatological times. Each of these temporalities will be represented by various educational

96 *The time and space of study*

philosophers. Thus the prophet will be played by Ivan Illich, the apocalyptic by Peter McLaren, and the messianic apostle by none other than Paulo Freire More than the others, Freire approaches the threshold of the messianic with his insistence on dialogic pedagogical practice, yet even he retreats into the false security of a strong utopian image of the future that ultimately sacrifices the present for a historical dialectic and its logic of deferral. As such, we must use Agamben to clarify the messianic dimension of Freire's work, which otherwise becomes obscured by Freire's own utopian desire for a beautiful, humanized utopian future that negates the present as a mere moment within a larger teleology leading toward the full realization of human potentiality. Such a narrative of becoming erases the much more radical interdependence of impotentiality and potentiality that, as I have been arguing, offers the key to human freedom in present, messianic, now time.

Once I have cleared a time for the messianic, I will then turn my attention to the question of messianic space. As a complement to the temporality of full time, messianic space will offer us a place to study that is inside of yet outside of the traditional architectural form of the classroom. Together, the space and time of study suggest a suspension rather than a destruction of the coordinates of learning and its concrete cartographic inscription in the grammar of the schoolhouse, thus opening up an alternative spatiotemporal understanding of education that does not fall into either dystopian prognostications of the end of education or the utopian longings for total negation of the present in the name of a distant future. Messianic or weak utopianism grounds the possibility for study within the very nihilism of the present conditions of learning within biocapitalism and neoliberal politics, offering the slightest of shifts in time and space that nevertheless make all the difference. Here utopianism does not result in an image of the future but rather in the de-completion of the present in the name of educational im-potentiality.

In short, weak utopianism in the design of educational time(s) and space(s) undoes the strong tendency in education toward functionalism (to orient practice toward predetermined ends) and authority (to prescribe what these ends are and how best to achieve them). Unlike functionalism, which transforms time and space into meaningless, abstracted resources used in the maximization of educational outcomes, and authority, which always assumes expertise, weak utopianism opens up indeterminate educational coordinates for a type of study that cannot be measured, made into an instrument of learning, or controlled in advance by expertise. As such, the educational designer cannot, in the last instance, be either the bureaucrat or the prophet, and must instead be an apostle of study, giving time and space over to new possibilities and new practices.

Messianic time *as* study time

Before we can adequately understand the messianic temporality of study, we must define what the messianic is not. In Agamben's work on Saint Paul, he makes a crucial distinction between the messianic apostle and the prophet. This distinction concerns the relation between agency and time, which for Agamben are conceptualized differently for both subjects. While Agamben's division is useful for thinking about the relation between the present and the future, this division also obscures another dominant relation to time which is embodied within the figure of the bureaucrat. Thus I will add to Agamben's list the contemporary bureaucrat who operates within the field of secular as opposed to theological time.

The bureaucrat is asked to identify him or herself as the subject of secular, homogenized, chronological time. He or she acts as the principle agent for maintaining social relations through instrumental logics that increase efficiency in an inverted proportion to existential meaning. Here we have the iron-clad logic of Michel Foucault's (1979) disciplinary society, obsessed with the time-table, punctuality, exhaustive use, through which time is measured, policed, charted, captured, seized upon and simultaneously made empty, homogenous, and meaningless. We also have the time of E.P. Thomson's (1966) analysis of the birth of the working class in England, where the cyclical time of feudalism empties itself into the linear temporal structure of the work day. If the future exists, it only exists as an extension/intensification of the present moment (either for better or worse). Thus, Agamben writes, the "homogenous, rectilin-ear and empty" notion of time found in contemporary society "derives from the experience of manufacturing work and is sanctioned by modern mechan-ics, which establishes the primacy of uniform rectilinear motion over circular motion" (2007a: 105). Dead and abstracted from human experience, this notion of time is the secularized version of Christian time now divorced from any sense of an end. Indeed, the substitute for eschatological closure is nothing else except the Promethian myth of infinite "progress" and "development" (ibid.: 106). For schooling practices, this means a regimented formulation of educa-tion according to the schedules, deadlines, performance goals, annual reports, and other prescripted timetables that collectively conjoin to form the appara-tuses of learning. This regimentation is prescribed by bureaucratic experts, or the professional/managerial middle class, in accordance with a technocratic approach to institutional efficiency and school reform (Apple 2006). In other words, bureaucracy reduces time to an indifferent force, a reified and abstracted entity that *happens to us* above and beyond our immanent control. There is little time left for creative possibilities within the strictures of bureaucratic time for time itself seems to escape us. All that concerns the temporality of progress is the actualization of potentiality in the form of measurable outcomes that can be organized and interpreted according to the logic of development.

If the bureaucrat has, in certain ways, become the key figure for the regulation and maintenance of the temporality of learning, there is another opposing tradition that exists on the far left: prophetic education and its strongly utopian imagination. According to Agamben, the prophet "is first and foremost a man with an unmediated relation to the *ruah Yahweh* (the breath of Yahweh), who received a word from God which does not properly belong to him" (2005b: 60). In other words, the prophet receives a message directly and with certainty

98   *The time and space of study*

from a transcendental sovereign. The temporal orientation of this message is also of paramount importance, for the "prophet is essentially defined through his relation to the future" (ibid.: 61). The message is about a time to come, never the time of the present. The prophet offers a utopian message about the coming of salvation, emancipation, or equality which is deferred for a future time. Within the prophetic tradition, Utopia serves both a cognitive (critique of the present through the imaginative reconstruction of the future) and affective (opening up the possibility for hope, for desiring differently) function.

In educational discourse we see the prophetic most clearly in the work of Ivan Illich, who studied theology and philosophy and from 1956 to 1960 acted as vice-rector to the Catholic university of Puerto Rico. As is well known, Illich largely rejected the hope for transformative action within the current educational system, which he saw as corrupted and counter-educational: "All over the world the school has an anti-educational effect on society" (Illich 1970: 8). In fact, the established normalization of schools as a universal gatekeeper is destructive and only acts to divide the world against itself into the "academic" and the "pedestrian." Thus the result is schooling for schooling's sake as an instrumental and self-justifying activity: it produces those whom it then endows itself with the power to "save." The result is the transformation of secular bureaucracy into its own form of religious ritual.

In an effort to return education to the hands of the people, Illich turned to a radical reconstruction of education based on the premise of "learning webs" or "networks" in which individuals could find educational resources for themselves outside the strictures of compulsory and age-specific schooling. Although Illich turns against the role of the teacher as secular priest and prophet, his own utopian vision—a postindustrial, "convivial" society—is predicated on a prophetic authority delivered from within the visionary core of faith. Drawing on the image of the Old Testament prophets, Illich argues faith

> founds certainty on the word of someone whom I trust and makes this knowledge which is based on trust more fundamental than anything I can know by reason. This, of course, is a possibility only when I believe that God's word can reach me. It makes sense only if the One whom I trust is God.
>
> (Illich 2005: 57)

As with Agamben's description of the prophet, Illich emphasizes the certainty that the mystery of faith brings and the immediacy of the calling that unites the human and the transcendental. This faith acts as a bridge between God and the community, creating a telos between word and flesh that enables the prophet to critique current society. Illich states,

> So what did these prophets have to say to the Church that the other teachers and preachers mentioned in these first Christian documents could not say? I think they had to announce a mystery, which was that the final

The time and space of study   99

evil that would bring the world to an end was already present. This evil was called Anti-Christ, and the Church was identified as the milieu in which it would nest.

(ibid.: 59)

It is Illich's vocation to return to this prophetic position in order to combat the institutionalization of the Gospels in the form of the Church, and ultimately, the instutionalization of education in the form of the school.

The problem with Illich's prophetic theory is twofold. Summarizing his analysis of the prophet, Agamben writes, "The prophet speaks of the future, and not in his own name, but in the name of something else" (2004a: 119–120). In other words, the prophet addresses what is to come (in the future) and speaks in another's voice (in the voice of God's authority). As such there is a distinct closure of the present that must be rejected in full as a negative totality in order for this future to emerge, thus there is little room for resistance within institutionalized schools. There seems to be a gap between the present and the anticipated utopian future that Illich imaginatively creates, a gap that lacks a clear notion of creative time in the now. As an apophatic theologian, Illich's utopia can only be realized through a radical renunciation of the present and the assertion of a positive salvation in the future. Second, there is the question of authority. Unlike the bureaucrat who wields authority through a certain arbitrary will to power, the authority of the prophet for Illich is decoupled from the question of power over others. It is the notion of Christian friendship that ultimately transforms authority. As opposed to Greek notions of friendship which are predicated on a shared *ethnos*, "Jesus discloses a new unrestricted ability to choose whom I want for a friend, and the same possibility of letting myself be chosen by whoever wants me" (Illich 2005: 147). Here Illich suggests that authority is never to impose one's view onto the other but rather to open up a space of conviviality—which for Illich is defined as "autonomous and creative intercourse among persons, and the intercourse of persons with their environments" (1973: 11)—through which authority authorizes the other to speak and to be heard. The riddle of authority is solved through an analysis of Christian friendship and a recuperation of the radical dimension of the Good Samaritan. While Illich thus repositions authority outside of imposition, the question of the sovereign remains problematic, for what legitimates us to speak in the name of a future, positive utopia if not a "divine will" or a "gift from the Creator"? Illich's prophetic theory fails to achieve a state of immanence with human practice and instead falls back on a transcendental will from which a personal revelation is guaranteed. In short, the time of action seems missing in Illich's prophesy as well as a form of authority that does not in the last instance once again rely on a personal obligation to the gift of faith from a transcendental will.

While prophetic time is the time of the future, messianic time is "the time that remains between time and its end" (Agamben 2005b: 62). Neither chronological nor secular time, it is the time of the now. This moment presents time as a remnant, wherein "the division of time is itself divided" (ibid.). The messianic present is a creative time that exceeds chronological time by introducing future eternity as an internal surplus to the everyday and likewise bleeds the chronological as excess into the eternal. It is, in other words, a zone of indistinction or undecidability that short-circuits definitive boundaries between the past, present, and the future. Hence, as Agamben states, "the messianic world is not another world, but the secular world itself, with a slight adjustment, a meager difference" (ibid.: 69). In other words, the messianic reveals an immanence between this world and the future world. Stated differently, the messianic is not simply waiting for a Messiah to come to save human history. Rather the messianic is beyond the discourse of deferral (perpetual waiting) or historical dialectic that posits the completion of humanity's self-realization in a future temporality.

The time that opens up in the gap between chronology and the end of time is the time of the now, or *cairos*. The *cairos* is "an incoherent and unhomogenous time, whose truth is in the moment of abrupt interruption, when man, in a sudden act of consciousness, takes possession of his own condition of being resurrected" (Agamben 2007a: 111). As opposed to homogenous, empty, and linear chronology, *cairos* is the time of authentic history in which the past returns to the present. The now is neither the end nor the beginning but rather the contraction of all time in the beginning of its own end. Such a time allows the past to break through to be retroactively redeemed in the present. Rather than a new chronology, this radical interruption of the division of time results in "a qualitative alteration of time (a *cairology*)" (ibid.: 115).

The messianic time of the now produces what Agamben refers to as a "state of exception." In this state of exception there is an indiscernability of the law, in that the law ceases to operate in relation to an inside and an outside. The suspended law neither gives a commandment or a prohibition. It is a "being in force without significance" (Agamben 1999c: 169). Here Agamben points to Paul's treatment of the relation between the Jew and the non-Jew. In the moment of the now, Paul argues that a third figure is produced that breaks down the division of the Jew and the non-Jew constituted by the law—a division within the division that renders it inoperative. Between the Jew and the non-Jew resides the Jew of the flesh and the Jew of the breath. For Agamben this division of the division means "the partition of the law (Jew/non-Jew), is no longer clear or exhaustive, for there will be some Jews who are not Jews, and some non-Jews who are not non-Jews" (2005b: 50). The remnant is the non-non-Jew who cannot be fixed either within or outside the law, cannot be defined either as a Jew or a non-Jew. Throughout Agamben's work, the figure of the remnant appears and reappears as a destabilizing figure always on the margins of the social and the theoretical. The remnant for Agamben includes *homo sacer*, the sacred individual from Roman law who can be killed without the charge of murder, those held in the concentration camp whose existence hinges between life and death and between life and speech, and finally the refugee who exists without the guarantee of human rights by civil rights granted by the nation-state. In such states of exception, the result of legal

The time and space of study   101

suspension is not the closure of the law but rather its fulfillment in its very deactivation. The law that separates is held in potentiality, giving itself back to itself, and thus potentially opening up a space for a radical rethinking of community beyond the logic of the sovereign ban that founds the law.

Here it is important to point out that Illich's theory of the Samaritan who embodies a Christian notion of friendship also opens up a space to receive the roadside Jew (as a *homo sacer*) and thus creates a community beyond divisions. Yet it is crucial to note that this correspondence only takes us so far, for as I have indicated above, in the last instance, this community is *guaranteed* by a sovereign who grants us certainty in the form of faith—a sovereign whose position outside the contingent grants us access to community as the embodiment of love, compassion, and wholeness. Thus the state of exception intimated by Illich does not fully succeed as long as it is founded on the figure of the prophet and his or her relation to a transcendent law. For Illich the law cannot be institutionalized (as with the bureaucrat) without negating itself. It must remain active on an interpersonal level for a new community to arrive, and it is this personal activation of the law that grants friendship its meaning. Missed here is the true state of exception wherein the law operates through deactivation in the form of a suspension—only then can the law be returned to the human community as an object of free use (rather than an object animated and secured by a transcendental will). As Lorenzo Chiesa argues (2009: 161), the messianic in Agamben's work opens community to a state of grace which renders inoperative Roman and Mosaic laws and, in turn, resists the transformation of the Gospel into a set of normative precepts.

Returning to Agamben, the sign under which the messianic suspension operates is not the "as if" but rather the "as not." Philosophies of the "as if" function to negate the present from the perspective of redemption in the future. For educational prophets, the "as if" is often articulated as the ethical injunction: "We must act as if the sign of equality can be realized in a future education." Yet the messianic moment in which the future, past, and present coalesce in the now speaks to the *as not*. Quoting Agamben:

> The messianic tension thus does not tend towards an elsewhere, nor does it exhaust itself in the indifference between one thing and its opposite. The apostle does not say: "weep *as* rejoicing" nor "weeping as [meaning =] not weeping," but "weeping *as not* weeping" . . . In this manner, it [messianic time] revokes the factical condition and undermines it without altering its form.
>
> (2005b: 24)

The messianic does not cancel out this world in relation to a possible future so much as it pushes this world to itself through itself, and thus prepares this world for its end in the form of the "as not." In short, if the prophet represents the "as if"—contemplating the present from the position of redemption and the future

102 *The time and space of study*

realization of that which has been lost—then the apostle of the messianic moment represents the now as not now, containing both the past, present, and future in a state of indistinction. To be contemporary means to be untimely in a Nietzschian sense—to perceive the imperceptible time within time that cannot be fixed by the chronology of before and after. Messianic time does not destroy or annihilate, as in the apocalypse, but rather deactivates and suspends efficiency, thus giving potentiality back to itself. Through this inoperative suspension of the law, nothing changes and yet everything changes all at once. This is the moment of radical transformation within the very immanence of the presence that characterizes the messianic "as not." The "as not" overcomes the sovereign act of division between the Jew and the non-Jew—rendering the sovereign inoperative—precisely through the capability to live in im-potential. The "meager difference" of the "as not" is therefore opposed to the prophetic or the apocalyptic, in that its disengagement from the law which results in its deactivation occurs without the movement of dialectical negation. While prophetic time is characterized as a waiting for a future Messiah to arrive and save the fallen, Messianic time is the time of the now where there is no need to wait because the Messiah has always already arrived through the meager difference of the "as not."

If there is a messianic opening to be found in educational philosophy, perhaps it is Paulo Freire's rather shocking proclamation that all participants in dialogic education are "simultaneously teachers *and* students" (2001: 72). Such a maxim introduces a division that splits the division between teacher and student, opening up a sphere of indistinction characterizing the dialogical classroom. If "banking education" for Freire represents a hierarchical division between student and teacher, where the teacher is the one who knows and the student is a passive, empty vessel, then problem-posing education introduces a remnant that exists in surplus of such a relation. Rephrasing Freire's maxim we can state that the teacher who is also a student is the non-non-teacher, a teacher as not a teacher but also not completely a student either—a teacher pushed to the very limit of what a teacher is without moving beyond the form of the teacher. In short, teaching as not teaching is a messianic moment of indistinction. Teaching as not teaching puts teaching in tension with itself without simply canceling it but rather making it pass towards its own end. The remnant that divides the division of the banking classroom does not produce a new subject position beyond or outside of the student-teacher relation, but rather remains immanent within such a division while simultaneously suspending the division, making it inoperative. Teaching as not teaching is an experience of withdrawing from within the subject position of the teacher. In other words, the teacher remains a teacher while no longer being a teacher. Thus Freire writes, "The teacher is no longer merely the-one-who-teaches, but one who is himself taught in dialogue with the students, who in turn while being taught also teach. They become jointly responsible for a process in which all grow" (ibid.: 80). Unlike the bureaucrat who sustains the division between student and teacher, and unlike Illich who supersedes the division through the constitution of networks of friends/learning communities outside of traditional divisions of expert and ignorant, Freire's messianic moment enables us to imagine the teacher–student relationship in a state of potential, of active deactivation, of inoperative operation within the now.

In Agamben's description of the messianic, the apostle—as opposed to the prophet—is uncertain, constantly searching for a language to express his or her message. If the authority of the prophet relies on his or her ability to say "And thus speaks Yahweh," the apostle "must carry out his assignment with lucidity and search on his own for the words of the message, which he may consequently define as 'my announcement'" (2005b: 60). This uncertainty is transformed through Freire into a pedagogical enactment of mutual partnership in the act of education where student and teacher struggle in the world to name that world. Hence the importance of genuine dialogue in the pedagogy of the oppressed wherein the "teacher" becomes a "humble and courageous witness" that emerges from "cooperation in a shared effort—the liberation of women and men" (Freire 2001: 176). The teacher does not have the language of emancipation, which must rather emerge through a mutual search, a quest for the meaning of experience.

The resulting opening is the time of the now that rests between secular time (the time of everyday experience that in schooling means bureaucratic testing) and the event of prophesy (where schools become learning webs). Freire's messianic tendencies become clear in that dialogue transforms our experiences of the everyday into a means of "extraordinary re-experiencing the ordinary" (Shor 1987: 93). This educational time is not an eschatological vision of the end of time but is rather immanent to ordinary time, unlocked through only a slight shift in vision that nevertheless changes everything. It is dialogue that offers the meager difference through which sacred time and chronological time overlap and produce a creative nexus. This time of the now is a "precarious adventure" because it lacks certainty, it lacks a blueprint to a utopian future or a manifesto that outlines transformative action. The precarious adventure that is dialogic pedagogy is in the end a *quest*, which according to Agamben is the "recognition that the absence of a road (the *aporia*) is the only experience possible for man" (2007a: 33). Dialogue is an educational quest for humanization without recourse to a set road certified by expert/critical knowledge or a sovereign decision. As Freire and Myles Horton argue, *We Make the Road by Walking* (1990) without recourse to the map of that road. Thus the future opens up not through prophesy but rather by plunging into possibilities as they exist now, in the present moment.

Although this messianic kernel in Freire's work offers a sound corrective to bureaucratic and prophetic temporalities, this messianic kernel is, in the end, a latent potentiality. In particular, if Freire's emphasis on dialogue inaugurates a state of im-potentiality that suspends divisions between the student and the teacher, dialogue is nevertheless *a means to another end* and never a pure means in and for itself. In the last instance, the end that Freire emphasizes is transformative praxis or action for the realization of our true human potentials. In

104 *The time and space of study*

fact, Freire often refers to humanization as the "ontological vocation of the oppressed" (2001: 43). The mythological unconscious informing Freire's activist orientation is Prometheus, who, in the Marxist tradition, is the allegorical figure of *homo faber* or "man the maker." We can locate Freire's Promethean impulse in his continual calls for action, political revolution, and progressive humanization through the work of the oppressed to overcome their limit conditions. Thus the potentialities experienced through dialogue must be actualized through concrete attempts to humanize social relations for a communist future. Through this narrative, the language of fulfilling one's innate potentiality returns. Against oppressive dehumanization, Freire argues that praxis will bring about "human completion" (ibid.: 47) and thus enable us to "become fully human" (ibid.: 56). Here the remnant of im-potentiality that defines weak utopianism is once again sacrificed. If neoliberalism sacrifices impotentiality through spatial displacement (as discussed in the introduction to this book), then Marxism sacrifices it through *temporal displacement* into the past of a utopian future. The emphasis on fullness in an undefined, utopian future absorbs the messianic moment in Freire's work into the chronological time of Marxist developmentalism and teleological becoming. The problem here is precisely that Freire has *no concept of study* and thus no practice through which we can redeem im-potentiality as a pure educational means. We can never *have time* to study. Rather we must *realize time* through our actions *on* the world. What is ironic here is that the utopian vision to end sacrifice *sacrifices* precisely that which makes us human: our im-potentiality to be and not to be. Instead of positing a past, present, and future in terms of developmental narratives that fulfill our ontological vocation, studying is the indistinction of past, present, and future, suspending our ontological vocation, thus freeing the student *right now* to experience his or her im-potentiality as a form of immanent freedom. Interrupted time, in Agamben's final assessment, "is resolutely revolutionary: it refuses the past while valuing in it, through an exemplary sense of the present, precisely what was condemned as negative . . . and expecting nothing from the future" (2007a: 111).

Messianic space *as* studious architecture

While Agamben's work on the messianic is overtly concerned with time, space does play a minor role in his analysis. In fact, before Agamben's theorization of messianic time, he first turns his attention to messianic space through the analysis of the poetic stanza. Agamben writes,

> European poets of the thirteenth century called the essential nucleus of their poetry the *stanza*, that is, a 'capacious dwelling, receptacle,' because it safeguards, along with all the formal elements of canzone, that *joi d'amor* that these poets entrusted to poetry as its unique object.
>
> (1993b: xvi)

The stanza, for Agamben, is a *potential* space or a third space between subject and object, animal *phone* and human *logos*. The space opened by the stanza is a space of *harmonia* or a "laceration that is also a suture, the idea of a tension that is both the articulation of a difference and unitary" (ibid.: 157). It is, in other words, an impossible synthesis that separates and conjoins criticism and poetry, pleasure and reason, gathering and concealing. Uniting phantasm, word, and desire, the stanza is a chamber or site in which "the beatitude of love is celebrated" (ibid.: 128) through a kind of Borromean knot that heals the fracture between desire and a phantasmal or unattainable object. It is this impossible synthesis between corporeal and incorporeal in the space of the stanza that ties it to messianic redemption.

The stanza, an unreal space of an impossible unity, appears in Agamben's *Coming Community* as the ambiguous space of limbo—a kind of theological architectural enclosure for unbaptized children. Rather than a dystopian figuration of abandonment, Agamben turns this image on its head and argues that the lack of a relation to God and salvation is actually a weak utopian longing. "The greatest punishment," writes Agamben, "thus turns into a natural joy: Irremediably lost, they [the children] persist without pain in diving abandon" (1993a: 5). Beyond perdition or salvation, the forgotten children "remain without a destination . . . [and] are infused with a joy with no outlet" (ibid.: 6). Limbo emerges in this analysis as a space of ease wherein all destinations are suspended. Without such predefined destinations (or the hope for future salvation), those in limbo are free to experiment with unimpeded free being. As the space for a coming community, limbo, like the stanza, is a potentiality that is not determined in advance for this or that use. If the law exists here, it is a law that is left idle or held in suspension and therefore open to new appropriations and unforeseen articulations. Limbo is an indeterminate space or impossible space that exists despite attempts to separate the sacred and the profane.

A third image of weak utopian space is found in Agamben's repeated analysis of the threshold. He writes,

> It is important here that the notion of the "outside" is expressed in many European languages by the word that means "at the door" (*fores* in Latin is the door of the house, *thyrathen* in Greek literally means "at the threshold"). The *outside* is not another space that resides beyond a determinate space, but rather, is the passage, the exteriority that gives it access—in a word, it is its face, its *eidos*.
>
> (1993a: 68)

The doorway is a threshold that paradoxically holds together and simultaneously separates two binaries (inside and outside, real and unreal, phone and logos, salvation and perdition). The threshold as a door is the *architectural form* of potentiality—an impossible suture that is neither outside nor inside but rather

106 *The time and space of study*

a state of exception where such distinctions are rendered inoperable. In another discussion, this time related to Kafka's novel *The Castle*, Agamben reflects on the nature of the door hinge. For him, the hinge is "where the door that obstructs access is neutralized" (2011b: 36). The hinge is thus the apparatus of the door that suspends the function of the door to separate high and low, inside and outside, proper and improper. Importantly, the threshold or hinge is not a *transitional* space used to get from A to B, but rather a point of indistinction between divisions, or a prolongation/extension of their indeterminacy. Here I would also like to return to my previous examination of Bartleby (see Chapter 2). In Melville's story it is important to note that while the office separates or divides employees from employers, Bartleby's desk is located in the master's inner office space. Thus Bartleby confounds or suspends divisions between inside and outside that underlie the hierarchies of the office. Dwelling on the threshold is uncanny precisely because Bartleby becomes an included exclusion, not a transition between spaces of power but their interruption or contamination by a kind of recalcitrant remnant that "prefers not to" be located here or there.

The most exacting theorization of the threshold as an architectural chamber of potentiality is, interestingly enough, found in Agamben's examination of operational time—or the time it takes for an individual to create an image of an experience. According to Agamben's reading of the philosophical linguist Gustave Guillaume, humans experience time but do not have a representation of it. To represent time, the mind must "take recourse to constructions of a spatial order" (2005b: 65). The time that thought has to travel between the temporal experience and the time image (its spatialization) is "operational time" or, as in Agamben's reading, "messianic time" (ibid.: 66). Summarizing, Agamben writes,

> It is as though man, insofar as he is a thinking and speaking being, produced an additional time with regard chronological time, a time that prevented him from perfectly coinciding with the time out of which he could make images and representations. This ulterior time, nevertheless, is not another time, it is not a supplementary time added on from outside to chronological time. Rather, it is something like a time within time—not ulterior but interior—which only measures my disconnection with regard to it, my being out of synch and in noncoincidence with regard to my representation of time, but precisely because of this, allows for the possibility of my achieving and taking hold of it.
>
> (2005b: 67)

This time within time that is nevertheless outside of chronological time is also a space outside of space. It is a topos "as not" a topos—a spatial excess. Such a space lacks a determinate end, and thus remains *operational*. Operational space is, in other words, a state of exception that is neither here (in this spatiality) nor over there (in a utopian vision). "Utopia," writes Agamben, "is the very topia of

The time and space of study   107

things" (1993a: 103). This topia is the slightest of differences between what is and what ought, between Nirvana and the world. It is the operational time and space of action without deferral or without waiting.

The perfect example of an operational image is the "empty throne" Agamben analyzes as part of his archaeology of glory in political theology. The empty throne reveals the vacuity at the very center of the Western governmental apparatus—a threshold wherein the division between the Kingdom of God and the Government of Humanity enters into a state of suspension. This is the spatial inscription of Glory as what remains when human life and divine life are indistinguishable from one another. The purpose of the empty throne is therefore, according to Agamben, "to capture within the governmental machine that unthinkable inoperativity ... that constitutes the ultimate mystery of divinity" (2011a: 245). In this messianic space, the ceremonies and the symbols of power are left idle, open to new uses and appropriations that fail to compartmentalize themselves into either the divine or the secular. The empty throne—with its discarded liturgical implements—is akin to the paradoxical space of limbo. Both are spaces that have been abandoned—surplus spaces or spatial remnants that lie outside the topography of religious binaries in inoperative zones of indistinction. Weak utopianism is the operational image—the open potentiality of the utopian image before the image is actualized in terms of a concrete representation, political manifesto, or architectural blueprint. The empty throne (with its suspended symbols of Glory) is a kind of potentiality or infinite openness for creative appropriation or repurposing.

As such, weak utopianism is neither a process of reform nor a concrete materialization of a utopian blueprint, but is rather a *constant emergence* of the possibility of new uses within the space and time of the now. In other words, utopianism is no longer about achieving a future determination for Agamben but about experiencing a collective im-potentiality that is always already here. Messianic or weak utopianism is a potentiality breaking out of and into the present, arresting both everyday chronology and narratives of progress, opening up the full presence of the time and the space of *cairos*. Suspending the present from within the present, weak utopianism is not the replacement of the "is" with the "ought," but rather the revelation of the potentiality of whatever from within the present itself.

The space of weak utopianism I have been developing in this chapter is, importantly, connected directly with the question of education. For Agamben, the action which more than any other represents the messianic moment is the act of studying. The temporality of weak utopianism is not simply the messianic time of the now, but also the temporality of perpetual study where the student holds judgment in suspension in order to touch the im-potentiality of thought itself—the weakness in thought that cannot be made into a form of knowledge. Likewise the space of weak utopianism can be thought of as an educational space. In other words, the spatial and temporal dimensions of messianic utopianism are not so much about positing a model for a future perfection (as with many classical Utopias). Rather, *messianic utopianism is an education in our own*

108 *The time and space of study*

in-capability for utopian imagining within the present without committing to any one determinate form. In conclusion, I will now illustrate the educational importance of weak utopianism through several examples of educational architecture that are situated on the bureaucratic, prophetic, and messianic registers.

Educational space—like educational time—is largely ruled by the measure of the will of the bureaucrat or the imagination of the prophet. The bureaucratic space of the schoolhouse is perhaps best illustrated through Foucault's careful genealogy of institutional forms whereby he charts the network of disciplinary power relations which function through the arrangement of chairs, tables, clocks, blackboards, and so on in the common, everyday schoolhouse. Such arrangements discipline the body to sit in a particular way, hands to move in accordance with certain norms of efficiency, heads to turn in a uniform direction, activities to be organized according to maximum outputs. In other words, such a space is itself a "social orthopedic" for managing and making manifest each student's potentiality. These spaces are hierarchically ranked and ordered according to the overall logic of the panopticon, which functions under the rule of optimal visibility and transparency of all actions. Through this ranking, classifying, and surveying students, *disciplinary power produces subjects* recognizable by the educational apparatus (Foucault 1979: 170). The space of the panopticon is therefore the *space of learning*, for producing an efficient and self-regulating subject who has the capabilities necessary to realize his or her full potentiality according to the needs and interests of the state.

Yet it is also important to remember that for Foucault, there are two types of disciplinary spaces. The first is, as outlined above, the most widely commented upon: the panopticon. The goal of the panopticon is to "improve the exercise of power by making it lighter, more rapid, more effective, a design of subtle coercion for a society to come" (Foucault 1979: 209). It renders all actions and behaviors visible through examination, careful cataloging, and recording so as to produce a normalized and normalizing subject. The other image of discipline is the "discipline-blockade" which is an "enclosed institution, established on the edges of society, turned inwards towards negative functions: arresting evil, breaking communications, suspending time" (ibid.: 209). Stated differently, Foucault's distinction between eighteenth-century institutions which "reinforce marginality" and nineteenth-century institutions which "aimed at inclusion and normalization" (2000: 79) is interupted. Urban schools appear to resemble the discipline-blockade of the eighteenth century. Agamben's work pushes us even further and suggests that schools serve as a particular kind of disciplinary blockade: the camp. According to Agamben (1998), it is the camp that has replaced the panopticon as the paradigm of biocapitalism, exposing all life to the logic of abandonment and exclusion. While it might seem absurd to suggest that schools today function in a grey zone between panoptic spaces of normalization and camp-like spaces of abandonment, there is evidence that strongly suggests that below the seemingly banal power of the panopticon rests a more obscene sovereign injunction predicated on the threat of violence against educational life.

Thus, in 1988 Ivan Illich made the following provocative observation concerning inner-city Chicago schools:

> I had come to Chicago to speak about schools, not camps. My theme was educational crippling, not Nazi murder. But I found myself unable to distinguish between Oskar Schindler in his factory in Crakow and Doc Thomas McDonald in Chicago's Goudy Elementary, where he is the principal. I know Doc as indirectly as Schindler, I know him only from the Chicago Tribune, but I cannot forget him. And for some weeks now I have asked myself: Why does he stay on the job? What gives him the courage?
>
> In a sense there is no way of comparing the class of historical events that go under the name of Hiroshima, Pol Pot Cambodia, Armenian Massacre, Nazi Holocaust, ABCstocks, or human geneline engineering on the one hand, and, on the other hand, the treatment meted out to people in our schoolrooms, hospital wards, slums, or welfare. But, in another sense, both kinds of horrors are manifestations of the same epochal spirit. We need the courage and the discipline of heart and mind to let these two classes of phenomena interpret each other.
>
> (1988)

Here Illich clearly recognizes both the danger in making an analogy between schools and concentration camps and the necessity of thinking through these links (no matter how mediated) for understanding the logic of abandonment that lies at the heart of the learning society. If panoptic space includes students by *investing* into their potentiality, then the space of the camp includes students by their exclusion through divesting students of their potentiality, leaving only an impotence that they must bear as their own burden. In both the space of the camp and the space of the panopticon, there is no room for im-potentiality and the freedom to be this and that beyond learning imperatives or the force of abandonment.

Against this dystopic space of the contemporary schoolhouse (poised as it is between panopticon and camp), authors such as David Kennedy have turned toward a *strong* utopian vision of radical and complete transformation of the form and function of educational space. Not unlike Illich's prophetic turn, Kennedy also gazes into the future to glimpse the emergence of the New and bring it back to us in the present via a poetically imbued clarion call to "reimagine the school" in order to actualize the latent potentiality of adult–child dialogue. This reimagining project begins with a normative claim concerning the importance of dialogue in overturning hierarchically reified relations between children and adults. Such intersubjective restructuring demands an equally ambitious restructuring of the school as a whole. In other words, dialogue—as a transformative activity—must be reflected in and enhanced by spatiality. Kennedy summarizes, "Reimagining the praxis of school on this side of the 'revolution not unlike that introduced by

Copernicus' means imagining an institution that creates the conditions for dialogical relations between the forms of intentionality of childhood and adulthood" (2006: 165). It is not simply that the school as we know it today is antithetical to dialogical relations between children and adults (in terms of standardized curricula and certain administrative and bureaucratic impediments), but also that the space of the school limits the kinds of relations that can emerge in classroom settings. The utopian vision that emerges in Kennedy's work is a complex design that integrates curricular reform, new structures for governance, a pedagogical emphasis on dialogue, along with a blueprint for school design.

Kennedy highlights the centrality of spatial transformations in his utopian imagination: "The reconstruction of physical space to accommodate this reconstruction in practice and in the theory-practice relation is a crucial aspect of the shift itself" (2006: 170). He continues,

> The built environment is a reification in space—in boundary, pathway, wall and sector—of the social roles and relationships that gave rise to it—which in turn are influenced and determined by the built environment, and so on in a circle.
>
> (ibid.)

The first architectural principle for a dialogical space is that it must balance the differential lived experiences of children and adults. On the side of the child, the space must be open to the potentials of play and exploration of the world. Thus the traditional delineations between school and community and school and university are to be rejected for a much more permeable ideal wherein the school hosts the intellectual resources traditionally contained and controlled by the university. If the traditional schoolhouse emphasizes a spatial logic of *distance*—distance both metaphorically from the life-world of the students and physically from the community and the university—then Kennedy's utopian imagination replaces the spatial logic of distance with that of *immanence*. On the side of the adult, the logic of immanence would mean opening up the partitions of the school and classroom to the possibility for adult meetings, community organization, and collective practice. According to Kennedy, traditional school architecture focuses on specific details of design in order to solve isolated problems and maintain budgetary efficiency. Yet his utopian plan begins with an appreciation for the interconnectedness between all elements of design. Kennedy summarizes:

> The configuration of classrooms, offices, seminar and conference rooms, shop and studio areas, lounges and eating areas, large and small meeting areas, must be imagined within the larger context of design variables like the overall construction of pathway and route, the interface between indoor and outdoor spaces and the concomitant construction of a combination of natural and artificial light, the juxtaposition of "open" and

The time and space of study   111

"closed," "noisy" and "quiet," "hard" and "soft," public, semi-public and private spaces—of spaces designed for large groups, small groups, intimate groups and individuals.

(ibid.: 173)

Rather than discipline, surveillance, and normalization at a distance through panoptic technologies, Kennedy suggests an "emergent, systemic balance of multiple pedagogies and curricula, from the most open to the most closed forms of structure and organization" (ibid.: 174).

The resulting architecture is the spatialization of constructivist learning theory—an intentional community of actors inhabiting a shared, dynamic space of dialogue. Rather than a preexisting form imposed from the outside (a standardized design model), the school space is an organic expression of a living community. Although Kennedy does not directly argue this point, we could infer that one of the central reasons for the failure of constructivist learning theory to take hold in schools is that its reforms have been limited to curricular choices alone. Yet space is a vital part of the dialogical relation. Therefore constructivists must have a truly utopian horizon for their project: one that envisions the dialectical totality of curriculum, pedagogy, and architecture. Without this dynamic and totalizing vision of utopian transformation, constructivism will never fully take root, will never become fully embodied in practice and habit. Dialogue must become spatialized and space must become dialogical. The result is a blueprint for a new type of school—a laboratory school or, as John Dewey might say, an embryonic society of the future existing *today*.

Kennedy's vision is an expression of the strong utopian imagination at work. It emphasizes the need for total negation of the present—the space of the panopticon, the imposed curriculum, and the reification of adult–child relations into a hierarchy of command and control. This negative totality should be replaced with a utopian alternative of grand proportions that redesigns the school from the ground up. This redesign will unleash the playfulness of childhood and the democratic potentialities of education, restructure the relationship between school and society, and, in the end, reach out to impact our very notion of the space of community. In this sense, the politics of strong utopianism in educational architecture is akin to the goals of Le Corbusier's ambitious projects, the experimentalism of early Rem Koolhaas, and the futurism of Buckminster Fuller.

While Kennedy's utopian vision has many merits, the temporal displacement of educational equity, freedom, and playfulness to an indefinite future is highly problematic. This deferral to the future results in a kind of perpetual waiting for salvation. Only the prophet can offer a strong utopian message about the coming of salvation, emancipation, or equality that is postponed for a future time after the present has passed and judgment is upon us. In educational discourse we clearly see a prophetic dimension in Kennedy's work, which rejects the hope for transformative action within the current educational system—a system he sees as corrupted and counter-educational. The school, with its

112 The time and space of study

hidden curriculum and its panoptic architecture, becomes an institution of mystification, a ritual performance whose outcome is the normalization and reification of the adult–child binary and thus a complete denial of the trans-formative and democratic potential of dialogue. The present is locked within a totalitarian space–time structure that cannot be challenged from the inside. The only solution, according to Kennedy, is a dialectical leap into a qualitatively dif-ferent future. Akin to Herbert Marcuse's great refusal—a concept Kennedy draws direct inspiration from—the dialogical school of Kennedy's utopian imagination is a latent possibility that can only be actualized through the total rejection of schools as they exist today.

The irony here is twofold. First, although emphasizing spatiality and its importance for the concretization of dialogical relations, the laboratory school Kennedy imagines lacks a historical space of its own. While gesturing toward Dewey and Reggio Emilia it is uncertain whether or not he is recommending their *actual* schools as models or not. Thus the speculative turn in Kennedy's writing de-materializes his own attempt to materialize the laboratory school of his dreams in a space of its own. The result is paradoxical: on the one hand the laboratory school (for which we have no example) is supposed to act as the "valuable stranger" or "outpost" (Kennedy 2006: 186) in the present for a more democratic future, and on the other hand, it can only exist in an undefined future. While the logic of traditional schooling is, for Kennedy, based on distance and the logic of the laboratory school based on immanence, his prophetic turn reinstitutes a seemingly unfathomable gap or distance between what is now and what is to come, between actual spatial relations and non-existent spatial relations. If we are to struggle to realize the potentiality of the laboratory school, there is neither in-depth analysis of the specific kind of agents/collectives that could bring about such change nor a description of the kinds of political, economic, or social situations that could act as catalysts for massive school restructuring. The laboratory school and its intentional community are without grounding in actual movements or actual locations. If there is a force driving us toward this Utopia, it is the strong, gravitational force of the invisible hand of the dialectic itself as it moves through history.

The prophetic space of strong utopianism thus leaves us with an abstract vision. All the while, it denies the spatial and temporal logic of the present any specifically political or educational importance. The present is nothing more than a phase in a dialectical history of the adult and the child, which is charted through various historical constructs and summarized in a list of epochal distinctions, each equally unstable, each necessarily unfolding into the next. For Kennedy, the present is reduced to yet another moment within this overarching teleological narrative of becoming that must be negated through the advent of the laboratory school that, in Hegelian fashion, will solve the crisis in adult–child relations in a form of mutual recognition. And, although striving for determinate and thus clear and transparent negations, Kennedy's sublation is in the end magical and unreal—a kind of prophetic pole-vault into a qualitatively different future. The dialectical structure to his argument subsumes the present

The time and space of study   113

within a telos that is *not its own*. And here the final irony of Kennedy's project becomes viciously clear: if he rejects the contemporary intrusive curriculum imposed on schools from the outside, then so too his dialectic seems equally intrusive and forced, sacrificing the present for a delayed, prophetic vision. This vision attempts to fully actualize the utopian imagination and thus misses the messianic turn completely: a turn that does not emphasize the determination of the utopian imagination in any one particular form but rather the im-potentiality to imagine difference as such.

As opposed to either the dystopianism of the panopticon or the strong utopianism of Kennedy's school, we should instead ask what educational space available now, in the present, enables us to study. Study must be located within the time and space of weak utopianism, otherwise potentiality becomes subservient to actuality, means to ends, and education to instrumental learning. Certainly the many paradigms of messianic time and space Agamben provides are useful for constructing a constellation through which the various dimensions of study can be apprehended and conceptualized. Yet it might be helpful to end this chapter with a simple example of weak utopianism directly drawn from educational architecture. As historians David Tyack and Larry Cuban argue, a critical question after years of policies to "revolutionize schools" or "build the schools of tomorrow today," New York architects commissioned to design six new elementary schools in the 1990s took a radically different approach. Instead of starting from scratch and constructing a radical new blueprint based on their own utopian visions of the perfect school, the architects instead focused on a simple detail within the classroom. Taking the square classroom as their inspiration, they introduced a notch that created space for a new bay window as well as a small space for introducing new learning technologies, bookshelves, and so on. Tyack and Cuban summarize: "By combining both tradition and flexibility in their design, with teachers at the center, the architects promoted reform from the inside out rather than imposing it from the top down" (1995: 137). The result of this remarkably simple alteration of an existing floor plan was a new notion of teacher-centered innovation.

The notch in the classroom wall example is a clear example of weak messianic time and space at work. As with the messianic, this notch was the smallest and most insignificant of details that nevertheless altered everything from the configuration of the classroom to pedagogy to student interactions with peers. Rather than the classroom today "as if" it were the classroom of tomorrow, it is the classroom of today "as not" the classroom of today. In other words, the notch suspended the logic of the classroom within the form of the classroom, and thus was an alteration from within rather than from without. This meager transformation of space is not a grand utopian design, but rather preserves the traditional classroom layout in suspended form, opening it up for new uses. Using Agamben's terminology, I would argue that the notch is the "unpre-presentable space" or "space adjacent" (1993a: 25) to the functioning classroom which opens up to new, collective experimentation. Like the halo in messianic

114 *The time and space of study*

theology, the notch is an "inessential supplement" (ibid.: 55) or "supplemental possibility" (ibid.: 56) that is poised at the very limit of the grammar of the schoolhouse. As an unrepresentable space and time, the notch cannot be fully mapped in terms of radical reform or simple repetition of preexisting forms. Rather it is a suspension of the law of classroom design without destroying or negating this design—it is the empty throne of education, a kind of diagonal line that introduces an educational limbo into the highly codified and regimented classroom space. The notch is a positive manifestation of nihilation, not as destruction or negation but as suspension of the classroom from within the nihilism of the standardized, technologically enframed classroom. Indeed, if messianic time suspends the authority of the teacher then so too does messianic space suspend the authority of the grammar of the classroom. This suspension is not a rejection of the school (as in Kennedy's model) but a profanation of what exists: the notch is not any one's property, is not in anyone's control, and is not destined for any one particular use. It is the classroom as not a classroom. It is the space of study.

While Tyack and Cuban must be given credit for recognizing the importance of this event in educational architecture, the way in which they frame their discussion of such innovation is problematic precisely because it erases the messianic dimension of the notch. For Tyack and Cuban, the notch is a form of ground-up reform. As the title of their book suggests, it is a way of "tinkering toward utopia." In this sense, the notch is *oriented toward a future yet-to-come* that, in the end, erases the present moment as a now. "Tinkering toward" reintroduces a telos to school reform that always defers educational freedom for a future time/space. If the operational image enables us to reach the time–image, then this operational image, as Agamben would argue, also and equally *delays its arrival*. It is this delay and the immanent freedom to invent and experiment with the present as a constant emergence that Tyack and Cuban all too quickly reabsorb back into the long century of public school reform with its strong utopian promise.

Tinkering should instead be thought of as a *pure means* rather than simply a *means to another end*. Instead of tinkering *toward*, I would emphasize tinkering, full stop. The time and space of the operational image is a time and space of a pure means that releases potentiality from its submission to future actualization/determination. It is here—in this messianic now—that we can locate the notch. In short, the surplus space of the notch does not anticipate anything beyond itself. No specific learning outcomes are called for and no specific learning activities are inscribed in its form. Rather, it merely introduces a new dimension into the square space of the classroom for free use, for new innovation within the present. Because Tyack and Cuban lack such philosophical distinctions, reform drains their analysis of the notch of its utopian potentiality, and in turn miss-recognizes the messianic space and time of tinkering. Like the door for Agamben, the notch becomes the "weak" architectural form of im-potentiality without predefining the specific social or educational ends which must be fulfilled.

Conclusion: weak utopianism as tinkering

If Tyack and Cuban have missed the mark, we can nevertheless take seriously the concepts and examples they deploy—even if this means that we must radically re-interpret such concepts and examples in light of weak utopianism and its messianic time and space. Thus I would like to end with a reconsideration of the importance of tinkering—a concept that, in passing, has been connected with Agamben's theory of bricolage (Kishik 2012: 64).

Educational design should first and foremost be conceptualized as a form of tinkering with the time and space of education. Design as tinkering moves beyond functionalism—in terms of the prescriptive educational use of time and space to achieve predetermined outcomes—while remaining within the grammar of the schoolhouse. Appropriating a useful concept from Gert Biesta's analysis of educational architecture, I would like to argue that weak utopianism is a kind of "negative functionalism" that "is not aimed at trying to prescribe how a building should be used and how its users should behave, but instead aims *not* to make some actions and events *im*possible" (Biesta 2006: 111). Instead of destroying, design as tinkering preserves but only for the purpose of opening up the possibility for exploring potentiality anew. To enable study in the classroom, educational design should itself be a stupid practice, one always engaged in study with the temporal and spatial grammar of the classroom and of the schoolhouse, and thus open new forms of time and space beyond bureaucratic functionalism or prophetic authority. The potentiality of the design should remain latent (rather than determinant) and thus primordially generative for those who study within the space to tinker with. If Tyack and Cuban have the right example (the notch in the wall), they have the wrong theoretical framework (the language of progressive reform). And if Kennedy has the right theoretical framework (emphasizing immanence, playful study, and free use of educational materials and spaces), he has the wrong example (the utopianism of the laboratory school). The difficulty here is precisely the difficulty of the time image suddenly corresponding with the experience of time (the diachronic and synchronic intersecting in the explosive space-time of the now). Stated differently, the central issue that these scholars face is one that is inscribed in the very nature of weak utopianism itself and the perplexing, if not paradoxical, spatial–temporal relations which it folds into the contemporary moment. More tinkering is needed here . . .

6 The work of studious play
The problem of transmission revisited

The fracture defining education can be traced back to Plato's *Republic*. When discussing childhood education, the character of Socrates argues in Book III that "we must subject them [children] to labors, pains, and contests" (1992: 413d) in order to observe key character traits revealing the special nature of the child. The description continues: "Like those who lead colts into noise and tumult to see if they're afraid, we must expose our young people to fears and pleasures, testing them more thoroughly than gold is tested by fire" (ibid.: 413d). Through a battery of tests, the potentiality of the child will actualize itself, enabling the teacher to determine the student's exact nature. In this sense, testing becomes a kind of rite of passage, the child's first entrance into the division of labor that defines the ideal harmony of the city-state. The quasi-religious nature of ritualized testing appears all the more powerful when told through Plato's myth of the three metals, which divides the future workforce into gold, silver, and bronze, each with their attending attributes and particular qualities. The child, like metal in a blacksmith's shop, must be submitted to fire in order to determine his or her properties—properties that necessarily correspond to certain social and economic roles within the city-state. Thus education becomes a form of ritualized testing, a gauntlet children must endure in order to make manifest their potentiality in a determinable form. Yet later in the same text, Socrates returns to the issue of early childhood education, this time from a radically different perspective. In relation to teaching the highest levels of mathematics and dialectics, Socrates states, "all the preliminary education required for dialectic must be offered to the future rulers in childhood, and not in the shape of compulsory learning either" (ibid.: 536d). Compulsory testing should not be allowed because "no free person should learn anything like a slave. Forced bodily labor does no harm to the body, but nothing taught by force stays in the soul" (ibid.: 536e). In contradistinction to his earlier claim concerning the priority of ritualized testing, here Socrates suggests that educators "don't use force to train the children in these subjects; use play instead. That way you'll also see better what each of them is naturally fitted for" (ibid.: 536e–537). The relation between playing and testing remains obscure throughout this work. It would seem that testing is given a certain educational priority—a necessary technology for determining who is fit to rule—and that

The work of studious play 117

play only emerges later as a specific pedagogical practice for higher-order mathematical thinking reserved for those with golden souls. Yet at the same time, it is clear that Socrates encourages some form of play in order to determine "what each of them is naturally fitted for." Thus play is integral to the evaluative process itself. Indeed, it would make little sense to submit the child to harsh testing if, as Plato suggests, play more easily and directly manifests the soul of the child. Either way, my main point is that a problem emerges here that educational philosophy has inherited and passed down throughout the centuries: the ambiguous relation between rituals of testing and the freedom of play.

If, for Plato, ritual and play hang together—no matter how tenuously or awkwardly—in schooling today we see a sharp separation of the two. On one hand, we have the ritual of standardization and high-stakes testing. If Peter McLaren once argued that schooling is a ritual performance (1999), then this is perhaps now more true than ever before. Likewise, for Ivan Illich, institutionalized schooling acts like a modernized, secular church, full of rituals and mystical incantations that have little to do with actual education and everything to do with preserving the sanctity of this most cherished institution through testing, accreditation, and graduation ceremonies. Illich writes,

> The school system today performs the threefold function common to powerful churches throughout history. It is simultaneously the repository of society's myth, the institutionalization of that myth's contradictions, and the locus of the ritual which reproduces and veils the disparities between myth and reality.
>
> (1970: 37)

Here the school, with its hidden curriculum, becomes an institution of mystification, a ritual performance whose outcome is addiction to compulsive teaching and thus passive submission to an external authority—the teacher or, as Plato might argue, the golden soul of the philosopher king—who acts as a "priest" looking out for the flock. The net result: "School makes alienation preparatory to life, thus depriving education of reality and work of creativity. School prepares for the alienating institutionalization of life by teaching the need to be taught" (ibid.: 47). Stated differently, the major effect of schooling is the "progressive underdevelopment of self- and community-reliance" (ibid.: 3)—a removal of education from an immanence with social life as such. Jan Masschelein and Maarten Simons (2010) add another important dimension to this argument. For them, schools function as a form of secular baptism that offers children a *Logo* or orientation for entering a specific world. Thus baptism transforms the child into a "not yet" who "must be" (by adopting a certain language, style, and set of cultural norms and values). But perhaps the true measure of ritual testing and social baptism in the contemporary era has been the elimination of recess, the reduction in many play-based classroom activities, and the demolition of playgrounds to make room for more school buildings, trailers, or sport fields in primary school all in the name of educational

118　*The work of studious play*

efficiency (Olfman 2003). The ritualization of education through schooling as a secularized church has turned its back on the relation between education and play, squeezing it out of curricula and replacing it with skill and drill task-oriented activities. Play ceases to have any educational value and becomes a private affair rather than a public concern.

On the other hand, we have theories of play such as those represented by A.S. Neill's notorious Summerhill School in which play is the only worthwhile educational activity. Famously, Neill once wrote,

> Summerhill today (1971) is in essentials what it was when founded in 1921. Self-government for the pupils and staff, freedom to go to lessons or stay away, freedom to play for days or weeks or years if necessary, freedom from any indoctrination whether religious or moral or political, freedom from character moulding.
>
> (1992: 3)

On this view, school ritual is a form of indoctrination and is an obstacle to maintaining the radical freedom and individuality of the students. For Neill, "the evils of civilization are due to the fact that no child has ever had enough play" (ibid.: 38). By tapping into the instinctive "play-drive" (ibid.) of children, Summerhill allows individual freedom and creativity to flourish, setting the grounds for personal happiness. And while certain rituals, rules, and protocols might appear even at a place like Summerhill, such rituals emerge from within the innovative powers of the players themselves as contingent and immanent (rather than necessary and transcendent) tools for maximizing (rather than minimizing) more play. We see the influence on Summerhill and the idea of free play on more contemporary approaches to play as an "(un)curriculum" in the work of Denita Dinger and Jeff Johnson (2012). Such pedagogies are direct attacks against schools and the learning society as such, and while progressive educators might not be as drastic as Neill and abolish all ritual performance for the total spontaneity of free play, they would undoubtedly argue that some form of play is a necessary corrective to an over-emphasis on ritual testing in contemporary public schools. Under pressure to increase test scores and measurable progress, schools are drastically cutting back on all forms of play— free play or otherwise—with shocking results including measurable decreases in brain and muscular development, communication, problem solving, social skills, creativity, and an increase in violence, health risks such as childhood obesity, and ADHD (Chmelynski 2006; Lauer 2011). Supporters of play in all its manifestations and the (un)curriculum thus pick up and intensify Plato's later comments on play as a more natural evaluative tool for exposing the child's real nature.

At first, it may appear that Agamben would endorse free play as a solution to the ritualization of high-stakes testing. As opposed to cultural petrification through schooling as a ritual performance, Agamben, in several important passages, turns to play as a possible alternative. "The passage from the sacred to the profane can, in fact, also come about by means of an entirely inappropriate use (or rather, reuse) of the sacred: namely play" (2007b: 75). To play is to neglect to follow the rules of the ritual and to liberate things from their "proper use" according to a certain, predetermined *Logos*. Importantly, play does not destroy but rather preserves ritual in a kind of suspended form, rendering ritual inoperative. The result of playful profanation is "a new dimension of use, which children and philosophers give to humanity" (ibid.: 75). In this sense, play is the exact opposite of ritual: "Ritual fixes and *structures* the calendar; play, on the other hand, though we do not yet know how and why, changes and *destroys* it" (2007a: 77). In the time of play, "man frees himself from sacred time and 'forgets' it in human time" (ibid.: 79). Thus play seems to embody a solution of petrification and sacrifice found in the ritual performance of schools, redeeming education for new uses that are not held above or against life but define a form-of-life that is immanent to life.

Much of the secondary literature on Agamben has played-up the role of play in his philosophy, finding in play a kind of utopianism (both in a positive and negative sense). Thus Catherine Mills argues that for Agamben, play offers a messianic time of redemption which "can also be used to free humanity in relation to economics, law, and so on" (2009: 125). Play, in Mills' reading, offers Agamben "a means of resistance to the conditions of the current 'extreme phase' of capitalism, and most particularly to the spectacular cultural regime of consumption that is integral to it" (ibid.: 126). Masschelein and Simons (2010) agree with this reading, emphasizing that play liberates objects for free use and as such is essential for a coming education, or an education without specific destination. Joanne Faulkner has likewise focused on Agamben's theory of play, only this time less as a utopian alternative to capitalism and more as an overly romantic fantasy of childhood innocence. It is worthwhile citing Faulkner at length here:

> the child signifies potentiality for Agamben as a purely creative, experimental, and speculative way of being, without which nothing could come to pass into actuality . . . Yet [this description] still conforms to a disturbing tendency to signify in the child a separation from the remainder of the community. Agamben evokes the figure of the child at play, in *Infancy and History*, in order to represent the possibility of a break from the metaphysics of everyday life. Through play, the child plucks objects from their historico-material context, transfiguring everyday things into toys . . . Yet, in so doing, we might understand Agamben to recapitulate the very same gesture that places the child within a conceptual zone of exclusion.
>
> (2010: 210)

In this passage, Faulkner argues that the very gesture of play granted to the child merely replicates the very schism between bare life and the life of the citizen subject that Agamben attempts to breach. Stated differently, the "innocence" of childish play becomes a convenient fantasy for projecting adult anxieties concerning the fragility of their powers and their worlds onto the other.

120 *The work of studious play*

Although these two readings of play—positive and negative—are interesting, they both miss the central point of Agamben's argument. The human being is not a *homo ludens* but a "*homo profanes*" (de la Durantaye 2009: 27). This difference becomes clear through Agamben's analysis of the structural necessity of funerary and initiation rites in cultural transmission. In order for society to enter into continuity with the past without simply collapsing into this past as mere repetition, special ceremonies are needed. Funerary and initiation rites "do not entirely fit into either the schema of ritual nor that of play, but seem to partake of both" (2007a: 91). Expanding Agamben's argument further, I would point out that education is a kind of initiation rite which cannot and should not be thought of as either ritual or play but as a profanation of the distinction or a kind of suspension of the opposition. Furthermore, in *Profanations* it is not play *as such* that Agamben endorses. Following his analysis of play, Agamben immediately states the following: "It [profanation] is the sort of use that Benjamin must have had in mind when he wrote of Kafka's *The New Attorney* that the law that is no longer applied but only studied is the gate to justice" (2007b: 76). Commenting further on Benjamin's reflections on Kafka's short story (where the lawyer, Dr. Bucephalus, studies rather than practices the law), Agamben continues,

> In the Kafka essay, the enigmatic image of a law that is studied but no longer practiced corresponds, as a sort of remnant, to the unmasking of mythico-juridical violence effected by pure violence. There is, therefore, still a possible figure of law after its nexus with violence and power has been deposed, but it is a law that no longer has force or application, like the one in which the "new attorney," leafing through "our old books," buries himself in study, or like the one that Foucault may have had in mind when he spoke of a "new law" that has been freed from all discipline and all relation to sovereignty.
>
> (2005a: 63)

Suspended, the law that is studied is deactivated, no longer in force, and thus open to play. In this sense, it is not play but rather the relation between play and study that is most important. Summarizing, Agamben writes,

> And this studious play is the passage that allows us to arrive at that justice that one of Benjamin's posthumous fragments defines as state of the world in which the world appears as a good that absolutely cannot be appropriated or made juridical.
>
> (ibid.: 63)

Studious play is the moment when melancholy becomes inspiration, when undergoing becomes undertaking, when the old is opened up again to the possibility of the new.

The qualification of play as *studious* is absolutely important, especially when positioned in relation to Agamben's larger social critique of biocapitalism. In a world full of play, play has lost its profanity.

> Play as an organ of profanation is in decline everywhere. Modern man proves he no longer knows how to play precisely through the vertiginous proliferation of new and old games. Indeed, at parties, in dances, and at play, he desperately and stubbornly seeks exactly the opposite of what he could find there: the possibility of reentering the lost feast, returning to the sacred and its rites, even in the form of the inane ceremonies of the new spectacular religion or a tango lesson in a provincial dance hall.
>
> (Agamben 2007b: 77)

Biocapitalism profanes the world, but this profanation turns out, in the last instance, to be a kind of re-sacralization in the forms of ritual consumption, ritual testing, and so on. The task at hand is not simply to suspend ritual through play but rather to suspend the ritualization of play through playful study. Masschelein and Simons come close to this observation, but they make a clear distinction between play and study which, in turn, impoverishes both concepts. They write,

> the playing child who is imperturbably, and to a certain extent disconnectedly, given over to the play, absorbed by it, and the student who is completely absorbed in his or her study—also without destination at the very moment of reading and writing.
>
> (2010: 546)

My claim here is stronger. Dividing play and study into two separate forms of profanation misses exactly what is profane: their immanence in the act of studious play, which is a rhythmic turning between undertaking and undergoing.

What play and study have in common, and what enables us to conceptualize something called studious play, is that both are a form of *bricolage*, a kind of poetic process that "uses 'crumbs' and 'scraps' belonging to other structural wholes" (Agamben 2007a: 81) in order to gather them together in a constellation. Indeed, when children play with toys and with other objects discarded from the world of adult use and exchange, they do not simply play with crumbs but with "crumbness" (ibid.). Here we should be reminded of my earlier discussion of the archaeology of signatures. Through the creation of constellations of crumbs and scraps, children, like the one who studies in the archive, map the underlying network of background signatures that enable signs to signify, that ensure the efficacy of signs, that guarantee the transmission of culture through the maintenance of an impossible relation between rituals and events. The constellation is a kind of conjunction between signifying systems both in the present and in the past, enabling us to chart the lines of flight of various signatures as they spread out over a temporally and spatially vast terrain. In both play and study, there is a concern not for crumbs themselves (signs) but with the crumbness (signatures), the efficacy of the crumbs to potentially signify differently. The signatures of crumbness thus guarantee the "basic rule of the play of history," which for Agamben is that "the signifiers of continuity accept and exchange with those of discontinuity, and the signifying function is more important than the signifiers themselves" (2007a: 95). The signifying function is the efficacy of the underlying signatures which are excavated from the crumbs of history when we engage in studious play.

As such, Agamben is not suggesting that we leave behind us the world of ritual for the infinite variety and chaotic events of "Playland." In an essay dedicated to Claude Levi-Strauss, Agamben argues that what must be avoided is either a collapse into a "hot society" or a "cold society." Hot societies are nothing less than endless play, which trumps all rituals and submits them to the rush and excitement of constant invention. Fast capitalism and its promise of constant, hubristic productivity and invention approximate the "hot society." In the economy, we find that the ludic nature of play has been fully embraced by hot, transnational capitalism wherein adult playgrounds on corporate campuses and playful work cultures have become trendy management strategies, especially in high-tech firms such as Google. In such examples (especially in relation to Google), play itself has become ritualized or bureaucratized, thus losing any of its profanity. On the other extreme, there are cold societies where ritual dominates over play. This leads to a truly static society, frozen in time, mummified in a perpetually claustrophobic relation to the past. In today's world, we see this strange cultural mummification in the rise of a series of religious fundamentalisms that want to return to a mythic golden age of traditional values cut off from the promise of new possibilities for conceptualizing a coming community. What is important here is that both are the result of a single problem: a crisis in history and human experience which cleaves the cold from the hot. As Agamben argues, "In both cases there would be a lack of that differential margin between diachrony and synchrony in which we have identified human time—in other words, history" (2007a: 86). History emerges as a differential remnant between synchrony and diachrony, between ritual and event. Without holding the two in tension, human time—as a messianic time of the now—evaporates. For Agamben, history is located in the disjunction or break between play and ritual, the minimal gap that both separates and conjoins synchrony and diachrony. What Plato and his inheritors have missed is precisely the nature and function of playful study—not as a mediation or sublation between play and testing, but as their profanation.

The question of transmissibility

On an educational level, we can now return to my opening set of oppositions between the rituals of standardization and the unstructured playfulness of the ludic classroom. For the standardized or fully ritualized classroom, experience is smothered by the oppressive weight of a world that appears completed or fully determined and actualized in advance. Through ritual baptism, the student is anointed into a determined community and his or her potentiality is submitted to the *Logos* that binds that community together. The result is a prevailing sense of absolute necessity: the world must be the way that it is. If one classroom collapses education into a return of the same, then the other releases utopian value as a set of free-floating signifiers without the ability to connect the event of play with the past. In other words, in a purely diachronic classroom of play, there would be no trace of activity inscribed in the world after the play of signifiers has begun. The stain of synchrony would not enter into the equation, and the toys would never be put away. The result is a kind of infinite deferral that leads to its own strain of impossibility: the impossibility to take action or assume responsibility. Without the exchange between play and ritual, the movement of signifiers into signifieds would be lost and, as Agamben warns, children would come to be seen as threats and "bearers of subversion and disorder" (2007a: 94–95) rather than as agents in the process of history. Such a warning is most useful for diagnosing the current, paranoid view of young adults (especially poor minorities) in schools today as violent school-shooters, criminals, lazy dropouts, or deadbeats leeching off their parents. This phenomena is well documented by scholars such as Henry Giroux (2012) who have convincingly demonstrated that youth and youth culture are effectively demonized and criminalized throughout multiple sectors of the media.

Studious play is precisely the state of exception between play and ritual, between child and adult that binds them together as much as it separates them. Studious play resists both hot (a collection of disparate instances) and cold (perpetual and unchanging continuity) extremes. It is the location through which the translation of free signifiers can enter into exchange with signifieds and thus diachronic and synchronic structures communicate across time, opening up the space and time of the now. To engage in studious play is thus an experience of the difference and continuity between independent systems, becoming the measure of maturity (discipline) only in the moment of touching our collective infancy (freedom). It is this rhythmic exchange across systems that defines the poetically profane nature of studious play, and reclaims education from learning in the name of history.

In this sense, we can use Agamben's theory of play, ritual, and studious play to return to a central question of this text: how is transmission of culture possible in an age where hot and cold societies are in perpetual political and economic war, where there has been a bifurcation of logics between continuity and interruption? As suggested earlier in Chapter 1, the discourses and practices of learning concern themselves with the *transmission of specific content and skills*. Indeed, learning concerns the reproduction of the community through baptism of students into the *Logos* that defines a particular identity: the identity of the worker/consumer within a global market. This model of learning concerns the maintenance of values and norms in the name of perpetual progress, perpetual profits, and perpetual growth. Transmission of a particular *Logos*, in this sense,

124 *The work of studious play*

submits im-potentiality to the tyranny of the old, leaving no space for studiers to introduce the possibility of the new. Ironically, in a capitalist society that runs on the hot side of the equation, the turn back to learning as an apparatus of transmission speaks to an unstated anxiety concerning the ungrounded grounds of a community lost in the throngs of its own Promethian hubris. The more playful capitalism destroys the past in the name of infinite productivity and profitability, the more its educational system reverts back to the lost rituals of baptism through high-stakes testing. In other words, learning is a continual search of the authority of certain signs, laws, and customs to guarantee the unity of meaning, the certainty of plans, and the rightness of virtues that have lost their authority under hot capitalism's ludic propulsion. Thus learning is oddly anachronistic, a repetition that is not a solution to the problem of the hot society so much as one more symptom.

Play on the other hand seems to offer a model of education based on nothing more than the accumulation of events or instances without any connection to the past. In this sense, play suggests the *impossibility of transmission*. Students live in a perpetual present cut off from the past or the future, exposed to moments that are free-floating. Here the good-old-fashioned Marxist critique of the pre-dominance of ludic postmodernism throughout the humanities and the social sciences in higher education gains a new urgency and relevance (Zavarzadeh and Morton 1994). Yet we need not go to Marxists for this observation. Agamben himself stakes the claim that the university has become a kind of playland for ghosts (2007a: 95). Although a postmodern playground, the university has, ironically enough, forgotten how to play—has forgotten how to accept signifiers of discontinuity by returning them to the past for the sake of transmitting them to the future. What is at stake here is not play as such but rather the profanation of play which can only be redeemed through a close encounter between play and study.

As a third option, studious play is neither the transmission of specific content (specific norms, values, and ways of being in the world), nor is it the impossibility of transmission (toppling over into endless events and creative destruction). Rather studious play transforms the impossibility of transmission into the *transmission of im-possibility*. In such a model, transmissibility is liberated from transmitting any definitive message or law that would ground the identity and unity of a community in an essence. Although the transmission of tradition as a ground for community identity is an impossibility, this impossibility is also *the possibility* for new uses that open up through a constellation of signatures. The deactivation of the signs of *Logos* leaves the empty efficacy of signatures open to new uses beyond those perceived by the community thus far. Studious play is not therefore the transmission of some content/body of knowledge that guarantees cultural continuity, nor is it the production of new knowledge that expresses the genius of the will to manifest itself to itself. Rather it is the poetic *transmission of transmissibility* in the form of the effective powers of the signatures. It transmits transmission itself while the message, tradition, *Logos* remain pending, forgotten, deactivated. Another way of describing this phenomenon is that studious play is the transmission of *whatever* signatures remain effective within the crumbs of tradition, the fragments of a collapsed world. If our traditions have fallen ill (igniting a crisis in transmission or, as Arendt argued, a crisis in authority) then this crisis is not to be lamented. Again, commenting on Kafka, Agamben writes, "Kafka renounced the truth to be transmitted for the sake of not renouncing its transmissibility" (1999c: 153). It is this strange operation whereby the impossible is given back to itself as a positive ground that once again opens up a space for history to emerge against the backdrop of fundamentalist religiosity and fundamentalist capitalism. In short, to learn is to transmit signifieds down through the generations and to play is to unleash new signifiers into circulation. Yet to engage with studious play is to trace the contours of whatever signatures—neither signifiers nor signifieds—enable this exchange to happen, the underlying textual gesture which gives the exchange its efficacy. Just as the ultimate "lesson" of poetry is the very appearance of language itself, so too the ultimate lesson of studious play is the appearance of transmissibility produced when we pay attention to the efficacy that remains even when there are no focal practices which orient our projects toward this or that "for-the-sake-of."

Without appreciation for the role of studious play in Agamben's work, commentators misunderstand the nature of profanation itself as a form of resistance to what Agamben refers to as "thanatopolitics" (1998). At this point, I am compelled to take a bit of a detour in order to demonstrate the repercussions when studious play—and therefore the problematic of education—is not acknowledged as a foundational concept in Agamben's work. In his book on thanatopolitics, Timothy Campbell argues that Agamben inherited the distinction between the proper and the improper from Heidegger's work on technology. Technology, on Heidegger's reading, is linked with processes of dehumanization, producing an improper form of life that places humankind in danger of losing a relationship with its being-in-the-world. Campbell argues that this division is the root of thanatopolitics, which, most recently, has appeared in Agamben's distinction between *zoë* (natural life) and *bios* (the life of the *polis*). Drawing distinctions between improper and proper, biological life and the life of the citizen subject, results in the abandonment or sacrifice of the former— the production of bare life exposed to the direct threat of violence without mediation by the law. In Campbell's reading, we find an intensification and exaggeration of Heidegger's fundamental division between proper and improper in the extreme thanatopolitical conclusion that the world is accelerating towards absolute abandonment of life. Summarizing the catastrophe, Campbell writes, "First, these desubjectified subjects [bearers of bare life] may be killed or abandoned in greater numbers than ever before" and "Second, attempts by governmental machinery to administer life that has already been made docile, depoliticized, and desubjectified are, in a word, destined to fail" (2011: 56). These two catastrophes come together in Agamben's work, especially in his fundamental thesis that the new *nomos* of the world is the concentration camp wherein all life becomes bare life.

126   *The work of studious play*

As far as it goes, Campbell's reading of Agamben is correct, and highlighting the relation between Agamben and Heidegger is insightful. Yet the conclusion Campbell draws from this basic summary of Agamben's critical analysis of the contemporary moment are misguided. The central claim here is that

> If we are to locate an ontology of the actual in the present, the problem with Agamben's reading of life is that it becomes difficult, if not impossible to discover where the thanatopolitical drift enacted by a critique of technology ends and an effective ontology of the actual begins.
>
> (Campbell 2011: 82)

While Campbell continues on to argue that Agamben offers no solution to the thanatopolitical problem of abandonment, he misses the reconstructive dimension of Agamben's project. Certainly Agamben highlights the intensification of the deadly effects of the management of bare life, yet this does not mean that Agamben falls into the trap of nihilism as Campbell seems to suggest.

Rather than examine this second half of Agamben's project, Campbell prematurely moves beyond Agamben, in order to theorize his own alternative to thanatopolitics. Through the work of Freud, Deleuze and Guattari, Winnicott, and, most importantly, Foucault, Campbell argues for a new relation between technology and *bios* through attention and play. At stake here is redefining a practice of life that is not based on the mastery and judgment over and against life. Rather than simply capture, test, and ultimately sacrifice life, a new practice of *bios* is possible through attention and play. First, Campbell argues that unlike the test and the quest for mastery over life (both of which lead to thanatopolitical catastrophe), attention is a practice of life that opens the protected borders of the self to objects without capturing these objects within the self's compulsion to judge or to seize upon difference. Drawing on Deleuze and Guattari's concept of haeccetic space, Campbell writes that attention "holds open a space in which potentialities for becoming are allowed to emerge ... in which elements move into composition with each other" (2011: 145). Avoiding seizing or judging the object, attention affirms differences by "hold[ing] together elements in a kind of compositional space" (ibid.: 147) that does not separate between proper and improper but rather orchestrates differences in a set of relations. "A practice of attention," summarizes Campbell, "as immanent critique would not seize by judging, incorporating, or expelling but would allow one to uncover the relationality inherent in the elements that make up the haeccetic space" (ibid.: 148).

Along with attention, Campbell argues for a positive function of play as a practice of life over and against thanatopolitics. Play is a creative art of living that invents new modes of becoming beyond capture within the split pair of the proper and improper. Looking toward children for inspiration, Campbell points out how we can

> make out the horizon of a living art in play that would allow us to see how the self, by withdrawing to play as *bios*, might be able, if not to block, then

The work of studious play   127

to slow down the speed with which borders and defenses and, with them, the instinct for destruction are made manifest.

(ibid.: 154)

Thus with attention and play Campbell gives us a possible alternative to mastery, judgment, and capture which define Agamben's notion of thanatopolitics.

What is most peculiar in Campbell's argument is that the alternative which he provides is nothing less than Agamben's own theory of studious play! Although Campbell is at pains to include all major theorists of play in the twentieth century into his analysis, Agamben's name does not appear at all except in the latter part of a footnote. In fact, I would argue that Campbell's whole project is nothing less than a series of false problems that do not lead away from Agamben but rather back to Agamben. Not only is the occlusion of any discussion of Agamben's work on play a rather strange oversight for a book that, for all intents and purposes, appears to be well researched with an exhaustive bibliography, but also Agamben's theory of studious play, which I have been elaborating upon, is, in the end, superior to Campbell's theory of attention and play in two respects. First, while Campbell separates attention and play into two separate though overlapping practices of life, Agamben effectively combines them into one practice of profanation: studious play. Studious play *is* attentive play. It is attentive to the composition of signatures that underlie divisions between signifiers and signifieds and in turn guarantee their exchange. Rather than judge, divide, or attempt to master life, a constellation of signatures opens the world up to new possibilities through the transmission of transmissibility in its nudity or purity. Second, Campbell's concept of play falls prey to Faulkner's critique of the romanticization of childhood play. In a desire to provide an alternative to the distinction between the proper and improper of thanatopolitics, Campbell all too quickly misses how play itself has been co-opted by thanato-technologies. Thus the issue here is not play in and for itself, but rather maintaining its profane dimension through *studious play*.

If I have spent some time critically analyzing Campbell's argument, this is not simply to demonstrate a misreading of Agamben. Rather it is to demonstrate a larger point: the need to rethink education as a *central terrain for fighting against thanatopolitics as the obscene supplement to biocapitailsm's investment into life*. Instead of to play, it is to the question of study that we must turn our attention. As such, I would like to end with an example of studious play at work. While this example concerns children, it should not be mistaken as an argument for the playful nature of children as such. Rather, similar examples could be found in a host of disciplines and practices germane to adults just as much as to children.

Tinkering as studious play

Studious play is not so much a synthesis of play and study as it is a state of productive tensions between moving toward and withdrawing from, melancholia

128 *The work of studious play*

and joy, hesitation and inspiration. It is neither the linear, chronological time of enlightened progress nor is it the infinite creative destruction of punctuated instances divorced from the past and future in a ludic moment. It is rather the suspension of time in a messianic moment that both propels forward into the future while also recursively returning to the past. But what would this look like as an actual practice? How can education encourage studious play without dipping into either sheer playfulness or ritualistic repetition? Educator Gever Tulley calls the state of studious play "tinkering," and has opened up a series of "tinkering schools" across the United States. For Tulley, the purpose of education is to expose children to a broad theme (such as "wind") and then give them the opportunity to explore this theme through tinkering (building kites, gliders, and so on). In other words, he encourages students to be attentive to the signatures of wind found within a host of activities and seemingly unrelated objects. There are three functions of the teacher in tinkering schools: supply students with time, space, and materials. In other words, the teacher does not transmit *this* or *that* body of knowledge. Nor does he or she promote the creation of new knowledge per se. Rather, what the teacher does is provide resources that open up to signatures which underlie the potentiality for connections to be made without predetermining what these connections need to be.

The time of tinkering is a time of suspension, where the rules prohibiting certain behaviors ("Don't play with fire!") are left idle. Indeed, what is most controversial about the tinkering school is that Tully allow students to transgress a series of taken-for-granted laws that usually divide proper from improper behaviors. Suspension of these rules and laws offers a time of free use wherein time is no longer held above students but rather returns as immanent to their actions and the collective rhythms of their projects. The very concept of "tinkering" has a certain *temporal* dimension suggesting a loss of definitive ends, uncertainty of outcomes, and the simultaneous rhythms of withdrawing and progressing. Rather than marching forward toward the evaluation of the test, tinkering suggests a practice of being attentive to the activity in and for itself, of finding pleasure in tinkering as a pure means. The end is no longer the priority so much as the experimentation with the signatures, their possible combinations and relations. Even if one tinkers in order to achieve a specific goal, what is unique about tinkering is that its meandering and its improvisational pacing push toward a goal while also delaying its eventual arrival. In this sense we can make a critical distinction between tinkering and "testing out" or "trying out." Both testing and trying are concerned with trial, evaluation, and eventual judgment. If testing means *deciding upon* then tinkering with means *experimenting with*—the former erases what is potential while the latter retains a relationship to this potential indefinitely. Thus it is not uncommon to find "perpetual tinkerers"—those who resist closure, measure, or judgment over whatever they are doing. Outside of chronological unfolding (where "trying out" pushes toward

The space of tinkering is a space open to constant reconfiguration—a free space defined by the actions it houses. Neither a Utopia existing in an abstract future or the panoptic space of the contemporary school defined by the surveillance of ritualized testing, the tinkering school is an *atopia*. This atopic space is a common space, open to all. As a common space, the tinkering school is no longer predefined in terms of specific uses. Rather all uses lay open for exploration. This free time and free space house the freedom of a community that does not yet have a name, only a set of signatures to be collected, composed, and attentively studied.

In terms of materials, the tinkering school redeems the most ephemeral bits of trash for thematic exploration. According to Agamben, children are "humanity's little scrap dealers," preserving "profane objects and behaviors that have ceased to exist" (2007a: 79). Walter Benjamin likewise noted that children are "irresistibly drawn by the detritus generated by building, gardening, housework, tailoring, or carpentry," through which they "bring together, in the artifact produced in play, materials of widely differing kinds in a new, intuitive relationship" (1986: 68–69). As with Agamben's theory of studious play, the work of tinkering is a transformative one that unleashes free uses from discarded relics (the crumbness of crumbs). In the tinkering school, the teacher offers a *collection* of remnants, traces, and discarded objects which, when brought into the space and time of tinkering become alive, or are made effective. Altogether, the space, time, and materials of tinkering suspend the logic of ritual baptism which separates and abandons. In other words, tinkering separates itself from the logic of separation.

Through the process of tinkering, students simultaneously feel the push and pull of both their potentiality to innovate and construct a new world and also the finite and precarious nature of their plans (their collective im-potentiality). As Tulley states, "nothing ever turns out as planned ... ever" (2009, n.p.). In fact, students quickly learn that "all projects go awry" and learn to accept that all projects can end with success or "gleeful calamity" (ibid.). On my reading, tinkering becomes a kind of quest, which, for Agamben, is the "recognition that the absence of a road (the *aporia*) is the only experience possible for man" (2007a: 33). The results of studious play are not what are important so much as the quest itself as a pure means for experiencing the rhythmic sway of collective and collaborative tinkering. Tinkering is, in the end, precisely the experience of "gleeful calamity" described by Tulley—the recognition of the fleeting nature of projects coinciding with a profound joy and freedom in these very contingencies. It is, after all, the calamity which introduces contingency into the process, opening up the possibility that things could be different than what they are, that plans can change, that the unexpected turn of events inevitably occurs. Calamity is the indeterminate moment of suspension that keeps open the time, space, and free use of tinkering, therefore postponing tinkering from becoming

130   *The work of studious play*

a teleological process culminating in particular ends and purposes outside of tinkering itself.

In the face of gleeful calamity, children do not simply stop their tinkering. Rather, as Tulley points out, they "decorate" their machines, structures, and contraptions. And in that temporary withdrawal from building and constructing (wherein students lay down their saws, hammers, drills, and nails), the children have time to contemplate, reflect, and dream. Decoration is a gesture loosened from a predetermined ends—it is a kind of hesitation that is no longer thrusting forward toward a definitive end or judgment yet not withdrawing from the study of materials either. In other words, decoration presents the tinkerers with a potentiality suddenly loosened from any particular destination/fulfillment. Rather than willful manifestation of a capability to make and do, decoration slows down the march toward completion and evaluation and withdraws from an undertaking to an undergoing that is indefinite. Here the will is not what is at stake so much as an openness to listen to what is offered up by the calamity itself. Thus the one who tinkers is less concerned with externalizing an internal power than in withdrawing into the im-potentiality of the moment in order to become responsive to *whatever is left when calamity happens and the world seems to collapse.* Perhaps the most dangerous item children are exposed to when tinkering is not, in the end, the power tools, pocket knives, or saws so much as the possibility of studying, of im-potentiality, which interrupts narratives of "fulfilling one's potentials" or "educational progress" or "learning for success." Exposing one's self to the im-potentiating calamity of tinkering interrupts certain progressive myths that form the backbone of education. Tulley's ultimate gambit is that tinkering (as the sway between progress and regress, discipline and freedom, potentiality and impotentiality) should not be restricted to the philosopher's chamber or to the "pure research" of the ivory tower. Rather, the danger of tinkering should be given a space and time within the child's educational life—even if this means exposing them to the dangers of calamities. Tinkering in this sense—with all its fits and starts, its rhythmic suspension—is the experience of the transmission of transmissibility let loose from determinate ends, plans, and preexisting measurements that attempt to capture, judge, and evaluate outcomes. These children tinker in order to experience the sudden appearance of their collective im-potentiality. And when lost in the moment of tinkering, the children are little angels playing with an inoperative world—a world that, precisely because it is out of joint, could be otherwise than.

Notch: Stupidity

Stupidity (not error) constitutes the greatest weakness of thought, but also the source of its highest power in that which forces it to think.

Gilles Deleuze, *Difference and Repetition*

There is a certain tendency, especially in the learning society obsessed with maximizing proficiencies, to villainize stupidity by linking it with pathology or moral lassitude. Indeed, learning is in some ways an immunization against the pathogen of stupidity (see Lewis 2009). Despite this trend, Agamben argues that

> studying and stupefying are in this sense akin: those who study are in the situation of people who have received a shock and are stupefied by what has struck them, unable to grasp it and at the same time powerless to leave hold.
>
> (1995: 64)

Studying and stupefying are both forms of a collision that leave us without balance, without stability, without sense of orientation. The collision introduces a kind of vertigo poised between the inability to think and the ability to think, between learning to be a subject and undergoing a radical desubjectification that leaves one nameless and homeless. Only *after* the shock of studying can the student write down what he or she has come to know, thus exiting from the messianic moment of suspension. Yet in the time and space of study, such knowing is never fully actualized—only the "I can, I cannot" of im-potentiality. As calamitous as this experience might sound, it is also inspiring, returning us to our freedom—a freedom that is nevertheless "stupid." Agamben writes that the studier, "shakes off the sadness that disfigured it [study] and returns it to its truest nature: not work, but inspiration, the self-nourishment of the soul" (ibid.: 65). How are we to understand this statement? How can stupidity be a kind of virtue of study rather than the mark of a mere deficit?

Like Agamben, Avital Ronell has attempted to rethink the connections between stupidity, thought, and scholarship, making the surprising claim that "stupidity does not allow itself to be opposed to knowledge in any simple way, nor is it the other of thought" (2002: 5). Knowledge cannot be immunized against stupidity without exposing itself to the germ cell of stupidity's own im-potentiality. As an example, Ronell turns to

132   *Stupidity*

Kant's examination of stupidity in his *Anthropology*. For Kant, the stupid subject does not lack knowledge but rather is prone to over-studying and thus excessive reading. To block the super-saturation of the mind with information (what we would refer to today in our high-stakes world of testing as "cramming for the test"), reason intervenes and produces a kind of intellectual disgust. But it is here that Ronell pinpoints a certain aporia in Kant's immunizing logic. "At which point," observes Ronell, "of the terminable-interminable exercise of reading stupidity sets in is left indeterminable" (ibid.: 295). In other words, there is always the threat that we have read too much and that we have *already* become stupid. As with Agamben's description of study, Ronell argues that stupidity is "a structure of exposure" (ibid.: 9) to indeterminacy or im-potentiality. Drawing on Heidegger, Ronell suggests we read the inauthenticity of *das Man*, which is a structural facet of *Dasein*'s being-in-the-world as a kind of idiotic backdrop; an "unassimilable, and assimilating stupidity" (ibid.: 74) of experience as such. We have always already fallen into stupidity, which is the backdrop for thinking, some sort of background indeterminateness that we can never fully get a grip on or explain. Studying therefore does not deliver us from stupidity but rather returns us to a primordial experience of stupidity as a kind of ontological struc-ture—an ontological profanity at the very heart of *Dasein*. The resulting melancholic mood is not so much a psychological problem as it is an ontological atmosphere that opens *Dasein* to its ontological stupidity.

Rather than disavow this structure, Ronell suggests that we take "responsibility" (2002: 19) for this capability that is also an incapability—a responsibility for that which threatens and undermines the logic of learn-ing that utilizes a certain educational orthopedic to maximize measurable outcomes and overcome indetermination. The risk of studying is that we discover our perpetual stupidity (our idiotic thrownness in the efficacy of faint yet pervasive signatures underlying everyday things and signs), but it is this very stupidity that offers freedom to think, dream, perceive, and imagine differently. Only through our responsibility toward that which remains mediocre, stupid, and thus perpetually withdrawn from any determination can we glimpse a strange kind of new creativity.

It is interesting to note that at the end of his book on nudity, Agamben briefly turns to the question of knowledge. He writes,

> The ways in which we do not know things are just as important (and perhaps even more important) as the ways in which we know them. There are ways of not knowing—carelessness, inattention,

Stupidity 133

forgetfulness—that lead to clumsiness and ugliness, but there are others—the unselfconsciousness of Keist's young man, the enchanting *sprezzatura* of an infant—whose completeness we never tire of admiring.

(2011b: 113)

We must find new ways of valuing the "principles of an art of ignorance" (ibid.) that are found in the child. We have to revitalize our relationship with the zone of non-knowledge through the act of studious play. In studious play we find what is special: our impotent freedom. It is perhaps the hardest and most painful experience of all to bear witness to the darkness of non-knowledge, to our stupidity. Yet, as Agamben testifies, this pain is also a gift, an inspiration, a silent call of Genius.

Only when the individual is rendered stupid can the relationship to Genius be reconsidered. When we *stop overthinking*, when we *stop trying*, Genius suddenly appears as if from without to offer us a gift. According to the Greeks, Genius is a god whom we were all born with. While appearing as our most intimate guardian, the paradox of the Genius soon becomes clear. Agamben writes,

this most intimate and personal god is also that which is most impersonal in us; it is the personalization of what in us, goes beyond or exceeds us . . . If it seems to be identified with us, it is only in order to reveal itself immediately afterward as more than us, and to show us that we are more and less than ourselves.

(2007b: 11)

Thus the individual is not simply a will controlled by a self-sufficient, self-directing consciousness. Rather there is a part of the self that is no-part of the Cartesian ego—a strange visitor that always accompanies us. Studious play is our fraught relationship with this stranger who "escapes mastery" (ibid.: 12) and always introduces contingency into all our plans. Yet this very contingency also offers the possibility of experiencing im-potentiality less as a pathology and more as a gift. As "a part that is forever immature, infinitely adolescent, and hesitant to cross the threshold of any individuation" (ibid.: 15), Genius is the halo that shines through our stupidity, and in the process, gives us a glimpse into our im-potential freedom (our freedom to be *rather than* any determinate goal, end, or measure that has been set for us in advance). When Genius comes, we are empty, stupid minds, open and responsive to its efficacy. Thus when we are at our best (our most ingenious) is when we are attuned to what moves through us (Genius) beyond our willful control and influence. Agamben argues that brushing up against Genius as an "impersonal power" that exceeds the conscious subject results in a "desubjectivation" (2004a: 124). Desubjectification is precisely the state of stupidity wherein the conscious subject loses a sense of his or her self. Stupidity, as the impotence of the subject to know and control his or her actions, beliefs, and gestures, resides here in the desubjectification process at the very point where the power of Genius takes hold as a creative potency.

In this sense, the question of Genius separates Agamben's theory of stupidity from Jacques Rancière's theory of ignorance. According to Rancière, "I can't" is nothing less than a "sentence of self-forgetfulness" (1991: 57) which denies that intelligence serves the will and not the other way around. The primacy of the will means that all intellectual divisions between the smart and the stupid are not so much reflections of inherent traits as they are symptoms of a lack of opportunities for the will to express itself and focus the mind's powers. Indeed Genius, for Rancière, is nothing less than

> the relentless work [of the will] to bend the body to necessary habits, to compel the intelligence to new ideas, to new ways of expressing them; to redo on purpose what chance once produced, and to reverse unhappy circumstances into occasions for success.
>
> (ibid.: 56)

In other words, Genius is the *power of the will to command the intelligence*. It is a kind of sovereign injunction to do, to redo, and to produce. Perhaps we could even generate a crude formula to represent Rancière's position:

Genius = ignorance + will

Such a formulation stands in stark contrast to Agamben's theory of Genius. As argued above, Genius *cannot be commanded*; it exceeds the will and of the act of willfulness. It is the contingent force that is neither inside nor outside the subject, which exists in surplus of the individual will, which compels us to take responsibility for that which is not of our own making or doing yet nevertheless is inexplicably bound to our actions. For Rancière, what is at stake in his definition of Genius is the pure assertion of the power of the will, of "I can." Thus he desires to separate potentiality from the impotentiality of "I cannot" (which is for him a kind of reckless self-forgetting). Yet for Agamben, "I can" and "I cannot" are primordially indistinguishable, and any attempt to ground human ontology in "I can" simply *sacrifices* "I cannot." The structure of command therefore replicates the aporia of the sovereign decision over and against the inhuman, the other, the impotential remnant. Lost here is the *freedom* that im-potentiality (stupidity and non-knowledge) brings. At stake is an ethic of willful productivity of what a subject can do versus willing receptivity to what exceeds willful striving. If there is a principle of equality at work in Agamben's formulation it is not the equality of intelligences but rather the equality of stupidity as we stand, minds open and receptive to Genius. Only when accepting one's stupidity can the demand of Genius be heard. In this way, Genius is the halo of the subject under its own erasure (a subject *as not* a subject)—the faint glow of what remains when the will is left idle.

7   Studying with friends

The previous chapter opens up a new question that must now be directly addressed: With whom do we tinker? While my analysis to this point has ignored the question of community, my example of collective tinkering suggests that there is a social/political dimension of study. In this chapter, I would like to explore this question further, and in particular argue that we tinker with friends. Of course this is not a controversial statement. Ask any child or adult whom they study with and it will invariably include those we consider our friends (or at least potential friends). What I want to suggest is that there is something intuitively right about this common-sense view. But at the same time, what is right is not intuitively clear or obvious. Yes, we study with friends, but the nature of this friendship is what is at stake. For to tinker with friends, to engage in studious play with them, is not simply to "hang out" with other individuals we think are "cool" or "smart" (pleasure-seeking friendships, as Aristotle would say). In this chapter, I will argue that friends are not those whom we recognize, or reflect back our best-selves. Nor are friends those who share our special natures. Rather, we tinker with others whom we do *not recognize* but who are, nevertheless, our friends.

The common-being of friendship

For Agamben, the question of friendship lies at the very core of philosophical thinking. If he turns to Aristotle to link friendship first philosophy, then we can also make a similar connection between friendship and education. For example, the discussion of friendship in the *Nicomachean Ethics* is the final component of ethical education. Aristotle's educational theory moves from habituation (early childhood) to instruction (young adulthood) to friendship as the last phase of ethical life—a phase that opens up to political life as the sharing of all in the common project of creating and sustaining the life of the city. Indeed, the good citizen can only achieve a virtuous life in relation to the friendships he has. Aristotle famously argues that self-knowledge is best attained through the observation of the virtuous actions of good friends. "We can contemplate our neighbors better than ourselves and their actions better than our own," thus "the supremely happy man will need friends of this [virtuous] sort" (Aristotle

1941: 1170a) in order to reflect on what counts as the good life. In this sense, the friend emerges as a kind of *ethical study partner* who is not simply a private individual but also a public, pedagogical figure. Because action and speech are unpredictable, often inconclusive, and open to uncertainty, Hannah Arendt, drawing directly from Aristotle, argues that political dialogue should happen between friends. Indeed, she argues that Socrates' political (and ethical) project was an attempt to "make friends out of Athens' citizens" (2005: 16). Rather than community as bounded by laws or by territory, friendship bound Athenians to a common that existed *between* them. Through friendship, concludes Arendt, citizens became "equal partners in a common world" (ibid.: 17). As with Aristotle, it was not the idea of justice but rather the practice of friendship that created and sustained the common. Although Arendt is leery of introducing educational relationships into political relationships (see Arendt 1993), I would return to Aristotle here and suggest that friendship is an ethical and political practice that does not constitute inequality between teacher and student so much as equality between study partners.

On Agamben's reading, a friend is not someone (or something, for that matter) that has a certain set of defined predicates seen as "valued" qualities (from which the enemy deviates). Simply stated, if we were to enumerate all the qualities that make a certain individual a friend, the list would never reach the heart of the matter, for the essence of a friend cannot be represented. The friend is never someone who is simply an amalgam of particular qualities added together and then recognized as "desirable traits." "Friends," warns Agamben, "do not share some*thing* (birth, law, place, taste)" (2009b: 36). More primordially, a friend is—as in Aristotle's original analysis—someone with whom we share *sharing*. In other words, it is a relationship through which sharing is shared in common. Or even better, what is shared is the im-potentiality of sharing itself! Sharing an im-potentiality rather than actuality (of this or that set of clearly defined predicates) exposes a pure belonging to a being-in-common, which in the end, is beyond any distinction between belonging and not-belonging. For Agamben, this means that friendship "is the con-division that precedes every division, since what has to be shared is the very fact of existence, life itself" (ibid.). Friends share the sharing that is ontologically prior to the division between friends and enemies, prior to this or that set of culturally specific predicates.

If this is the case, then to have friends is to undergo a peculiar kind of desubjectification. Rather than an alter ego, the friend is, for Agamben, an other self, a *heteros autos*. The friend, on this reading, emerges less as another individual and more as a "becoming other of the self" (2009b: 34–35). Every sense of self is always already a sense of otherness within the self: the being-in-common of friendship. Instead of intersubjective recognition (which is popular today just as much in political as educational theory), what is recognized in friendship is a *whatever* ontology that exists in common and undoes divisions between self and friend, self and other. In sum, "Friendship is this desubjectification at the very heart of the most intimate sensation of the self" (ibid.). The pleasure of friendship is this sharing of a fundamental whatever that does not belong to anyone, that does not have any predestination of its own, that is not any one particular identity. It would not be ridiculous to answer the question "What is it about that individual that makes her your friend?" with the response "Whatever it is that she is." Stated differently, a friend is friends with the friend's whatever, and friendship is the sharing of this whatever as an indeterminating being-in-common.

Yet in the contemporary world, this primordial exposure to being-in-common has been misappropriated in the political sphere as consensus in which everyone reflects everyone else in a perfect symmetry of interests. For Jacques Rancière (1999), consensus is an ordering principle within society, which polices the *polis* by providing a place and station for all of its citizens so that no one is left uncounted within the count of the community. Within this order those who do not abide by certain performative rules are excluded as irrational, their voices reduced to mere noise, their lives to bare life exposed to the threat of violence. Consensus within this order demands the exclusion of the non-identical as "disruptive" or "threatening." The boundaries between the proper and improper, the organization of power relations, and the knowledge systems utilized to legitimate these divisions are all manifestations of "policing" the commons in the name of consensus.

For Agamben, the community of friends who study together have no destination, and are thus a kind of inoperative community. Here I am referring to Jean-Luc Nancy's work on the inoperative nature of being-in-common. The best way to understand inoperativity is against the backdrop of the operative community (or at least its myth). For Plato, the operative community is a kind of division of labor that assures the organic harmony/unity of the city-state. In such a community, everyone has one specific kind of special nature that corresponds without remainder to a particular occupation. The resulting community is a community of harmonious parts, each doing what it is intended to do. The consensus of parts is a kind of division of labor that ensures the perfect relationship between essence and appearance. The problem with such notions of community is that community is thought of not so much as an action (a sharing with) as an essence or substance that must be preserved or, alternatively, expressly made manifest through some sort of labor. Thus politics becomes the work of preserving *a people* or *a nation* with their specific identity, traditions, norms, and values that are exclusively theirs. The operative community as an expression of an essence results in the end of politics rather than its beginning—an end that is marked by a thanatopolitical war against life (Nazi genocide for instance).

For Nancy, as for Agamben, community is an "infinite lack of identity" (Nancy 1991: xxxviii). It is made by the lack of something, a gap, or subtraction of essence. Thus what is shared in being-in-common is precisely a space of ex-isting. Being-in-common is inoperative in the sense that it is not defined in terms of an essence that enables divisions between us versus them, friend versus enemy, smart versus stupid. Nor does it have an operative teleology that founds its identity through a process of determination (a kind of ontological vocation that orients it towards a predefined future). Instead of a teleological project of actualizing its full potentiality, the inoperative community is not, according to Nancy, "a project of fusion, or in some general way a productive or operative project—nor is it a project at all" (ibid.: 15). In other words, this community is not a means to another end, but is a pure means, a pure experiment in being-in-common, of sharing whatever remains when foundations are abandoned. Indeed, inoperative community is "nothing other than what it undoes" (ibid.: 4), the impossibility of every becoming immanent to its own absolute identity, the impossibility of counting all of its parts in an ordered whole, the impossibility of interpellating its subjects into their "proper" vocations. Such a community does not project its own impotentiality outside of itself onto the other but rather maintains an ethical relation to its own internal otherness, its internal surplus—it is a positive having of that which it lacks. In sum, it does not recognize itself in itself but rather recognizes only the *im-potentiality to be otherwise than* itself.

In terms of education, we can clearly see that the operative community is a learning community where everyone has his or her place within an ordered, measured whole. Everyone and everything is accounted for, assessed, and ranked according to educational outputs that are tabulated by a host of biometric technologies. This is a community of consensus-building, of harmonious parts that work together to collectively fulfill the potentiality of each individual. All potentiality is transformed into a quantifiable number to be administered through the social orthopedic of schooling which will transform it into a marketable skill, human capital, or other commodity. In this sense the learning community operates according to what Foucault once referred to as the maxim of "exhaustive use" (1979: 154). To make operative is to ensure the exhaustive extraction of potentiality through maximum speed and efficiency. The operative community is a hubristic community that denies its own impotence, its own sharing of a lack of identity. It is a community where *friendship is impossible* precisely because members cannot share in their own im-potentiality. Because impotentiality is separated from potentiality, inoperability from operability, the community of learning can only produce *individual* competitors who struggle for private goods (grades, degrees, teacher favoritism, etc.). Relationality is mediated through technologies of measurement that attempt to continually actualize potentiality into forms of useful or effective human capital, and thus ban impotentiality as educational waste or project it outward onto the educational other (see the Introduction to this book).

The tinkering community, the community of studious play, is an inoperative community that shares its own calamities (its impotential) with joy. Indeed, the calamities of tinkering are a gift: the gift of inoperability that sustains a shared exposure to one another in the moment of suspended decisions, aborted attempts, ambiguous results, unfinished schemes, unanticipated outcomes. This suspended state is, as argued in the previous description, not a mere laziness or passivity, but a state of decoration wherein the incapability to finish is

140   *Studying with friends*

transformed into a capability for prolonged reflection, observation, and aesthetic creativity. The inoperative community of tinkerers is a community of rhythmic sway, back and forth from an undertaking to an undergoing, from melancholia to inspiration without necessary end. In short, it always returns back to the proverbial drawing board, and when asked if its project is complete, the only answer possible is "I prefer not to judge just yet. . . ." To tinker is to tinker with friends in an inoperative community of equals.

The face of friendship

If the friend in such a community has any feature at all it is but one: a face. But this is not the particular face of a particular, recognizable individual. In the friend we recognize the appearance of a face *as* a face. On this view, to have friends, we must suffer from prosopagnosia (face blindness). If one suffers from face blindness, one cannot recognize particular, individual faces, only the generic appearance of faceness as such. In Oliver Sacks' memoir of his own "mild" case of prosopagnosia, he writes that "it is by our faces that we can be recognized as individuals" (2010: 82). For those with face blindness, the recognition of individuals becomes increasingly impossible, even to the point where one cannot recognize one's own face. Thus Sacks writes of several uncanny experiences wherein he practically "apologized for almost bumping into a large bearded man, only to realize that the large bearded man was myself in a mirror" (ibid.: 85). Normal functioning can only be achieved with such a condition through the development of little tricks through which the subject can "read" the features of a face like a text, highlighting certain unique features that can be associated with particular individuals (a big nose for instance, or a distinctive haircut). But what is most interesting for our discussion is how face blindness does not simply erase certain content. It also exposes the face as a pure face. Indeed, Sacks poetically muses that "even if I cannot recognize particular faces, I am sensitive to the beauty of faces, and to their expressions" (ibid.: 92). The beauty of pure expressivity let loose from expressing this or that particular personality/identity is a kind of miraculous, positive upshot of face blindness. Faces, now unhinged from the private property of specific individuals, become generic "configurations" (ibid.: 98). While the experience of one's own face is more often than not a sense of recognition (a subjectification of the body as one's own home), the patient suffering from face blindness does not recognize their face as belonging to them (a desubjectification of the body as an uncanny abode). At this most basic, most fundamental state of exposure to the configuration of the face, there is no preference, contemplates Sacks, for individual faces. Recognition thus is a higher-order brain function that overwrites/encodes the generic faceness of the face. Yet it is in the fundamental level of the face as an indeterminate and fully generic, un-recognizable configuration that beauty shines through. Each individual face, at its primordial point of emergence as a face, is a whatever face, an impersonal face that is nevertheless singular. The face is the signature of the body, which is the hidden efficacious backdrop necessary for the signification of individualization to occur. The face is revealed to be a nude face, a gesture of its own im–potentiality (its capability to express this and that expression, character, identity without expressing any one particular character or identity). If the study of signatures is the study the appearance of the world, then to study the face is to study the appearance of human infancy expressed on and in the body.

Still, the friend and the stranger do not become indistinguishable. While certainly the threshold of indistinction has been opened via my analysis, this does not mean that all friends are strangers. Indeed, Sacks offers a surprising and highly provocative observation at this point. Referring to his patients that suffer from extreme prosopagnosia, he argues that they often complain of having bouts of déjà vu. This experience of uncanny doubling is attributable to the fact that "one can have familiarity without recognition" resulting in a state of "hyperfamiliarity" (Sacks 2010: 105). Turning to his father as evidence, Sacks observes that "a patient may find that everyone on the bus or on the street looks 'familiar'—he may go up to them and address them as old friends, even while realizing that he cannot possibly know them all" (ibid.). Prosopagnosia—as the general inability to distinguish individuals of a class—does not reduce the world to a bunch of strangers who are unapproachable, intimidating, and thus radically different from us. Rather, it produces a world of friends *whom we nevertheless do not recognize*. These friends are those who only share one thing in common with us: the nudity of the face.

In sum, we cannot see a face unless we are struck blind. Blind to the grimace of the individual, which for Agamben, is the transformation of the openness of the face into a determinate identity. As opposed to the openness and pure visibility of the face, the grimace "rigidifies into a character" (1995: 128). A face lacks a destiny, a task, a name, an identity. A face as a face (not this or that specific face) is only familiar, not recognizable. Friends gaze into each other's faces, nude, without the mask of the grimace to hide behind. They are exposed to each other as radically naked, lacking the clothing offered by the grimace. In this sense, face blindness is actually blindness to the grimace that individuates and at the same time is a witnessing of the expression of the signature of the face.

When we encounter the face of the friend, we recognize not a reflection of ourselves as particular individuals, but rather a shared "special being" that belongs to both. For Agamben, special being "does not mean the individual, identified by this or that quality which belongs exclusively to it" but rather "a being insofar as it is whatever being [*essere qualunque*], a being such that it is—generically and indifferently—each one of its qualities, adhering to them without allowing any of them to identify it" (2007b: 58). Special being as whatever being shines through the face of the other as a kind of being-in-common that is not personal but prepersonal, is not individual but singular (and thus unclassifiable). In this sense, the face is the gesture of special being, and is therefore never the private property of any one individual subject.

142   *Studying with friends*

Here we can think of the first expressions of a young child. Gilles Deleuze writes, "very small children all resemble one another and have hardly any individuality, but they have singularities: a smile, a gesture, a funny face—not subjective qualities" (2005: 30). Thus their faces do not mark any individuality any personhood. Indeed, small children cannot grimace, they can only make faces! What shines forth in the face of the infant is an "impersonal yet singular life" (ibid.: 28) that is neither pure biological life nor a fully subjectified personalized life. Rather it is *a life*—a special life without destination or vocation. Although Agamben does not directly refer to Deleuze's analysis of the face of the small child, we can make an important connection here between the two in relation to the theme of infancy. According to Agamben, infancy is a paradoxical state of being inside yet outside of language. Rather than a state of biological development, infancy is retained throughout linguistic experience in the messianic "no longer" and "not yet." Only when we no longer lack the capability for speech but have not yet spoken do we *return* to our linguistic origins in a state of infancy. Agamben speculates that we have a pure experience of language expressing nothing except its own existence when we "lack names, where speech breaks on our lips" (2007a: 7). Precisely when speech breaks the lips, but before we have said anything particular, the arrival of language expresses itself through the face. Not this or that face, but the face of a pure arriving without any determinate destiny. Thus the face is always the face of the infant. Perhaps we could even argue that the face is the expression of our infancy through singular and not yet subjective qualities.

Face blindness recognizes the im-potentiality of the human to be this *and* that (to be rather than what it has been). For the learning society, the face is a problem for two important reasons:

1   The face is reduced to a biometric identification of the potentialities of a student. The face becomes a marker of learning potential—a potentiality (a not-yet) that must be made into a trace of the student's individual character (a must-be). In this way the face is catalogued, made into an individual grimace that can then be compared to other individual grimaces. When the face is made into a grimace, learning apparatuses can build a profile of the student as this or that kind of learner with these kinds of deficits needing these kinds of interventions in order to maximize these kinds of outputs. *Profiling is the technology of the grimace.* Without the ability to bear witness to the indeterminacy of the face (the im-potentiality of expression that is special), the learning society projects the face outward onto the proverbial other whose vacant stare "cannot be saved," whose eyes reveal an "incapacity to learn." The inoperability of the face becomes the impotence of a subject abandoned by the learning society as "non-responsive" or "at risk." It is the educational other that must bear the face so that the individually recognized grimace of the chosen can be saved (made to express the learning potentiality of the subject) through the managerial technologies of learning and testing.

2   In the first case, the face is lost, projected outward onto the other as a kind of vacuous mask. In the process, the state of exception between expression and inexpression, potentiality and impotentiality is sacrificed. The result is a division of the crowd of faces in the classroom into those who "express" the skills and talents to learn and those who lack such expressive character-istics and thus perpetually appear "dumbfounded." If this example demon-strates an inability to recognize the face within the grimace as its disavowed, im-potential support, then the second case all too quickly embraces the face in the form of "color blindness" (the face abstracted from any particu-larities, the face as a pure potentiality). Color blindness, for Eduardo Bonilla-Silva and David G. Embrick (2006), is a form of racism without racists. According to these authors, liberal whites use the language of equal-ity and freedom of the market to justify the retraction of affirmative action politics. If teachers "don't see color," the reality of discrimination can thus be conveniently ignored, and inequalities explained with reference to indi-vidual lack of effort. Here a key distinction must be made between face blindness, as I am discussing it, and color blindness. If color blindness does not recognize the relationship between a face and its predicates (reducing everyone to a single, homogenous "face"), then face blindness sees only whatever it is that makes the other a singularity. What shines forth in the face is an unquantifiable im-potentiality, a pure medium for transmission of this or that emotion, gesture, idea without being predetermined to express any particular emotion, gesture, idea. In this sense, predicates are not negated but rather loosened from predestined meanings. This does not deny the past, yet at the same time, it does not determine the future (the face of the student is not yet x, y, or z but is also no longer a, b, or c). Markers of a given identity can come to mean differently, mean *rather than* what they have meant. Any determinate and necessary connection between any given predicate and any given identity is rendered radically contingent. For color-blind pedagogy, such markers cannot come to signify differently precisely because they do not exist in the first place (or have no significant relation to the questions which preoccupy the field of education). If one erases differences, the other strives to assert the equality of differences through a sharing of whatever.

Yet those who have critiqued the discourse and practices of learning have also left little room for the infancy of the face. In alternative descriptions of educa-tion beyond learning, the face as an expressive signature is forced into the role of the sign—forced to speak the identity of the one who studies. According to Charles Bingham and Gert Biesta, "Emancipatory education can therefore be characterized as education that starts from the assumption that all students can speak—or to be more precise: that all students can *already* speak" (2010: 142). In other words, as against the assumptions of discourses and practices of learning, emancipation begins when we reconceptualize the student as a speaking subject rather than merely a lack or gap waiting to be filled. While Agamben would

144   *Studying with friends*

agree that we must view students as speaking beings, it is the question of *already* that is at stake here. The missing concept in Bingham and Biesta's model is that of infancy. As argued previously, infancy is the moment before the speaking subject speaks ("not yet") but after he or she has some sort of linguistic capability ("no longer"). Infancy is therefore both a potentiality (to speak) and an impotentiality (not to speak)—a privation that is not simply a lack but as a positive having of that which is absent. Infancy is the redemption of the incapacity of speech within speech. René ten Bos perhaps summarizes infancy best when he argues that infancy "interrupts language precisely at the moment when it is actualizing itself" (2005: 40). If speaking is an act of subjectification—as Biesta writes, speaking is a way "for newcomers to respond and come into the world' (2006: 150)—then the experience of infancy is a state between subjectification and desubjectification that opens us up to a capacity to be *and* not to be. This is the moment of withdrawing-from where we experience the surprising appearance of the impotential within our potential for speech. When speech breaks on our lips, it arrives, announces itself, while at the same time pausing, hesitating on the lips, de-completing the very gesture which brings speech into the world as *this* speech act. Thus if subjectification is an interruption of the socializing function of learning for Biesta, then infancy is the *interruption of the interruption* that makes appear not this or that specific communication ("I believe *x* or *y*" or "I am this or that subject") but rather the formless and impotent contingency of our im-potential. In short, if Bingham and Biesta argue that the best resistance to the learning society is the student as speaker, using Agamben's argument we can qualify this further and in turn refute the entrepreneurial focus of self-actualization found in neoliberal discourses of learning. The studier is not a speaker (as in Biesta's model) but rather the one who has an expressive face. This face conveys nothing in particular to the teacher beyond its own incapacity for speech. In his most recent work (2011), which places new emphasis on the moment of hesitation, Biesta has carved out a time and a space for infancy. Without this seemingly inconsequential supplement that is between times and between expressions, the face of study is lost, even in the most ardent critiques of learning.

The friend bears witness to the *infant face* of the one who studies, who sees the face of the studier not as a mere generic potentiality to be actualized in this or that form or as a simple impotence or deficit but as an im-potentiality and thus the mark of freedom. According to Agamben's analysis, a witness is someone who "lends the inhuman a voice" (2002: 120). In other words, the witness refuses to separate (and thus sacrifice) the impotential kernel from potentiality. In short, the witness separates him or herself from separation by testifying to the indestructible, co-originary relation between the human and inhuman, potentiality and impotentiality. Witnessing the impotential within the potential of the face (to speak or express) is the gesture of the friend. For Aristotle the friend modeled the good life, providing a mirror for the self to reflect on what counts as the good life. For Agamben, this mirror does not reflect back a positive image of the virtues so much as the im-potential ground for their existence in the first place: the nudity of virtue stripped of its positive features, of its various predicates.

To see the face of infancy and to bear witness to it in the classroom is to seek out those students who lean forward, raise their eyebrows, open their mouths, poise themselves to speak before speaking. In such fugitive moments, we glimpse their in-capability to speak and to not speak simultaneously. This is a moment of contingency and choice, where the "I can, I cannot" of im-potentiality shows itself showing itself. Most teachers would rush to complete this incomplete gesture, finishing the sentence for the student or pushing the student to speak and thus be heard as a subject with such and such a belief. Both reactions to the studious, infantile face demonstrate a certain anxiety over the indeterminacy of studying that interrupts the smooth transformation of potentiality into an actuality—whether that be in terms of a measurable outcome or in terms of an answer to Biesta's question "What do you think?" Both reject the face of *thinking*, which is a perpetually pensive, infantile face. As opposed to these models that push potentiality toward some sort of determination, the one who witnesses the face remains silent, listening to and looking for the infancy of the one who studies. In this manner, what is conserved here is the infancy of im-potentiality, of the specialness of each student. Thus the impotent assistant remains infuriatingly ambiguous, his or her only gift is a rather weak injunction: "Keep thinking about it, you don't have to tell me what you think just yet."

Dialogue as tinkering with thought

If in the former chapter I ended with an example of tinkering with material objects (the studious play of trash), here I propose a different kind of tinkering: tinkering with thought itself. We tinker with thought when we dialogue with friends. The importance of intellectual friendship and the genesis of critical theory has been explored by scholars such as John Ely (1998) whose work traces the intimate circle of friendship between Adorno, Benjamin, Bloch, Kracauer, and Sohn-Rethel, who all vacationed in Positano, Italy, where they found inspiration for key themes in critical theory such as aura, porosity, and ruin. Although Ely's research focused exclusively on the quasi-utopian retreat to Positano as a bastion for anti-capitalist musings, I would venture that friendship is even more "radical" when it is located precisely in the heart of instrumental reason itself, as the friendship between Adorno and Horkheimer in exile in Santa Monica, California, attests. Neither a family bond nor a form of economic association, this friendship in the sunny mecca of the culture industry finds a modicum of refuge in the mutual act of studying a state of shared displacement and disenchantment. This makes their odd intellectual affinity the ultimate form of profanity.

As an example of friendship in exile, I turn to the dialogues of Adorno and Horkheimer in the short book titled *Towards a New Manifesto* (2011). Taken down by Gretel Adorno in 1956, these discussions offer an intimate glimpse at two friends who are engaged in tinkering—tinkering with the fundamental

146 *Studying with friends*

terminology, form, and problematic of classical Marxism. Most startling about this exchange is that everything seems up for grabs. All presuppositions are suspended (presuppositions about the primacy of Marxism, the primacy of the party, and so on), the need to reach definitive conclusions and solutions is deferred, and the need to argue persuasively for preexisting theoretical positions is left idle. Even in this seemingly inoperative state between chronological time (the unfolding of events) and the end of time (the advent of the revolution) there is still time remaining to think. The result is a text that does not record a determinate actualization of a manifesto (that gives causes, explanations, and argues for *what must be done*) but rather the indeterminating im-potentiality of studious play—a messianic rhythmic sway between progression toward and withdrawing from. As such, friendship emerges as a kind of inoperative community that equally recognizes the urgency of reaching an end while also reveling in the pleasure of thinking as a pure means without an end.

The oscillation between affirmation and negation, undergoing and undertaking, melancholia and inspiration opens up the messianic time and space of study, dialectical reversals and punctuated silences, and sustains this space and time for the reader to experience for him or herself. Over and over, the two friends return to the same questions: the question of terminology, of audience, of the relationship between theory and practice, of style, of the usefulness/ uselessness of Utopia. These seemingly interminable questions push toward some resolution at the very moment when this resolution recedes from view and opens up to new, unanticipated problematics. What is left is the creative time of the now, the time of study wherein all thoughts are open, all cards are on the table, all deadlines are dismissed. In this sense, the extreme fertility of this dialogue (its many lines of inquiry that emerge suddenly like a flash of light in the darkness) offer a glimpse at the potentiality of studying, while at the same time, the frustration of the authors (the flashes of brilliance that just as quickly fade into the background darkness) captures the impotentiality of the very same gesture. They seem to testify to the possibility of saying everything without saying anything at all. Studying the potentiality for writing a manifesto is thus also and equally studying the impotentiality to complete such a proposal in the first place.

One illustration pulled from the text should suffice to capture the inoperative gesture of study. In a brief exchange concerning the nature and use of argument, the following statements are made in rapid succession:

HORKHEIMER: There is a theme I would like to tackle some day: the question of the nature of argument. . .

ADORNO: Thinking that renounces argument—Heidegger—switches into pure irrationalism.

HORKHEIMER: One can argue only if there is a practical implication behind it.

ADORNO: If there is a definite pull behind it. Kant.

ADORNO: The mistrust of argument is at bottom what has inspired the Husserls and Heideggers. The diabolical aspect of it is that the abolition of argument means that their writing ends up in tautology and nonsense. Argument has the form of "Yes, but. . ."

HORKHEIMER: But the "Yes, but. . ." remains in the service of making something visible in the object itself.

ADORNO: There is something bad about advocacy—arguing means applying the rules of thinking to the matters under discussion. You really mean to say that if you find youself in the situation of having to explain why something is bad, you are already lost. Alternatively, you end up saying like Mephistopheles: "Scorn reason, despise learning." Then you will discover the primordial forces of being.

HORKHEIMER: The USA is the country of argument.

ADORNO: Argument is consistently bourgeois. (2011: 67–73)

In this excerpt, the negative dialectic leaves us with an aporia concerning the ambiguous nature of argument which turns in on itself and ultimately devolves into nothing more than a tool of the bourgeoisie. In this sense, the dialogue seems to wither on the vine, and the text is reduced to nothing more than a remnant of missed opportunities (if not the musings of a privileged class of elite intellectuals who have the time and space for chit-chat). Yet the dialogue does achieve a certain kind of work: it reveals not the actualization of *a thought* but rather the creative chaos of *thinking* that opens when one studies. If Adorno thus states that "thinking is a form of practice" (ibid.: 75), at stake is the *particular kind of practice that thinking is*. Studying is the practice of thinking, of continually circling and being encircled by the im-potentiality of special being, of a being that cannot be instrumentalized or classified according to pre-existing criteria.

Friends who study lack an audience, or rather, the audience turns their backs on such friends. Horkheimer worries that "What these people want from us is partly pernicious, partly well-intentioned. It is the belief that the intellectual must be someone who can really help. It is not enough to say 'I am thinking'" (2011: 88–89). Thinking is neither simply a pure, abstract activity divorced from practice nor is it a "gadget" for putting forth solutions or ten-point plans. Rather it is an activity that de-completes itself. Studying suspends ends yet does not retreat into pure potentiality. It is the ambiguous state of recessive sway that holds within itself this and that without choosing either. As such, studying holds within it both the pleasure of undertaking (a new project) and the interminable pain of undergoing (an indefinite process). What is most important here is not simply what is said (a collection of statements that testify to the ability of the participants to speak and think) but rather the gaps that also permeate the dialogue as so many enabling absences or silences. This dialogue renders Adorno and Horkheimer vulnerable because it presents study in its nudity, in its infancy. In its nudity, thinking emerges as a kind of inoperative gesture without guarantees, without clear origins or goals, without specific destinations. Who is the audience for the enactment of im-potentiality, of an inoperative community of impotent friends, of the fits and starts of studying? Certainly not an audience who expects to *learn* anything. Certainly not an audience who *identifies* with the speakers. The only audience remaining is a kind of anonymous audience of singularities who witness the im-potentiality of the work of this dialogue.

What is revealed in the end is the surprising face of friendship. All predetermined positions, all individual habits of mind are oddly suspended, and the two friends meet as singularities whose being-in-common is nothing more than the im-potential experience of studying. In this sense, the personal grimaces of the friend give way to his or her specialness (a specialness that does not eradicate particularities, but rather resists the urge to reduce specialness to any one particular set of traits, habits, tics, patterns, or features). What opens is the possibility of being at ease with one's friends. For Agamben, ease designates "the empty place where each can move freely" (1993a: 25). To be at ease is not to feel the need to put on the grimace to mask one's special face. Around friends who study, the face shines forth in all its contradictions, all its inconsistencies. To study with a friend is to love one with all his or her predicates, his or her *being as such*. When reading this dialogue, the reader feels the freedom of Adorno and Horkheimer to express this and that view without need to be consistent or "living up" to certain expectations that have been projected onto them (both by each other and by their phantom audience). In other words, they come to embody the law of good neighbors, and the book that their dialogue produced embodies the poetic rhythm that unites and separates the ease of friendship and the effort of study.

The historical materialist question that such dialogue seems to call for would be something like this: Is it possible, given this historical constellation, to write a new communist manifesto? My response would simply be that the task has changed. Rather than simply transmit an old manifesto (as so many dogmatic Marxists are prone to do through their endless repetition of old Marxist terminology that has become totally reified), and rather than write a new manifesto, what Adorno and Horkheimer have done is to suspend the writing of *a* manifesto for the study of the signatures (the heritage of theories, terms, concepts, and styles form the effective backdrop of writing, thinking, and acting) that make manifestos possible in the first place. They have chosen to dwell within the im-potentiality of these signatures (so many terminological options, so many different styles, so many different possible arguments) without transforming these signatures into actualized signs of a completed work or definitive political project. Thus all that are left are the impotent fragments of friends struggling with the only freedom that remains: the freedom to occupy the space and time of thinking.

8 Public, collective studying as an im-potential political gesture

Throughout this book, each chapter has attempted to unpack a specific dimension of studying. I have moved from the ontology of study (whatever being) to the aesthetics of study (poetic rhythm) to the method of study (collection of signatures) to the messianic space and time of study (the notch) to the intersubjective dimension of study (studying with friends). What has been produced is a kind of *tinkering phenomenology* of study in different times and spaces. Yet one essential question remains: is there a politics to studying? My examples of Bartleby, who does not take any kind of recognizable political action to defend himself and thus ends up dying in prison of starvation, or of Adorno and Horkehiemer's suspended and unfinished manifesto, or of children pausing to decorate a project after having experienced some kind of calamity all suggest *a deferral of (political) engagement*. Indeed, one might quickly assume that Agamben's oft quoted notion of a "coming community" suggests a kind of infinite waiting for a future that is perpetually yet-to-come. In this vein, Ewa Plonowska Ziarek has argued that Agamben fails to explain how "powerlessness can be transformed into possibility" (2010: n.p.)—especially for marginalized or oppressed groups who are suffering from real and immediate forms of oppression.

If Ziarek finds the theory of a coming community politically problematic, the issue appears to be compounded when it comes to studying and its apolitical implications. The hesitation of studying—and its rhythmic, indeterminate oscillation between profound boredom and inspiration and back again—seems to be a radical refusal of the call to be this or that type of political subject with this or that agenda and this or that set of specific demands. Isn't studying the ultimate expression of "I would prefer not" to engage in political action? And if so, is this retreat from direct political engagement something to be lamented, criticized, or suspicious of? As opposed to symbolic and systemic forms of objective violence within the current state of exception, Slavoj Žižek argues against proponents of a "fake sense of urgency" in the face of global warfare. In response to those like Hardt and Negri who place such faith in the labor of the multitude, Žižek argues that intellectuals should have the courage to say "There are situations when the only truly 'practical' thing to do is to resist the temptation to engage immediately and to 'wait and see' by means of a patient, critical analysis" (2008: 7). In other words we must draw our model from Lenin, who

150 *Public, collective studying*

in 1914 withdrew to Switzerland where he "learned, learned, and learned" (ibid.: 8) by reading and rereading Hegel's logic. The most radical gesture against violence is the non-violent violence of study which detaches itself from political urgency in order to collect signatures of efficacy, or signatures of what still remains possible within a state of world destitution.

Yet what I want to suggest in this last chapter is that studying is not simply a detachment from politics (which is either criticized by Ziarek or lauded by Žižek). Rather there is an *im-potential political dimension* to studying. In what might be considered a rather unorthodox move, I will argue in this chapter that the im-potential politics of study are thrown into relief in the first phase of the Occupy Wall Street (OWS) movement. Although it has morphed into a more directed, goal- and project-oriented movement since its eviction from Zuccott Park in November of 2011, the occupation, at its inception, offered a radical interruption of what has come to be expected from either political or educational activities. What OWS presented was a new thesis: when studying becomes a collective and public experience (an experience held in common), then studying becomes a kind of politically weak force—a force that "would prefer not' to settle on this or that agenda or demand and instead experiment within a suspended, whatever state of being. Indeed collectivization means that Agamben's phrase "I would prefer not to" (enunciated by a generic singularity) must be rearticulated as "*We* would prefer not to" (enunciated by a multitude or a coming community). To be clear, this is not (a) a political potentiality waiting to happen in the future nor is it (b) a political actualization in the present. Rather collective study is a political im-potentiality which is "no longer" simply education and "not yet" a political determination. The refusal to engage in political negotiation with existing power structures is precisely what makes the im-potential of study's politics so infuriating. In the end, public and collective study can be theorized as a new form of *communist study* that does not delay the arrival of a coming politics but is a messianic appearance of an inoperative community in the present. While Hardt and Negri come closest to this point, arguing that OWS was a kind of "encampment" for "self-learning" (2012: 39), their analysis is, in the end, lacking precisely because it is not grounded in a comprehensive theory of study and its connections to im-potentiality. In this final chapter, I will take Hardt and Negri's intuitive comments as a jumping-off point to further explore the connections between occupation, study, and politics in OWS.

In this way, collective, public study allows us to return to one of Benjamin's most cryptic formulations found in his essay "Critique of Violence." In this essay, Benjamin famously draws a distinction between mythic and divine forms of violence. For Benjamin, the latter refers to violence that is law-creating, whereas the former refers to a violence that is law-destroying. What is peculiar here is that Benjamin refers to divine violence as having an "educative power, which in its perfected form stands outside the law" (1986: 297). The educative power of divine violence has many manifestations, one of which is the general strike. Benjamin speculates,

These are defined, therefore, not by miracles directly performed by God, but by the expiating moment in them that strikes without bloodshed and, finally, by the absence of all law-making. To this extent it is justifiable to call this violence too, annihilating; but it is so only relatively, with regard to goods, right, life, and suchlike, never absolutely, with regard to the soul of the living.

(ibid.: 297–298)

In sum, divine violence de-activates the intuitive, familiar, everyday distribution of things, roles, norms, and values, opening up a space and a time of free use beyond the measure of any particular law. Such violence is ultimately non-violent because it does not annihilate these things, roles, norms, or values but rather suspends them in order to study them. The suspension offered by divine violence is its educative power. If learning is a kind of mythic violence over and against potentiality (sacrificing impotential for maximizing outcomes in the form of human capital development), then collectivized study is a kind of violence against violence, preserving im-potentiality as a pure means. In this formulation, Benjamin draws together the threads binding study—as an educational suspension—with the general strike—as a public and collective occupation of factories, schools, and institutions. While for Žižek, study is pre-political, and for Ziarek, study is apolitical, for Benjamin, the strike is a kind of suspension of the divisions that separate violence and non-violence, action from in-action, in an im-potential political gesture, producing a dialectic at a standstill. As my analysis will demonstrate, occupation is the *paradigm* fusing educative power to the politics of the general strike, generating a state of exception that would otherwise separate the two. And if the results appear to be "inconclusive" (according to the logic of learning and testing), it is precisely because of occupation's ontological status as an indeterminate, pure means. As such, the event of occupation returns politics to the luminous spiral of the possible that is discovered through study, and study turns outward from solitude to solidarity amongst friends who have gathered in public spaces to collectively "prefer not to."

OWS as collectivized study

It is interesting to note that one of the first destructive acts waged against OWS was the destruction of the library facilities. As was widely reported in the press, during the eviction of protestors from Zuccotti Park in the fall of 2011, over $47,000 worth of damage was done to the 3,600 books, computer equipment, and furniture that made up the "People's Library." The library was not simply the "property" of the protestors who had to be removed from the park by the police. Rather, it was an example of the collective nature of study that defined the OWS from day one. In this sense, it is most appropriate that the police removed the library first and foremost from the site: it represented the studious nature of an im-potential politics. If Bartleby the Scrivener was the first to occupy Wall Street (see Chapter 2), then OWS transformed his singular and

152   *Public, collective studying*

largely private/solitary act of study into a public event that embodied a coming politics. In order to demonstrate the connections between occupation and the messianic space and time of study, I will turn to the first person accounts of OWS collected in the book *Occupy! Scenes from Occupied America* (Blumenkranz et al. 2011). This book is a unique, on-the-ground perspective of what happened in Zuccotti Park in the early days, and as such, provides great insight into the complexities of the first phase of Occupy from the inside. It is my contention that these complexities are best explained in references to my theory of study that I have been developing throughout this book, and in particular the im-potential freedoms which are paradigmatically embodied in study. While OWS would describe itself more in relation to the theory and practice of anarchism rather than study, what I want to argue that is when we think of the relationship between phase one of OWS and study, new understandings of both are made possible which disrupt expectations, revealing deep, ontological connections between overt anarchistic political values and the whatever being experienced through study.

To be precise, phase one of OWS in its various forms was a manifestation (sometimes explicitly but more often implicitly) of what I would call communist study. As Astra Taylor recalls from her experiences at OWS:

> I hooked up with a group of friends and we had an 'assembly' with a bunch of strangers and talked economics for two or three hours. It was kind of nice to be at a protest and, instead of marching and shouting, to be talking about ideas.
>
> (Blumenkranz et al. 2011: 3)

While the media as well as the politicians were losing patience waiting for OWS to define its agenda and its list of definitive demands, the occupiers themselves were busy dialoguing, studying the situation at hand. Eli Schmitt thus reported from the ground that "Someone asked what the action was, what we were going to do, and someone else responded that this was the action, that we were there to talk and organize" (Blumenkranz et al. 2011: 4). Instead of putting forth a specific agenda, OWS spent most of its time *preferring not* to commit to any one demand over and above any other. And this preferring not caused a kind of prolonged suspension of the order of political negotiation. This suspension of ends for the experience of pure means is the im-political gesture of public, collective study, which interrupts expectations for actualization of certain potentialities. Continuing his narrative, Schmitt recalls

> In the middle of our discussion, we debated why it was problematic to make a demand, how in order for a demand to be meaningful, one must have some power to leverage . . . We talked about what criteria made for good demands.
>
> (ibid.: 5)

The demand that emerged here was not a demand for such and such but rather a demand *as not* a demand: a demand to withhold demands so as to listen and reflect in the time and space of study.

Toward the end of the discussion, Schmitt noted

> We still don't know exactly what are the demands. One of the members of our group, in discussing the criteria for a good demand, noted that Americans like to "get something" out of a political action. Repeal, enact, ban. We want visible, measurable outcomes.
>
> (Blumenkranz et al. 2011: 6)

This insight into the nature of politics should be read on an ontological level of potentiality itself. The model of status quo politics in the U.S.A. consists of actualizing certain potentialities and thus submitting potentiality to the reign of what can be made determinate. If politics is dominated by demands—indeed I would argue that contemporary political and educational debates consist of nothing but demands (to raise or lower taxes, to improve test scores, to bring back American jobs from overseas, and so on) without substantial analysis or critical reflection—then OWS ruptured the prevalence of demands. In all cases, the demand is an explicit demonstration of a willful power over and against another will. The demand is either a reconstitution of a hierarchy or the inversion of a hierarchy through a battle of forces. When spoken from above, it constitutes the fundamental gesture of biocapitalist command. When spoken from below, it offers an insurgent if not revolutionary clarion call against such commands. Certainly the agonism of demands is fundamental to political struggle (without the pronunciation of demands, politics would cease to be a struggle and transform into a kind of post-political consensus building). Yet OWS suspended the form and function of the demand as well as the underlying political ontology of its willfulness. Instead of the combative will powering a set of demands, OWS organized itself according to a weak power of open willingness to listen, think, and study without the rhetorical force of the demand. As McKenzie Wark argued,

> It is an occupation which, almost uniquely, does not have demands. It has at its core a suggestion: what if people came together and found a way to structure a conversation which might come up with a better way to run the world?
>
> (3 October 2011)

The suggestion has no status in politics today precisely because it remains open to an ethic of listening to others and of being flexible to what appears in a situation. Thus, the suggestion interrupts and suspends the unidirectional force of the demand, making the inoffensive gesture of suggestion into an offensive tactic of subversion. At the same time, it is not simply "soft" politics or a politics of accommodation, negotiation, or compromise. Rather the suggestion remains

154 *Public, collective studying*

absolutely steadfast, uncompromising, and militant, refusing to set demands, engage in negotiations, play certain tactical games to achieve an agenda and thus sacrifice its potentiality to be and not to be this and that kind of movement. In this manner, the ontology of public, collective suggestion is an im-potential political form positioned betwixt and between study and political action, suturing the two together in an impossible synthesis. The first phase of OWS was threatening (as well as confusing) not because of a specific or exact demand but precisely because it destabilized the ontology of political thinking and acting through the enigma of preferring not to make demands. The preferring not to enacts the rhythmic sway of study between progressing toward and withdrawing the solidification of demands, agendas, and manifestos. This oscillation is the time it takes to formulate and reflect on suggestions brought forth for public, collective study. Tinkering with options becomes the quintessential im-potential political gesture.

Sarah Resnick captured the rhythmic sway of study when she noticed a tension in the occupation between a push toward real, substantial action guided by a clear plan and directed at specific goals and a withdrawal from such action into a more immediate experimentation with the possibilities of living and thinking together as an indeterminate group, defined less by demands and more by the circulation of suggestions. Resnick wrote

> I noted a commonality among these various criticisms: and anxiety toward idleness. And it struck me that this idleness could potentially be redeemed. Acts of protest wouldn't—needn't—always meet a preordained objective or outcome, a prompt reaction or result, cause and effect. We were taking up space, filling up time—and inaction, boredom, even listlessness would sometimes play a part, and they too have value.
>
> (Blumenkranz et al. 2011: 95)

Letting things idle through occupation stops or interrupts the incessant need for "results" and is itself a kind of impotent result, or a result that withdraws from calculation and measure. The inaction, boredom, and listlessness are here redeemed as part of a larger rhythm of the im-potential politics of collective study. The redemption of melancholic remnants is part of the work of study, which returns the studier to a primordial state of stupidity—stupidity that is itself an opening to radical possibilities for new uses that make their fleeting appearance via the weak power of the suggestion.

Instead of simply detaching itself from politics (as Lenin's injunction to learn, learn, learn seems to indicate), study is resolutely involved in and immanent to the appearance of the occupation itself, pushing forward toward the horizon of becoming a political movement and simultaneously withdrawing or pulling back from this same horizon. The result is a dialectic at a standstill that opens the space and time for dwelling together and thinking together in the now. In this peculiar zone of indistinction, study emerges as an atopia without determinate goals beyond its own self-appearance. The complexity of both space and time that OWS as collective study generated in Zuccotti Park is therefore completely missed by both Ziarek and Žižek, who remain incapable of thinking the im-potentiality of study. It seems that the either/or choice offered between total detachment from or total submersion in politics is too reductive to understand the neither/nor logic of collectivized study.

In the end, as Marina Sitrin aptly stated, the real demand of OWS became a demand to "be left alone in our plazas, parks, schools, workplaces, and neighborhoods so as to meet one another, reflect together, and in assembly forms decide what our alternatives are" (Blumenkranz et al. 2011: 8). This quote is important for several reasons. First, "to be left alone" should not be read as an anti-political, utopian desire to end politics. Rather it should be read, again, as a valence of Agamben's "I would prefer not"—a great refusal to engage in negotiation with power and instead dwell in a kind of im-potential, atopic space and time of study wherein friends can "meet one another" and in turn "reflect together." The coming community that Sitrin imagined was not so much oriented toward future utopian desires or blueprints as a reflection on the present—the present as a continual coming rather than a waiting. She continued "We all strive to embody the alternative we wish to see in our day-to-day relationships" (ibid.: 9) right now in the now time of OWS. The park, which is actually privately owned by Brookfield Properties, became "our plaza" precisely through the public act of study which returned the park to the commonwealth. Thus OWS splintered the American political ontology of time which is always oriented toward a future point of dialectical negation or a progressive telos of overcoming. Rather than overcoming, OWS was a coming that always already manifested in their actual assemblies and actual practices.

Messianic suspension means a release of means from ends, a release of potentiality from the measurement and evaluation of judgment. As Natasha Lennard wrote in her article "Occupy and failure," "Occupy—the weird, ever shifting assemblage of actions, gatherings, and connections that it is—technically avoids the logic of success and failure altogether" (27 April 2012). Preferring not to set demands has the effect of suspending judgment or evaluation of what OWS meant, or what it amounted to in the broader history of political "movements." Even the original gathering of Occupy at Wall Street was not definitively planned or guided by predetermined definitions of what "success" might constitute. Thus OWS embodied a fundamental refusal of all political ontologies to *measure* and *calculate* the effects of actions in terms of specific goals or agendas. It is not a passage to an act but a passage pure and simple. This is also a suspension of the fundamental educational logic of biocapitalism which quantifies outcomes according to economic needs or political aims. Occupy became a pure means—it withdrew when it pressed forward, it offered a kind of weak power in the face of global exploitation, and it seemed to subtract itself from the calculus of measure that narrowly defines success versus failure in instrumental terms.

Here it is important to emphasize the centrality of the term "occupation." In her short but powerful contribution to *SFOA*, Angela Davis argued that we

156 *Public, collective studying*

must remain cognizant of the long legacy of brutal and violent colonialist occupations of indigenous places. In light of this oppressive history of top-down occupation, OWS must "transform the meaning of 'occupation'" (Blumenkranz et al. 2011: 133) from connoting appropriation to connoting dis-appropriation of private ownership in the name of the commonwealth. Using Agamben's theory of the messianic, I would argue that OWS actually embodied occupation *as not* occupation. We must remember that for Agamben, the messianic offers the slightest of shifts within the present in order to open up new possibilities and usher in a coming community. The messianic is not acting *as if* equality and freedom *might* be possible in a world *beyond* capitalist occupation. Rather it occupies occupation itself, unleashing a radically different set of possibilities from within the destitution of the world simply by appropriating occupation as *no longer* the occupation of the world by the 1 percent. Stated differently, the im-potential political gesture of collective study suspended the logic of exploitative occupation in order to tinker with the meaning of occupation from inside. To occupy as not to occupy was to open up an atopic space that was neither the dystopia of Wall Street high finance nor a future-oriented Utopia, but rather a coming education. If for Agamben a camp is a state of suspension designated from above by the power of a sovereign, then the OWS camp was a state of suspension from below designated by the weak messianic power of a multitude to prefer not to abide by a sovereign decree. In this sense the OWS camp was a real state of exception that suspended the sovereign's suspension in the name of a coming community beyond all separations, divisions and exclusions. Zuccotti Park thus became a kind of inoperative notch in the side of the financial district.

The occupiers were a multitude of singular "studiers" or "study groups." Marco Roth recalled a tumblr titled "We Are the 99 Percent" which listed the diversity of the protestors:

> indebted, often over-educated for the few jobs and salaries available to them, stripped of dignity, tormented by anxieties over how to care for themselves and their families, laid off from jobs, non-unionized, clinging precariously to the idea of middle-classness that seems more and more to be a chimera of the past.
>
> (Blumenkranz et al. 2011: 25)

The 99 percent was not a party, nor was it an identity based on race, gender, or sexual orientation. As Jodi Dean pointed out (Blumenkranz et al. 2011), the 99 percent was a radical departure from democratization, moralization, and individualization. Thus it exchanged American electoral politics for direct democracy, ethical reform for economic critique, and individual choice for collectivity. OWS was not an identity politics based on a *particular* political subjectification or hegemonic suturing under a single, shared platform. Rather, the 99 percent was a radical desubjectification lacking fixed, definable predicates that exclude some and include others. If statistics are normally used to impose

Public, collective studying   157

a process of desubjectification onto the masses, in this case, it is precisely the nihilism of technological enframing that became a potentiality for a new kind of desubjectification that reconnected with possibility and contingency against impossibility and necessity. Through OWS, 99 percent became a totally generic yet absolutely irreducible singularity. The exclusion of the 1 percent was interesting in this respect. If the 1 percent represented the sovereign power to exclude, to abandon, and to pass judgment, then here we see the exclusion of the agent of exclusion, a separation from the source of separation. The 99 percent was therefore the primordially chaotic ontology of *whatever* being—a radical *declassification* of all subject positions. Because it was whatever it was without division or classification as this or that kind of political subject, the questions that Roth posed are again open to an ontological reading:

> Is OWS a movement calling for the people to be bailed out too, or a movement of noble anger against the corporate welfare state we've been living in? Or is it, in fact, an actual liberation movement, aimed largely at reclaiming the freedom of the streets for popular assembly, against tourism and a managed public sphere? Is this, in fact, the largest homeless rights movement on the planet?
>
> (Blumenkranz et al. 2011: 29)

The only answer to this question is "yes": OWS was indeed whatever.

The refusal to create a set of demands, to align with specific political parties, to put forward a clear agenda of reform might very well remind us of another important occupation: Tiananmen Square in 1989. As Agamben argues,

> What was most striking about the demonstrations of the Chinese May was the relative absence of determinate contents in their demands (democracy and freedom are notions too generic and broadly defined to constitute the real object of a conflict, and the only concrete demand, the rehabilitation of Hu Yao-Bang, was immediately granted).
>
> (1993a: 85)

Between April 15 and June of 1989, Beijing students initiated one of the largest student protests in modern history, spreading outward to include multiple student groups from various universities throughout Beijing and beyond, urban workers, and residents of Beijing. During this period of time, the world witnessed direct demonstrations on multiple campuses, the occupation of Tiananmen and a massive, ongoing hunger strike, as well as military backlash that ended in an unknown number of deaths and prison sentences. Early on the occupation was marked by multiple power struggles amongst students to define the scope of demands to be made, tactics to be deployed, and political line to be taken with the Chinese Communist Party. But what interests Agamben the most is perhaps the last days before the forceful military seizure of Tiananmen. As Dingxin Zhao argues (2004), after martial law was declared in the square and

158 *Public, collective studying*

leadership lost control of the hunger strikers, radicals, and energetic new arrivals, a period of chaotic experimentation opened up that included the creation of the Statue of the Goddess of Democracy as well as the opening of the Democracy University. Various attempts to consolidate interests under the Joint Federation of All Circles in the Capital or the Beijing Students' Autonomous Union failed to articulate a clear vision or exercise control over the continually shifting and dynamic range of participants in the occupation and hunger strike. While Zhao finds this period to be more or less the failure of the occupiers to elect representatives and negotiate with the government for change, Agamben sees something very different: the emergence of a new notion of community.

For Agamben, the messianic time after initial attempts by leaders to curb the protest toward certain interests and before the military crack-down, the remaining occupiers of Tiananmen in Beijing did not seem to have any conditions of belonging, nor any definitive demands addressed to the state, nor any identity (beyond general demands for more democracy) which could represent specific interests to a broader community. It was precisely a coming community composed of a multitude of singularities studying its own possibilities, and tinkering with the free use of speech that had been set loose from determinate ends. In this sense it is interesting to note the return to more or less traditional metaphors, images, and rituals used by the occupiers (see Zhao 2004). Rather than marks of a conservative desire to return to a mythic past, the occupiers were de-propriating such signs and performances, releasing them for new uses. Thus the underlying method to the occupation was one of suspension: suspending the function of the square as well as the power of the state without destroying either.

And what provoked the Chinese leaders was the radical gesture of preferring not to negotiate or settle on a particular plan, manifesto, or list of complaints. Such "agendas" can be managed by the state, but what the state cannot tolerate is a preferring not to engage with the status quo, with the abrupt suspension of politics-as-usual by and through studious play. Remember, studious play is semi-indifferent to any determination, to any destination beyond or outside of itself. As such, it interrupts the efficiency of any police order, grinding the present (as defined by a chronological unfolding) to the zero-point of the now (which exists in surplus of chronology). Such a gesture provokes violence from the police precisely because it refuses to abide by the rules of lawful conduct. Agamben warns, "Wherever these singularities peacefully demonstrate their being in common there will be a Tiananmen, and, sooner or later, the tanks will appear" (1993a: 87). It would appear that the overt police brutality against OWS and various manifestations of occupation across the globe is precisely a reminder of this warning.

Because of the ontological commitment of OWS to whatever—a collective of generic singularities—the "homeless question" was repeatedly brought to the foreground of daily assemblies. Christopher Herring and Zoltán Glück argued that for OWS as well as other Occupations around the country, the homeless question was of paramount importance for defining OWS's stance toward "exclusion, legitimacy, and belonging" (Blumenkranz et al. 2011: 166). Rather than reproduce the exclusive logic of capitalism, OWS had to deal directly with the "bare life" of the homeless. It is at this point that OWS more than any other protest opened itself up to the necessary study of the relationship between the survival of the homeless and the politics of protest. This is a quintessentially *biopolitical* question concerning the relationship between *zöe* and *bios*. Through its ontological commitments to the multitude of whatever singularities, OWS blurred the lines of the debate: it made survival a political issue and in turn politics a matter of survival. Occupation, self-organization, and self-management became interconnected through a shared practice of studying the very possibilities for forming a coming community. In this state of exception where dichotomies and divisions were left idle, the homeless, the middle class, and a host of other intermediary groups (including students) met in an atopic space and time to *study* the sublime art of discussing across differences and living across class divisions. What emerged was precisely the *question* (and not the answer) of inclusion and exclusion facing not only OWS but the contemporary learning society as such. While the learning society cannot question its own logic of exclusion, OWS made this questioning a central tenet of its own self-study, of its own possibility to exist. Those involved in OWS were therefore learning to study *as friends* who shared the sharing of Zuccotti Park despite their differing appearances, different levels of cultural capital, different expectations, and different states of biological thriving. Such friendship, far from a romantic ideal of mimetic unity, was precisely the most intense and most controversial aspect of life in the park, pushing OWS to the limits of its own self-identity as an "all inclusive" or "pluralistic" collective. In this sense, friendship does not lead to consensus but rather to further study, and study does not end but rather continually complexifies itself, undermining any notion of closure or completion or realization of this or that identity or this or that political platform. Thus Jodi Dean (2012), despite her many insights, is fundamentally wrong in her prescriptions for OWS. Dean argues that to become truly revolutionary, OWS needs a party to orient it. Such prognostications enact the classic role of the prophet who can foresee the future using a philosophical divining rod. Yet this turn back to the party denied precisely what was most unique and important about the first phase of OWS: that it was an im-potential gesture that was no longer merely education and not yet a political movement. With the focus on the structure of the party as a solution to the aporias of OWS, Dean cut occupation from its ontological commitments to the collective and public study of whatever. What Dean did not recognize was that OWS was not a symptom of the fragmentation of the left (such fragmentation only happens when there are no longer friends but anonymous strangers who can go separate ways) but rather solidarity in sharing the burdens and privileges, the melancholic sadness and inspirational joy of militantly studying.

160 *Public, collective studying*

As Peter Murphy aptly reminds us,

> Just as philosophy is the activity of friends, so also is politics. Neither a species of kinship system nor a creature of the state, politics is modeled on the relationship among friends. Friendship, conversely, is akin to a "little republic."
>
> (1998: 170)

For Murphy, friendship is not simply a privative affair between like-minded individuals, but is rather a relationship between commoners who share a public place (the market, the café, the school, gymnasium, and so on) and a particular orientation toward a mediating, common thing, idea, or condition that rests between the two. The common element in a friendship equalizes the relation. Despite differences and distinctions, the common, mediating element produces a proportional equality between friends. Although Murphy does not stress this point, I would extend his analysis and argue that the activity of friendship is always an activity of studious play with whatever conjoins friends. Murphy's own examples of friendship point in this direction: the relationship between novelist Mary McCarthy and philosopher Hannah Arendt as well as the relationship between George Thomson and Ludwig Wittgenstein. Both sets of relations involved intense periods of study, dialogue, and letter writing concerning the common space (intellectual, emotional, aesthetic, and so on) that conjoined them. And it is precisely through the activity of public, collective study that friendship becomes political. Murphy concludes that friendships represent "an *equality of difference*" (ibid.: 172) that is analogous to political justice. Friends, despite differences, engage in studious play with the common that rests between them, and this activity of play prefigures a coming justice. Returning to OWS, Zuccotti Park could be read as a little republic, a kind of primitive communism between friends, a notch in Wall Street's seemingly impervious armor, precisely because of the seriousness of the studious play that developed and the dedication of the studiers to the analysis of the common that joined them across differences.

Study and free university

Since Zuccotti was forcibly dispersed, OWS has taken many shapes—several of which have moved more toward goal-oriented projects. Various working groups such as Empowerment and Education have morphed into Occupy Student Debt as well as Occupy University. Occupy Student Debt and Occupy University both make explicit the implicit educational dimension of OWS and its direct connections to the struggle to study. The first is largely a question of refusal. In fact, Occupy Student Debt has a pledge that essentially calls for occupiers to "prefer not to pay" their debt. This is a kind of rejection of the economics of learning that is based on the calculation of education as a good to be bought and sold to consumers who are, in the last instance, nothing more than potential human capital value waiting to be made actual. The clearest example of preferring not to can be found in Quebec's *le printemps érable* (or Maple Spring) which is the longest lasting student strike in Quebec history. Beginning in 2012, the Maple Spring, although much closer to a movement than an occupation, similarly suspended the logic of economic debt in the name of a *social debt* to the commonwealth. The logic of suspension in both cases does not destroy the concept of debt but rather *collectively and publically plays with this concept* in order to return it to free use. In this case: the free use friends make of the university when they study.

As Alia Al-Saji reported from the front lines of the Maple Spring:

> Walking, illegally, down main Montreal thoroughfares with students in nightly demonstrations, with neighbors whom I barely knew before, banging pots and pans, and with tens, if not hundreds, of thousands of people on every 22nd of the month since March—this was unimaginable a year ago. Unimaginable that the collective and heterogeneous body, which is the "*manif* [demonstration]", could feel so much like home, despite its internal differences. Unimaginable that this mutual dependence on one another could enable not only collective protection from traffic and police but the affective strength and audacity to take back the street—a mutual dependence that includes the masked demonstrators ready to help when gassed by police. Unimaginable too that we would be breaking the law daily, that blocking traffic and seeing the city from the center of the street would become habit, and that as the "*printemps érable*" becomes summer, we would be investing our time in neighborhood assemblies, in weaving social bonds, and in sustaining and deepening the mobilization.
>
> (2012: n.p.)

In other words, *we would prefer not to* opens up a space and a time for a new notion of social debt to emerge that renders inoperative economic logics of tuition. To study together in public, collectivized spaces is to recognize that friendship is not simply a bond between those with whom we identify but rather a co-belonging of "heterogeneous" bodies (some wearing masks) that cannot be recognized and yet to whom all owe a debt. The primitive communism between friends that emerges when a collective proclaims "we would prefer not to" opens to the potentiality of study, which, as Al-Saji argues, is not simply an incapacity to reach decisions, but is a form of hesitation (withdrawing from) that is internal to direct democratic participation (which surges forward). In other words, the hesitation of preferring not to and the following debt of friendship should not be unjustly stigmatized as "ineffective" tools for achieving set goals but rather seen as the rhythmic flow of public, collective study. Hesitation in Occupy Student Debt and the Maple Spring is therefore not simply an incapability but is an in-capability or im-potentiality unleashed when preferring not to be or do or pay x, y, and z is collectivized amongst friends.

The second offshoot of OWS—with its evocations of a horizontal pedagogy—offers a radical restructuring of the very space and time of education. While sharing certain features with Illich's learning webs or David Kennedy's utopian school discussed in Chapter 5, there is an important and fundamental difference between these prophetic visions of de-centralized educational institutions and the actual practices of Occupy University. As Hardt and Negri have argued (2012), one of the most important and influential aspects of new movements such as Occupy is that they have demonstrated the obsolescence of the prophet. Instead of the prophetic imagination, which is guided by strong utopian visions of a future oriented life-to-come, OWS and the likes embody a radical messianic sensitivity to the now and the possibility to experiment with alternatives in this now. In other words, instead of a crowd led by a prophet, OWS becomes a multitude of apostles wandering in the newness of the now, occupying spaces and times *as not* the spaces and times they are intended to be.

On May 1, 2012, Occupy University participated in the Free University that occupied Madison Square Park and other spaces in the city to create an educational environment free and open to all. Without direct reference to the Democracy University of Tiananmen, the Free University seemed to once again emphasize the connections between democracy, politics, and collective, public study. This was an education that shifted debt from economic to social logics. As a collective educational experiment, the Free University enacted a kind of educational strike, withdrawing from the buying and selling of educational labor-power. Withdrawing from and preferring not to opened up a space and time of alter-education which broke free from the imperatives to realize one's latent potentiality in the name of human capital production. Through the indeterminacy of weak utopianism, the apostles of the Free University were experimenting to see what happened when they embraced the im-potential political gesture of study, transforming the city into a space of study. Without abandoning the idea of the University, such occupations enact a *minimal* displacement of its form from campuses largely owned and operated through capitalist, governmental, and military contracts to public spaces accessible to all. Yet, as Agamben argues, such minimal displacements contain the promise of messianic freedom. This freedom is not so much the actualization of latent potentials as the experience of the potentiality of the university to be a universe of study and for the city to be a collective of friends. Thus it was not necessarily any particular content taught that was most radical about the Free University so much as the studious play with the idea of the university as such.

The Free University *as not* the university in chains offered a clear expression of messianic or weak utopianism at work. Stated differently, the Free University offered a new notion of use beyond the discourse and practices of lawfully sanctioned rights and privileges. Drawing on the Franciscan movement, Agamben speaks of *usus pauper* or poor use as an alternative to property (and rights thereof). Although taking a vow of extreme poverty, the Franciscan brotherhood nevertheless made use of certain things. Instead of a right to use this or that thing, the Franciscans insisted, to quote Agamben, "It's not a right to use, it is a use without right" (2004a: 119). This *communal* or *communist* use interrupted any notion of public or private property without destroying the notion of use. What was at stake in the Free University as an educational strike was the liberation of the university from property right (the right of those who pay to enter or the right of those who invest to dictate research) or governmental control and an opening up of education to free use or poor use. The Free University was therefore poor, radically so, yet in this poverty, it was free. Only in the space and time of freedom can teachers and students meet as friends, as whatever singularities, as the blossoms of study.

In this sense, the Free University was a profanation of the apparatus of learning. "Profanation," for Agamben, "is the counter-apparatus that restores to common use what sacrifice had separated and divided" (2009b: 19). If the university divides the population into the expert and the novice and the learned from the ignorant through the technology of the exam and the cultural capital of the degree, the Free University separated the university from such separations, letting idle the technologies which support them. Indeed, anyone could propose a class for Free University, and likewise anyone could attend these classes. Rather than a university degree being the *privileged and private property* of individuals, the Free University or the *Communist University* de-appropriated the very idea of the degree, making previously unavailable objects, ideas, and concepts open for free usage. What was at stake in this liberation of common use was the idea of the university. Rather than occupy the physical space of the university, the Free University occupied the idea of the university, and reminded everyone of its ongoing efficacy within a world of media spectacle and biocapitalist appropriation. In this sense, there is an im-political bond that joined together the Free University and the student general strikes during Canada's Maple Spring which, argues Krista Geneviève Lynes, "prefigure[d] the poetic excess of the classroom unbound by the logic of calculation, by learning outcomes, skills training, or the measurable metrics of success" (2012: n.p.) creating a coming university, or a university that is not *not* a university.

Not yet a conclusion

What, in the end, are the "lessons" that educators can take from studying OWS, Free University, and other student occupations? Is this even a viable question to ask? Can lessons be learned and thus formulated into general rules to guide future occupations? Because occupations such as Tiananmen or Maple Spring suspend the question of success or failure, they cannot act as political models. Indeed like im-potentiality itself, they have a peculiar epistemological status. As pure means, they resist becoming lessons that can be tallied up in history books (which assess their merits and demerits), quantified by sociology (which abstracts the contingencies of events into general claims or structural architectonics), weighed by political judgment (which measures success in terms of tangible outcomes or met demands), represented as educational models (which always want to pass down the important lessons of life to the next generation).

164   *Public, collective studying*

Indeed, these occupations have a peculiar epistemological status as *paradigms* of collective and public study. Paradigmatic thinking is to be separated from either induction or deduction. As Agamben writes, "While induction proceeds from the particular to the universal and deduction from the universal to the particular, the paradigm is defined by a third and paradoxical type of movement, which goes from the particular to the particular" (2009a: 19). Stated differently, the paradigm thinks through analogy, rendering inoperative the dichotomy of universal and particular. Paradigms presuppose the impossibility of any rule that either (a) would guide judgment of particular cases or (b) result from the comparison of particular cases. What we are left with are cases without rule that nevertheless exhibit a "rule" that cannot be stated or applied.

If I have assembled a constellation of examples that collectively form a paradigm, it is to trace the intelligibility of the im-potential politics of study. This intelligibility cannot be formalized into a clear set of rules or principles to guide future occupations. Such formulation would transform a pure means into a mere means toward an end, thus forcing the withdrawal of im-potentiality into an actualized (and measurable) quantity. I cannot possibly end a book on study with such formalization—thus becoming a schoolmaster who, in the end, must assign a "grade" to OWS to see if it passed some sort of progressive litmus test. Such a gesture would be nothing less than an enactment of mythic violence that destroys im-potentiality in the name of preserving the law of measure.

But what I can offer in the end is a summary of the imprint that study as a collective and public event has left on the contemporary landscape. These spectral imprints can, perhaps, never be fully evaluated (thus transformed into preexisting success conditions for future occupations) but nevertheless present remnants of the practices of study that haunt hallways, parks, classrooms, and campuses. These phantasms sustain an opening for free use even in the darkness, even when the libraries have been destroyed by the police, the last residue of collective experimentation wiped clean off of park benches, and the sound of general assemblies silenced by the white noise of oncoming traffic. In other words, all that can be done is to assemble the traces of the underlying signatures of study left in forgotten spaces, atopic spaces that are neither here nor there, which speak to an ongoing efficacy despite signs that point elsewhere.

First, study is—as an im-potential political gesture—always shared amongst friends. These friends are not the ones we identify with ("Hey, you have similar tastes as I do" or "Hey, you share my political ideology") but rather those with whom we share the atopic space between desubjectification and subjectification.

Second, it is a collectively self-organizing event. The studier is an autodidact, and the study group is self-generating and self-sustaining. If the teacher is present, the teacher is a kind of impotent assistant who offers nothing more to the studier than the space and time (and sometimes the materials or collection) to study.

Third, it is ultimately an act that refuses (or prefers not) to be identified as labor (the reproduction of biological life), work (the production of durable things), or politics (the actions taken in public to secure one's citizenship, one's recognition by the state). Study is a state of exception, a state which suspends the biological imperative of labor, the finitude of work, or the actions of politics to create a public *bios*. As such, it is immeasurable and unquantifiable.

Fourth, the space of collective study is a public space occupied by individuals who "do not belong there." It ruptures the *functionality* of spaces, creating an opening for weak utopianism to emerge in the now as a kind of inoperative redemption of the present.

Fifth, unlike political movements, the occupation is deeply concerned with living together, caring for others in a shared space, circulating suggestions rather than making demands, and thus deeply invested in the process of self-study. As Aristotle argued, the defining feature of friendship is "living together" (*to suzên*), studying that which con-joins. In this sense, it is concerned with *understanding its own conditions of possibility*.

Sixth, the divine violence of occupations is an educative power to suspend the law and the force of willful demand. Suspension is a particularly effective educational power because it opens laws, norms, values, and object to new, free use by the studiers. Such violence is in essence a violence against the exclusive and destructive violence of sovereign command that always forces a division between potentiality and impotentiality.

To end a book with a small if not impotent constellation of six remnants is to end without conclusions, proclamations or even declarations. I end not at a destination but at a threshold—a threshold that returns us all back to the labyrinth for more tinkering.

Bibliography

Abbas, A. (1988) 'Walter Benjamin's collector: the fate of modern experience', *New Literary History*, 20(1): 217–237.

Adorno, T. and Horheimer, M. (2011) *Towards a New Manifesto*, trans. R. Livingston, London: Verso.

Agamben, G. (1991) *Language and Death: The Place of Negativity*, trans. K. Pinkus and M. Hardt, Minneapolis: University of Minnesota Press.

—— (1993a) *The Coming Community*, trans. M. Hardt, Minneapolis: University of Minnesota Press.

—— (1993b) *Stanzas: Word and Phantom in Western Culture*, trans. R. Martinez, Minneapolis: University of Minnesota Press.

—— (1995) *Idea of Prose*, trans. M. Sullivan and S. Whitsitt, New York: SUNY Press.

—— (1998) *Homo Sacer: Sovereign Power and Bare Life*, trans. D. Heller-Roazen, Stanford: Stanford University Press.

—— (1999a) *The End of the Poem: Studies in Poetics*, trans. D. Heller-Roazen, Stanford: Stanford University Press.

—— (1999b) *The Man Without Content*, trans. G. Albert, Stanford: Stanford University Press.

—— (1999c) *Potentialities: Collected Essays in Philosophy*, ed. and trans. D. Heller-Roazen, Stanford: Stanford University Press.

—— (2000) *Means Without End: Notes on Politics*, trans. V. Binetti and C. Casarino, Minneapolis: University of Minnesota Press.

—— (2002) *Remnants of Auschwitz: The Witness and the Archive*, trans. D. Heller-Roazen, London: Zone Books.

—— (2004a) 'I am sure that you are more pessimistic than I am . . .': An interview with Giorgio Agamben', interviewed by Vacarme, *Rethinking Marxism*, 16(2): 115–124.

—— (2004b) *The Open: Man and Animal*, trans. K. Attell, Stanford: Stanford University Press.

—— (2005a) *State of Exception*, trans. K. Attell, Stanford: Stanford University Press.

—— (2005b) *The Time That Remains: A Commentary on the Letter to the Romans*, trans. P. Dailey, Stanford: Stanford University Press.

—— (2007a) *Infancy and History: On the Destruction of Experience*, trans. L. Heron, London: Verso.

—— (2007b) *Profanations*, trans. J. Fort, London: Zone Books.

—— (2009a) *The Signatures of All Things: On Method*, trans. L. D'Isanto and K. Attell, London: Zone Books.

—— (2009b) *What is an Apparatus?*, trans. D. Kishik and S. Pedatella, Stanford: Stanford University Press.

—— (2011a) *The Kingdom and the Glory*, trans. L. Chiesa and M. Mandarini, Stanford: Stanford University Press.

—— (2011b) *Nudities*, trans. D. Kishik and S. Pedatella, Stanford: Stanford University Press.

—— (2011c) *The Sacrament of Language: An Archeology of the Oath*, trans. A. Kotsko, Stanford: Stanford University Press.

Al-Saji, A. (2012) 'Creating possibility: The time of the Quebec student movement', *Theory & Event* 15(3 supplement): n.p.

Apple, M. (2006) *Educating the "Right Way"*, New York: Routledge.

Arendt, H. (1969) *On Violence*, San Diego: Harvest Books.

—— (1993) *Between Past and Future*, London: Penguin Books.

—— (2005) *The Promise of Politics*, New York: Schocken Books.

Aristotle (1941) *The Basic Works of Aristotle*, ed. and trans. R. McKeon, New York: Random House.

Arsenjuk, L. and Koerner, M. (2009) 'Study, students, universities: an introduction', *Polygraph* 21: 1–13.

Benjamin, W. (1968) *Illuminations*, trans. H. Zohn, New York: Schocken Books.

—— (1982) 'Eduard Fuchs: collector and historian', in A. Arato and E. Gebhardt (eds.) *The Essential Frankfurt School Reader*, New York: Continuum.

—— (1986) *Reflections*, trans. E. Jephcott, New York: Schocken Books.

—— (2002) *The Arcades Project*, trans. H. Eiland and K. McLaughlin, Cambridge: Belknap Press of Harvard University Press.

Biesta, G. (2006) *Beyond Learning: Democratic Education for a Human Future*, Boulder: Paradigm Press.

—— (2010) 'How to exit politically and learn from it: Hannah Arendt and the problem of democratic education', *Teachers College Record* 112(2): 556–573.

—— (2011) 'Philosophy, exposure, and children: how to resist the instrumentalisation of philosophy in education', *Journal of Philosophy of Education*, 45(2): 305–319.

Bingham, C. and Biesta, G. (2010) *Jacques Rancière: Education, Truth, Emancipation*, London: Continuum.

Blumenkranz, C., Gessen, K., Greif, M., Leonard, S., Resnick, S., Saval, N., Schmitt, E. and Taylor, A. (2011) *Occupy! Scenes from Occupied America*, London: Verso.

Bonilla-Silva, E. and Embrick, D.G. (2006) 'Racism without racists: "killing me softly" with color blindness', in C.A. Rossatto, R.L. Allen, and M. Pruyn (eds.) *Reinventing Critical Pedagogy: Widening the Circle of Anti-Oppression Education*, Lanham: Rowman & Littlefield Publishers.

Booker, K. (2002) *The Post-Utopian Imagination: American Culture in the Long 1950s*, Westport: Greenwood Press.

Borges, J.L. (2000) *Selected Non-Fictions*, trans. E. Weinberger, E. Allen, and S. Levine, London: Penguin.

Bush, G.W. (2001) *No Child Left Behind*. Washington: US Department of Education.

Campbell, T. (2011) *Improper Life: Technology and Biopolitics from Heidegger to Agamben*, Minneapolis: University of Minnesota Press.

Chiesa, L. (2009) 'Giorgio Agamben's Franciscan ontology', in L. Chiesa and A. Toscano (eds.) *The Italian Difference: Between Nihilism and Biopolitics*, Melbourne: re.press.

Chmelynski, C. (2006) 'Play teaches what testing can't touch: Humanity', *Educational Digest: Essential Readings*, 72(3): 10–13.

168 *Bibliography*

Clarke, C. (2003) *21st Century Skills: Realizing Our Potential.* Online. Available HTTPS: http://webarchive.nationalarchives.gov.uk/20040116235613/http://dfes.gov.uk/skillsstrategy/docs/fulldoc.pdf (accessed 10 September 2012).

Coleman, N. (2005) *Utopias and Architecture*, New York: Routledge.

Daston, P. and Park, K. (2001) *Wonders and the Order of Nature*, London: Zone Books.

Dean, J. (2012) *The Communist Horizon*, London: Verso.

De la Durantaye, L. (2009) *Giorgio Agamben: A Critical Introduction*, Stanford: Stanford University.

Deleuze, G. (1997) *Negotiations: 1972–1990*, trans. M. Joughin, New York: Columbia University Press.

—— (2005) *Pure Immanence: Essays on A Life*, trans. A. Boyman, New York: Zone Books.

Dickinson, C. (2011) *Agamben and Theology*, London: Continuum.

Dinger, D. and Johnson, J. (2011) *Let Them Play: An Early Learning (Un)curriculum*, St. Paul: Redleaf Press.

Dreyfus, H. (2005) 'Starting points: an interview with Hubert Dreyfus', interviewed by Z. Sachs- Arellano, *The Harvard Review of Philosophy* XIII(1): 123–152.

Dreyfus, H. and Kelly, S.D. (2011) *All Things Shining: Reading the Western Classics to Find Meaning in a Secular Age*, New York: Free Press.

Ely, J. (1998) 'Intellectual friendship and the elective affinities of critical theory', *South Atlantic Quarterly*, 97(1): 187–224.

Faulkner, J. (2010) 'Innocence, evil, and human frailty: potentiality and the child in the writings of Giorgio Agamben', *Angelaki* 15(2): 203–219.

Fine, M. (1991) *Framing Dropouts*, Buffalo: SUNY Press.

Foucault, M. (1979) *Discipline and Punish: The Birth of the Prison*, trans. A. Sheridan, New York: Vintage.

—— (2000) *Power*, ed. J. Faubion and trans. R. Hurley, New York: New York Press.

—— (2008) *The Birth of Biopolitics: Lectures at the Collège de France 1978–1979*, ed. M. Senellart and trans. G. Burchell, New York: Palgrave Macmillan.

Freire, P. (2001) *The Pedagogy of the Oppressed*, trans. M.B. Ramos, London: Continuum.

Giroux, H. (2007) *The University in Chains: Confronting the Military–Industrial–Academic Complex*, Boulder: Paradigm Press.

—— (2012) *Disposable Youth: Racialized Memories, and the Culture of Cruelty*, New York: Routledge.

Gombrich, E.H. (1986) *Aby Warburg: An Intellectual Biography*, Chicago: University of Chicago Press.

Hardt, M. and Negri, A. (2012) *Declaration*, New York: Argo.

Heidegger, M. (1984) *The Question Concerning Technology and Other Essays*, trans. W. Lovitt, New York: Harper Torchbooks.

—— (1995) *The Fundamental Concepts of Metaphysics: World, Finitude, Solitude*, trans. W. McNeill and N. Walker, Bloomington: Indiana University Press.

—— (2001) *Poetry, Language, Thought*, trans. A. Hofstadter, New York: Harper Perennial.

—— (2008) *Being and Time*, trans. J. Macquarrie and E. Robinson, New York: Harper Perennial.

—— (2009) *Pathmarks*, ed. W. McNeill, Cambridge: Cambridge University Press.

Horton, M. and Freire, P. (1990) *We Make the Road by Walking*, Philadelphia: Temple University Press.

Illich, I. (1970) *Deschooling Society*, London: Marion Boyars.

—— (1973) *Tools for Conviviality*, New York: Harper and Row.

Bibliography   169

—— (1988) 'The educational enterprise in the light of the Gospel,' Lecture, Chicago IL.

—— (2005) *The Rivers North of the Future*, Anansi: Toronto.

James, W. (1992) *William James: Writings 1878–1899: Psychology, Briefer Course, The Will to Believe, Talks to Teachers and Students, Essays*, ed. G.E. Myers, New York: Library of America.

Keefe, A. (2012) *Wordimage: Lyric Ekphrasis and Subjectivity in the Twenty-First Century*. PhD Dissertation, Rutgers University.

Kennedy, D. (2006) *The Well of Being: Childhood, Subjectivity, and Education*, New York: SUNY Press.

Kishik, D. (2012) *The Power of Life: Agamben and the Coming Politics*, Stanford: Stanford University Press.

Koslofsky, C. (2011) *Evening's Empire: A History of the Night in Early Modern Europe*, Cambridge: Cambridge University.

LaCapra, D. (2007) 'Approaching limit events: siting Agamben', in M. Calarco and S. DeCaroli (eds.) *Sovereignty and Life*, Stanford: Stanford University Press.

Lauer, L. (2011) 'Play deprivation: is it happening in your school?' EBSCO Online Submission. Available HTTP: http://www.eric.ed.gov/contentdelivery/servlet/ERICServlet?accno=ED524739 (accessed 10 June 2012).

Lennard, N. (2012) 'Occupy and failure', *Truthout*. Online. Available HTTP: http://truth-out.org/opinion/item/8780-occupy-failure (accessed 1 September 2012).

Lewis, T. (2006) 'The school as an exceptional space: rethinking education from the perspective of the biopedagogical', *Educational Theory* 56(2): 159–176.

—— (2009) 'Education and the immunization paradigm', *Studies in Philosophy and Education*, 28(6): 485–498.

Lynes, K.G. (2012) 'Poetic resistance and the classroom without guarantees', *Theory & Event* 15(3 supplement): n.p.

Masschelein, J. and Simons, M. (2008) 'The governmentalization of learning and the assemblage of a learning apparatus', *Educational Theory* 58(4): 391–415.

—— (2009) 'Towards the idea of a world university', *Interchange* 40(1): 1–23.

—— (2010) 'Schools as architecture for new comers and strangers: the perfect school as public school?' *Teachers College Record* 112(2): 535–555.

—— (2011) 'The university: a public issue', in R. Barnett (ed.) *The Future University: Ideas and Possibilities*, New York: Routledge.

McClintock, R. (1971) 'Toward a place for study in a world of instruction', *Teachers College Press* 73(2): 161–205.

McLaren, P. (1999) *Schooling as a Ritual Performance*, Lanham: Rowman and Littlefield.

Melville, H. (2002) *Melville's Short Novels*, ed. D. McCall, New York: W.W. Norton and Company.

Mills, C. (2009) *The Philosophy of Giorgio Agamben*, Montreal: McGill Queens University Press.

Murphy, P. (1998) 'Friendship's eu-topia', *South Atlantic Quarterly*, 97(1): 169–185.

Murray, A. and Whyte, J. (eds.) (2011) *The Agamben Dictionary*, Edinburgh: Edinburgh University Press.

Nancy, J.L. (1991) *The Inoperative Community*, trans. P. Connor, L. Garbus, M. Hooland, and S. Sawhney, Minneapolis: University of Minnesota Press.

Neill, A.S. (1992) *Summerhill School: A New View of Childhood*, New York: St. Martin's Griffin.

Noguera, P. (2009) *The Trouble with Black Boys: . . . And Other Reflections on Race, Equity, and the Future of Public Education*, San Francisco: Jossey-Bass.

170   *Bibliography*

Obama, B. (2009) *Promoting Innovation, Reform, and Excellence in America's Public Schools*. Online. Available HTTPS: http://www.whitehouse.gov/the-press-office/fact-sheet-race-top (accessed 18 September 2012).

Olfman, S. (ed.) (2003) *All Work and No Play: How Educational Reforms Are Harming Our Preschoolers*, Westport: Praeger.

Patrick, J. (2002) 'The botched book and the empty archive: Melville's Bartleby', in R. Comay (ed.) *Lost in the Archive*, Toronto: Alphabet City Media.

Pierce, C. (2013) *Education in the Age of Biocapitalism: Optimizing Educational Life for a Flat World*, New York: Palgrave Macmillan.

Plato (1992) *Republic*, trans. G.M.A. Grube, Indianapolis: Hackett Publishing Company.

Rampley, M. (2001) 'Mimesis and allegory: on Aby Warburg's writings on astrology and art', in R. Woodfield (ed.), *Art History as Cultural History: Warburg's Projects*, Amsterdam: G+B Arts International.

Rancière, J. (1991) *The Ignorant Schoolmaster: Five Lessons in Intellectual Emancipation*, trans. K. Ross, Stanford: Stanford University Press.

—— (1999) *Disagreement: Politics and Philosophy*, trans. J. Rose, Minneapolis: University of Minnesota Press.

—— (2003) *Short Voyages to the Land of the People*, trans. J.B. Swenson, Stanford: Stanford University Press.

—— (2009) *The Emancipated Spectator*, trans. G. Elliott, London: Verso.

—— (2012) *Proletarian Nights: The Workers' Dreams in Nineteenth-Century France*, trans. J. Drury, London: Verso.

Rich, A. (1975) *Adrienne Rich's Poetry and Prose*, eds. Barbara Charlesworth Gelpi and A. Gelpi, New York: W.W. Norton & Company.

Ronell, A. (2002) *Stupidity*, Chicago: University of Chicago Press.

Rousseau, J.J. (1979) *Emile: Or, On Education*, trans. A. Bloom, New York: Basic Books.

Sacks, O. (2010) *The Mind's Eye*, New York: Alfred A. Knopf.

Salzani, C. (2007) 'The city as crime scene: Walter Benjamin and the traces of the detective', *New German Critique*, 34(1): 165–187.

—— (2012) '*Quodlibet*: Giorgio Agamben's anti-utopia', *Utopian Studies*, 23(1): 212–237.

Santner, E. (2011) *The Royal Remains: The People's Two Bodies and the Endgames of Sovereignty*, Chicago: University of Chicago Press.

Scheffler, I. (1985) *Of Human Potential: An Essay in the Philosophy of Education*. New York: Routledge.

Schrecker, E. (2010) *The Lost Soul of Higher Education: Corporatization, the Assault on Academic Freedom, and the End of the American University*, New York: New Press.

Shor, I. (ed.) (1987) *Freire for the Classroom: A Sourcebook for Liberatory Teaching*, Portsmouth: Boyton/Cook.

Soini, H. and Flynn, M. (2005) 'Emotion and rhythm in critical learning incidents', *Interchange* 36(1–2): 73–83.

ten Bos, R. (2005) 'On the possibility of formless life: Giorgio Agamben's politics of the gesture', *Ephemera: Theory & Politics in Organization* 5(1): 26–44.

Thompson, E.P. (1966) *The Making of the English Working Class*, New York: Vintage Books.

Thomson, I.D. (2004) 'Heidegger's perfectionist philosophy of education in *Being and Time*', *Continental Philosophy Review* 37: 439–467.

—— (2005) *Heidegger on Ontotheology: Technology and the Politics of Education*, Cambridge: Cambridge University Press.

Tulley, G. (2009) 'Life lessons through tinkering', title of TED talk. Online. Available HTTP: http://www.ted.com/talks/gever_tulley_s_tinkering_school_in_action.html (accessed 7 July 2012).

Tyack, D. and Cuban, L. (1995) *Tinkering Toward Utopia: A Century of Public School Reform*, Cambridge: Harvard University Press.

Vlieghe, J. (2012) 'Experiencing (im)potentiality: Bollnow and Agamben on the educational meaning of school practices', *Studies in Philosophy and Education*. Online. Avaliable HTTP: http://www.springerlink.com/content/07718n87632q8738/ (accessed 10 August 2012).

Wall, T.C. (1999) *Radical Passivity: Levinas, Blanchot, and Agamben*, New York: SUNY.

Wark, M. (2011) 'McKenzie Wark on Occupy Wall Street: "how to occupy an abstraction"', London: Verso. Online. Available HTTP: http://www.versobooks.com/blogs/728 (accessed 9 September 2012).

Watkin, W. (2010) *The Literary Agamben: Adventures in Logopoiesis*, London: Continuum.

Whitehead, A.N. (1967) *The Aims of Education and Other Essays*, New York: The Free Press.

Woodhouse, H. (1999) 'The rhythm of the university: part one—teaching, learning, and administering in the Whiteheadian tradition', *Interchange* 30(2): 191–211.

Zavarzadeh, M. and Morton, D. (1994) *Theory as Resistance*, New York: Guilford Press.

Zhao, Dingxin (2004) *The Power of Tiananmen: State–Society Relations and the 1989 Beijing Student Movement*, Chicago: University of Chicago Press.

Ziarek, E.P. (2010) 'Feminine "I can": on possibility and praxis in Agamben's work', *Theory & Event* 13(1): n.p.

Žižek, S. (2008) *Violence*, New York: Picador.

Index

Adorno, Theodor and Max Horkheimer 145–6, 148–9
angel 57, 61–4, 130; *see also* Dürer, Albrecht and Borges, Jorge Luis
apostle 96, 101–3; *see also* St. Paul
Arendt, Hannah 125, 137, 160
aura 80–6, 90–2, 145; *see also* Benjamin, Walter
Aristotle: on potentiality 3, 7; on friendship 136–7, 165
atopia 8, 33, 129, 154–64, 159, 161

Bartleby the Scrivener 38, 46–52, 62–3, 77, 92–3, 106, 149, 151
Benjamin, Walter 1, 75, 78, 89–90, 145; on aura 80–6; on children 129; on collecting 79, 81–7, 91, 93; on mechanical reproduction 80; on studying the law 120; on violence 150–1
Biesta, Gert 26–8, 115, 143–5
Bildung 27–8
biocapitalism 3–6, 11, 13–15, 26–7, 96, 108, 121, 155
blindness 31, 68, 70–1, 73; face blindness 140–3
boredom *see* mood
Borges, Jorge Luis 61–2, 70–1
brown study 62, 69, 73

cairos 95, 100, 107
capability 7–9, 14–15, 28, 37–45, 93, 102, 107, 130, 132, 139–45, 161
collection: public 79, 81–2, 84, 86–7, 91; private 79–82, 84, 86–7, 90; *see also* Benjamin, Walter and Warburg, Aby
community 15, 101, 123–4, 129, 136–8: operative 138–9; inoperative 138–40, 146, 148; coming

95, 105, 122, 149–50, 156–9
consensus 138–9, 153, 159
contingency 6, 8, 11–12, 14–15, 42, 58–9, 129, 133, 144, 157

Dante 59
darkness 17, 36, 52, 68–73, 91–3, 133, 146, 164; *see also* night
Davis, Angela 155
Dean, Jodi 156, 159
Deleuze, Gilles 37, 51–2, 126, 131, 142
divinity 31, 33; *see also* sacred
Dreyfus, Hubert 16–17, 26, 29–31, 34, 36, 78
Dürer, Albrecht 61–3, 67

empty throne *see* space
endarkenment 74
Erasmus 13, 68
evil 8–9, 11, 34, 38, 99, 108, 118

face 140–4, 148, 155; *see also* nudity
Foucault, Michel 76, 78, 97, 108, 120, 26, 139
Free University 162–3
freedom 4–5, 16, 18–22, 25–30, 33, 35, 38–42, 44–5, 51–6, 58–60, 63–4, 72, 81, 87, 93, 96, 104, 109, 111, 114, 117–18, 123, 129–33, 135, 143–4, 148, 152, 156–7, 162–3
free use 92, 101, 114–15, 119, 128–9, 151, 158, 161, 163–5; *see also* tinkering
Freire, Paulo 96, 102–4
Freud, Sigmund 77–8, 126
friendship 99, 101, 136–40, 145–6, 148, 159–61, 164

genius 134

Index   173

halo 72–3
Hardt, Michael and Antonio Negri 149–50, 162
Heidegger, Martin 16–17, 25–33, 35–7, 41–2, 60, 62–3, 73–4, 77, 92, 125–6, 132, 146–7
Holmes, Sherlock 77

ignorance 134
Illich, Ivan 96, 98–9, 101, 103, 109, 117, 162
infancy 17, 36, 42, 119, 123, 141–5, 147
inspiration *see* mood

James, William 16, 20–2, 25, 27, 30–1, 33–4, 36

Kafka, Franz 106, 120, 125
Kelly, Sean Dorrance *see* Dreyfus, Hubert
Kennedy, David 109–15, 162

law of good neighbors 35, 90–2, 148
learning 1–15, 24, 26–8, 34, 37, 39–41, 44, 49, 53–4, 56, 58–9, 60, 64, 75, 84, 95, 98, 103, 108–9, 111, 113–14, 116, 118, 123–4, 130–2, 139, 142–4, 150–1, 159–60, 162–3
 learning society 5–6, 8, 10, 109, 118, 131, 142, 144, 159

Marx, Karl 29–30, 69–70, 104, 148
Masschelein, Jan 4–5, 13, 22, 117, 119, 121
McClintock, Robert 12–15
McLaren, Peter 96, 117
mechanical reproduction (age of) *see* Benjamin, Walter
melancholia *see* mood
Melville, Herman 46, 49, 106; *see also* Bartleby the Scrivener
messianic time *see* time
Mnemosyne 91–2; *see also* Warburg, Aby
mood: boredom 42–3, 60, 62–4, 79, 149, 159; melancholia 21, 25, 36, 46, 62, 64, 67, 69–70, 93, 120, 127, 132, 140, 146, 154, 159; inspiration 12, 14, 17, 23, 61, 64, 67, 75, 90–1, 93, 112–13, 120, 126, 128, 131, 133, 140, 145–6, 149, 159; sadness 12, 14, 17, 19, 64, 93, 131, 159

Nancy, Jean-Luc 138–9
Neill, A.S. 118

neoliberal democracy 4, 8–10, 96, 104, 144; *see also* biocapitalism
nihilism 16–17, 26, 34, 36, 64, 78, 96, 114, 126, 157
night 68–74
notch *see* space
nudity 51, 127, 132, 141, 145, 147

Occupy Wall Street (OWS) 150–65
ontotautology 42

Plato 68, 70–2, 74, 116–18, 122, 138
play 14, 69, 110–11, 116–30; *see also* studious play
poiesis 28–9, 55–6, 58–60
praxis 14, 28–30, 59, 104, 109
profanation 15, 34–6, 51, 66, 78–9, 81, 84–5, 90, 105, 107, 114, 118–25, 127, 129, 132, 145, 163

Rancière, Jacques: on consensus 138; on genius 134; on ignorance 134; on night and night knowledge 69–71; on will 22–5, 27, 30, 32–4
rhythm 12, 14, 35, 44–5, 53–64, 67, 88, 90, 92, 121, 123, 128–30, 140, 146, 148–9, 154, 161
Rich, Adrienne 64–7, 71
Ronell, Avital 131–2
Rousseau, Jean–Jacques 16, 18–20, 22, 25, 27, 30–1, 33–4, 36

Sacks, Oliver 140–1
sacred 17, 26, 30–1, 34–6, 62, 78, 80, 82, 84, 94, 100, 103, 105, 118–19, 121
Santner, Eric 49–50
Scheffler, Isreal 39–45, 47, 50, 52, 60
shadows 27, 62, 68–74; *see also* darkness
signatures 62, 72–9, 85–7, 91–4, 121–2, 124–5, 127–9, 132, 140–1, 143, 148–50, 164
singularity 7, 41, 50, 80, 143, 157; generic 63, 150
space: empty throne 107, 114; limbo 66, 105, 107, 114; notch 92, 113–15, 149, 156; stanza 104–5; threshold 57–8, 60, 77, 96, 105–7, 133, 141, 165
special being 141, 147; *see also* whatever being
stanza *see* space
St. Paul 67, 86, 96, 100
state of exception 156, 159, 165
studious play 120, 121–9

174　*Index*

Thomson, Iain D. 27–8, 97
threshold *see* space
Tiananmen Square 157–8, 162–3
technological enframing 16, 25–7, 30–1,
　34–6, 78, 157
time: bureaucratic 95–9, 101–3, 108, 110,
　115, 122; eschatological 95, 97, 103;
　messianic 15, 44, 53, 56–8, 64, 95–6,
　99–108, 113–15, 119, 122, 128, 131,
　142, 146, 149–50, 152, 155–6, 158,
　162; prophetic 95, 97–9, 102–3, 108–9,
　111–13, 115, 162
tinkering 88, 114–15, 136, 139, 145, 149,
　154, 158, 165; school 128–30;
　phenomenology 149

Utopia: weak 95–6, 104–8, 114–15, 155,
　162, *see also* atopia; strong 95–6, 99, 103,
　109–14, 162, *see also* time: prophetic

value: exchange 80–2, 85–6, 121; exhibit
　80–2, 84, 86–7, 89–90; cult 80–1, 83–4,
　89; study 84, 87, 90
violence: divine 150–1, 165; mythic 151,
　164; *see also* Benjamin, Walter

Wall, Thomas Carl 35
Warburg, Aby 35, 75, 87–92
whatever being 35, 41–3, 45, 51, 63,
　72, 81, 107, 125, 130, 137–41, 143,
　149–50, 152, 157–60, 163
Whitehead, Alfred North 53–9, 63–4
will: willfulness 5, 9, 12, 16–9, 21–2,
　24–38, 40, 46, 50–1, 79, 91, 93–4, 130,
　134–5, 153, 165; willingness 16, 29, 31,
　34, 79, 153
wunderkammer 82

Žižek, Slavoj 149–51, 155